Self-Publishing For Dummies®

D1481063

Walking through Major Steps in the Self-Publishing Process

The following are the major steps involved with the self-publishing process. The order in which you complete these steps and how long each step takes to complete varies based on the type of book, your time and financial commitment, and the publishing process used; see Chapter 1 for more details. The main steps are

- ❑ Develop an awesome book idea.
- ❑ Research the idea to make sure that it's viable as a full-length book.
- ❑ Define your target audience.
- ❑ Create a detailed outline for the book's content.
- ❑ Research the book's potential content.
- ❑ Write the manuscript.
- ❑ Establish your publishing company (if applicable).
- ❑ Have the manuscript edited.
- ❑ Choose a self-publishing option, such as offset printing or Print-On-Demand (POD), and then hire a printer and/or publisher.
- ❑ Apply for an ISBN, copyright, and other book-specific information, if necessary (this step may be handled for you, depending on the publishing process you choose and the company you work with).
- ❑ Set the cover price for your book.
- ❑ Select a publication date.
- ❑ Have the manuscript's interior pages designed and laid out.
- ❑ Hire a graphic designer to create your book's front and back covers.
- ❑ Develop press materials for your book.
- ❑ Plan and implement a comprehensive marketing, public relations, and advertising campaign.
- ❑ Develop a Web site to promote your book.
- ❑ Begin pre-selling your book (pre-selling includes sending out press materials, promoting the book to distributors, lining up booksellers to sell the book, taking out ads, and so on).
- ❑ Have your book listed with online retailers.
- ❑ Publish the book and ship it to consumers, booksellers, retailers, and distributors (as appropriate).
- ❑ Continue promoting and marketing your book as you take orders.

For Dummies: Bestselling Book Series for Beginners

Self-Publishing For Dummies®

Cheat Sheet

Interviewing Freelancers

Self-publishing a book requires a wide range of skills and knowledge, some of which you may not yet possess. To ensure that each step of the process is handled correctly and to avoid costly mistakes, hiring freelancers to help you often makes sense. Some of the freelancers you may need to hire include a ghostwriter, an editor, a graphic designer for layout and/or cover design, a proofreader, salespeople, a public relations/advertising specialist, and a Web site designer.

Interview the freelancers to ensure that they have experience working on book projects similar to yours. Ask the following questions:

- What previous experience do you have?
- Have you worked on similar book projects in the past?
- What are your fees? How do you want to be paid (by the hour or at a pre-defined set rate)?
- Can you complete the necessary work in a timely manner (based on the author's publication schedule)?
- Can you provide samples of your previous work or list projects you've worked on in the past and provide references?

More Tips for Hiring Freelancers

Here are some additional tips for hiring qualified freelancers:

- Make sure that the freelancer understands your book's target audience and knows how to reach them appropriately.
- Review education, training, and past work experience.
- Check references.
- Review the freelancer's portfolio of work.
- Negotiate the price or fees in advance. Payment can be based on a flat fee or by the hour. Get a written estimate from the freelancer about the time commitment necessary.
- Ensure that the freelancer has time in his schedule to work on your project that matches your time frame.
- Determine if you can work with the people you hire. Freelancers shouldn't compromise your creative vision, so from a creative and personality standpoint, try to pick people you can mesh with.

For Dummies: Bestselling Book Series for Beginners

Self-Publishing FOR DUMMIES®

by Jason R. Rich

WILEY

Wiley Publishing, Inc.

Self-Publishing For Dummies®

Published by
Wiley Publishing, Inc.
111 River St.
Hoboken, NJ 07030-5774
www.wiley.com

WILEY

About the Author

Jason R. Rich is the bestselling author of more than 32 books, including a few self-published titles. He has also ghostwritten several additional books for business leaders and well-known experts in their field. As a journalist, Jason continues to contribute articles to numerous national magazines and major daily newspapers, and he works as a freelance public relations and marketing consultant for companies in a variety of industries.

Some of Jason's recently published books include *The Unofficial Guide to Starting a Business Online,* 2nd Edition (Wiley); *Pampering Your Pooch: Discover What Your Dog Needs, Wants, and Loves* (Howell Book House); *The Everything Family Travel Guide to Walt Disney World, Universal Studios, and Greater Orlando,* 4th Edition (Adams Media); and *American Idol Season 4: Official Behind-the-Scenes Fan Book* (Prima/Random House). Jason is also writing a series of personal finance guides for Entrepreneur Press, the publishers of *Entrepreneur* magazine. His most recent self-published book is *The Bachelor's Guide to Life* (iUniverse).

Jason lives just outside of Boston with his Yorkshire Terrier, named Rusty (www.MyPalRusty.com). Yes, Rusty has his own Web site. Please check it out! You can also visit Jason's Web site at www.JasonRich.com or e-mail him at jr7777@aol.com.

Dedication

This one is for Ferras, Mark, Ellen, Sandy, Emily, Ryan, and my family.

Author's Acknowledgments

Over the years, I have read a handful of *For Dummies* books. I am very proud to now have the opportunity to contribute a book to the popular series. I hope you, the reader, find this book helpful on your quest to become a published author.

Thanks to Mike Lewis at Wiley for inviting me to work on this project. Thanks also to Georgette Beatty, this book's project editor, for her hard work and guidance. The work of Carrie Burchfield (copy editor) and D. Patrick Miller (technical editor) are also very much appreciated. Many people work extremely hard to make the *For Dummies* series so successful. I'd like to offer my sincere gratitude to everyone involved, including the editors, illustrators, designers, proofreaders, reviewers, editorial supervisors, and the sales team. This book truly is a team effort.

On a personal note, my never ending love and gratitude goes out to my close friends — Ferras, Mark, and Ellen (as well as Ellen's family), who are all extremely important people in my life. I'd also like to thank my family for all their support. (Congratulations to Ferras on signing a major record deal and having the opportunity to pursue his dreams! I am so proud of you, Ferras!)

Publisher's Acknowledgments

We're proud of this book; please send us your comments through our Dummies online registration form located at www.dummies.com/register/.

Some of the people who helped bring this book to market include the following:

Acquisitions, Editorial, and Media Development

Project Editor: Georgette Beatty

Acquisitions Editor: Michael Lewis

Copy Editor: Carrie A. Burchfield

Editorial Program Coordinator: Hanna K. Scott

Technical Editor: D. Patrick Miller

Editorial Manager: Michelle Hacker

Editorial Assistants: Erin Calligan, Nadine Bell

Cover Photo: © Alamy

Cartoons: Rich Tennant (www.the5thwave.com)

Composition Services

Project Coordinator: Tera Knapp

Layout and Graphics: Andrea Dahl, Denny Hager, Clint Lahnen, Barbara Moore, Barry Offringa, Melanee Prendergast, Jill Proll, Heather Ryan, Alicia B. South

Proofreaders: Leeann Harney, Jessica Kramer, Christy Pingleton, Aptara

Indexer: Aptara

Publishing and Editorial for Consumer Dummies

Diane Graves Steele, Vice President and Publisher, Consumer Dummies

Joyce Pepple, Acquisitions Director, Consumer Dummies

Kristin A. Cocks, Product Development Director, Consumer Dummies

Michael Spring, Vice President and Publisher, Travel

Kelly Regan, Editorial Director, Travel

Publishing for Technology Dummies

Andy Cummings, Vice President and Publisher, Dummies Technology/General User

Composition Services

Gerry Fahey, Vice President of Production Services

Debbie Stailey, Director of Composition Services

Contents at a Glance

Table of Contents

Introduction

You may have personal and/or professional reasons why you want to get published. Perhaps it's to supplement your income or generate an entire income as a writer. Maybe it's because you have important information to convey or a compelling story to tell.

For someone with good writing skills and a flair for putting words together in a way that's readily accessible to intended readers, becoming a freelance writer for newspapers, magazines, Web sites, and other media outlets is certainly a viable option. Becoming an author with a published book and working with a major publishing house, however, continues to be much more of a challenge due to the highly competitive nature of the book-publishing business.

In recent years, would-be authors have been given an entirely new way to have their work professionally published in book form and then have it distributed to the general public. The process is called self-publishing. *Self-publishing* is a fast-growing opportunity made available when new forms of printing technologies, called digital printing and desktop publishing, were perfected. Now, instead of having to print thousands of copies of a book at one time, as few as one copy of a book can be printed at any given time.

The price to self-publish a book has also dropped dramatically in the past few years. Now, publishing a book is extremely affordable for virtually anyone. Never before has the opportunity to publish a professional quality book been within reach of any aspiring author.

Self-Publishing For Dummies helps you take your idea for a book, develop the idea into content to fill a full-length manuscript, and have it published. This book describes the incredible opportunity self-publishing offers to aspiring writers and authors, business leaders, entrepreneurs, consultants, and anyone else with a great idea for a book.

About This Book

Self-publishing puts you in total charge of your publishing project. A successful publishing venture means properly dealing with each step in the publishing process. Without the proper knowledge and experience, costly mistakes can easily be made. The information in this book helps you avoid the most common mistakes made by authors and self-publishers and helps you properly cater your book to your intended readers. This book also lends a hand when you gather a highly skilled publishing team for your venture. By hiring freelance experts to help you with editing, design, layout, and marketing, your book more effectively competes with the tens of thousands of other books currently on the market.

Most importantly, this book shows you how to obtain distribution for your book and properly market it in order to generate sales. Using marketing, public relations, and advertising strategies, along with the power and capabilities of the Internet, you can transform your book into a successful publishing venture.

I've put the chapters in an order that makes sense if you're looking to transform your manuscript into a self-published book. However, each chapter focuses on one important aspect of the self-publishing process, so you can jump around to quickly obtain the specific information that you're looking for. For instance: Check out Chapter 11 for the scoop on Print-On-Demand (POD) and finding a reputable POD publisher. If you're looking to put together press materials for your book, skip ahead to Chapter 18. Want to know more about what an ISBN is and how to obtain one for your book? Check out Chapter 7.

Keep in mind that this book isn't a "how to write a book" book or an "improve your writing skills" book. Developing the writing skills and the necessary expertise on the topic you plan to write about is your responsibility. If you need to brush up on your writing skills, I recommend that you sign up for writing classes or workshops. This book helps you take the manuscript you've written or are about to write and transform it into the best book possible.

Conventions Used in This Book

I use a few conventions to help guide you through this book:

- ✓ *Italic* words point out defined terms or emphasize words.
- ✓ **Boldface** text indicates keywords in bulleted lists and the action part of numbered steps.
- ✓ `Monofont` text highlights Web addresses.

Each chapter of *Self-Publishing For Dummies* focuses on one important aspect of the self-publishing process. Within each chapter, you find many useful resources and companies that provide products or services for self-published authors. Keep in mind that the companies listed within this book are only a sampling of what's available. Feel free to shop around and research other companies or services before deciding whom to work with. Also, expect the prices associated with self-publishing to change as digital printing options become cheaper, more competition enters into the business, and a greater number of options become available to perspective authors.

What You're Not to Read

In many chapters, sidebars (formatted in gray boxes) are used to further explain certain topics or to provide interviews with various experts in their field. These interviews are designed to provide additional insight into specific steps in the publishing process, but reading them isn't essential to getting your book published. Therefore, if you're in an incredible hurry (and self-publishers can be extremely busy people!), the sidebars are informative but can be skipped over.

Foolish Assumptions

In writing this book, I've made a few assumptions. I know, making assumptions isn't always the best idea, but in developing the content for this book, I had to start somewhere. Here are my assumptions:

- ✔ You have basic writing skills and a great idea for a book. *Self-Publishing For Dummies* helps you evaluate your idea in terms of its suitability and marketability.

- ✔ You already have information to convey to your readers, whether it's a good story or valuable and informative content. Sure, this book helps you fine-tune your approach when it comes to communicating your content to your readers, but it's up to you to decide what information to include in your book, based on your book's target audience.

- ✔ You may even have already written a book, and you want to bypass the traditional publishing process and do it yourself. Or perhaps you've already approached major publishers to sell your book without success, and now you want to give self-publishing a whirl. If you already have written your manuscript, this book shows you how to publish it, market it, and make it available to its intended audience.

How This Book Is Organized

You need to complete many steps to ensure that your publishing venture is successful. This book is organized to help you find specific information easily. Each of the book's six parts is devoted to a particular topic and contains several chapters covering information that directly relates to that topic.

Part I: Do It Yourself: Getting Started with Self-Publishing

The first part of this book introduces you to self-publishing, explains what it is, and clarifies how self-publishing can be used to publish your book. You read about the pros and cons of self-publishing and discover if it's the right publishing option for you. This part also helps you gather all the tools you need to write and publish your book, while providing you with basic information about developing and fine-tuning your manuscript.

Part II: Pulling Together the Details: Administration and Design

After you've finished writing your full-length manuscript, a lot of work is still necessary before it's ready to be printed and sold. This part focuses on setting up your own self-publishing business and handling the book-specific tasks necessary before your book goes to press. Part II also focuses on taking your book's manuscript and creating a professional layout and design for its interior and delving into what it takes to create the best possible front and back cover.

Part III: Start the Presses! Examining Printing Choices

As a self-published author, you have a handful of options when printing your books. Which option you choose is best determined by a number of factors: your budget, your ultimate goals for the book, your distribution plan, and your audience. Each chapter in this part focuses on a different printing option, such as offset printing, Print-On-Demand (POD), and eBook publishing. I also show you how to work successfully with any printer.

Part IV: Making Your Book a Bestseller: Distribution Methods

Simply writing and publishing a book isn't enough to make it successful. One of your biggest challenges is getting your book into the hands of potential readers. You have a few options to distribute your book: selling your book online, distributing through booksellers, and marketing to other retail stores. This part focuses on different book distribution methods and how to best utilize each. I also discuss how to handle your own warehousing, order fulfillment, and shipping, and I explain how to gain even wider distribution for your book by choosing to sell it to a major publisher.

Part V: Creating a Buzz: Publicity and Marketing

Being able to inform readers that your book exists means the difference between selling thousands or tens of thousands of copies (or not selling any copies at all). Developing a comprehensive advertising, marketing, and public relations campaign and then properly implementing it requires a financial and time investment, plus a tremendous amount of creativity, planning, and initiative.

Whether you have a few hundred dollars or an unlimited budget to properly market your book, this part shows you how to utilize the media to generate positive reviews and editorial coverage and how to create effective advertisements. You also discover how to use the Internet to reach your book's target audience and how to develop spinoff products from your book.

Part VI: The Part of Tens

In this part, you discover how to avoid ten common mistakes self-published authors make and find a variety of resources where you can obtain additional information and guidance as you embark on your book publishing venture.

Icons Used in This Book

The icons used throughout this book help you quickly pinpoint important information, focus your attention on information that's worth remembering, and draw attention to things you should watch out for and avoid as you start your publishing project.

This icon appears when I convey information worth remembering. Sounds simple enough, right?

This icon appears whenever advice or tips are provided. The information listed with this icon can help save time and money or help you improve your overall productivity and chances of success.

Watch out for this icon. It accompanies information like common mistakes people make, misconceptions that need clarification, or potential pitfalls you in your publishing process.

Where to Go from Here

For an overview of what self-publishing is all about and to determine the best way to get started, Chapter 1 is definitely the best place to begin reading.

Never before has the opportunity to publish a professional-looking book been available to so many people at such an affordable price. After you've written your manuscript, by following the advice offered in this book, you can become a published author in a matter of weeks and begin selling your book. If you have something important, relevant, or entertaining to say, self-publishing is a viable option for distributing your message to the public.

Part I
Do It Yourself: Getting Started with Self-Publishing

The 5th Wave   By Rich Tennant

Working deckside, self–publisher Janine Walker mistakenly coats herself with writer's block instead of sunblock.

Dang!

WRITE NO MORE

In this part . . .

You've heard the phrase *self-publishing*, but what does it really mean? This part offers an introduction to self-publishing and helps you get your publishing project off the ground. I tell you about the pros and cons of self-publishing and explain how to equip yourself to start the writing process. I also give you the lowdown on assembling a winning manuscript and editing it carefully.

Chapter 1

Welcome to Self-Publishing!

*D*o you have expertise that other people can benefit from? Do you want to share an amazing story? Do you have basic writing skills and a good command of the English language? Do you have the discipline to write a full-length manuscript? If you answered yes to at least two of these questions, you may have the "write stuff" to become a published author. But there's one problem: Many major book publishing companies aren't willing to work with first-time authors with little or no writing experience. In the past, this fact could've kept you from achieving your dream of becoming a published author but not anymore!

Thanks to new digital printing technologies anyone with good writing skills and a great idea for content can have a book professionally published and made available to the general public. The process is called self-publishing. *Self-publishing* offers many awesome benefits and allows ordinary people, business leaders, celebrities, entrepreneurs, educators, students, retired people, stay-at-home moms, and just about anyone else to become a published author for a relatively low financial investment. What's required, however, is a tremendous amount of time, creativity, and discipline to write, edit, design, publish, promote, distribute, and sell your book (that is, if you want it to be successful, and who doesn't want to be successful?).

This chapter provides an overview of what becoming a self-published author involves. The rest of this book takes you step-by-step through the entire self-publishing process. By the time you're done reading *Self-Publishing For Dummies,* you can put your knowledge and ideas into writing and have them published in book form.

Figuring Out Whether Self-Publishing Is the Best Option for You

When you get hired as an author by a major publishing house, your job is to write the book's manuscript and perhaps gather some or all the artwork that's included within that book. For this work, you're typically paid an advance and a royalty on book sales. Various experts working for the publisher handle all the other steps (and there are many of them) in the publishing process.

Self-publishing is different. As the author, you're still responsible for writing your book's manuscript, but you're also responsible for every other aspect of the book publishing process. (Don't worry; as you delve into the self-publishing process, you're able to hire a wide range of freelancers and companies to handle some of the major steps in the publishing process, but you ultimately are the decision maker and person in charge of the project.)

In Chapter 2, you find out specifically why you should consider self-publishing, and you discover the benefits of the process. Chapter 2 also reveals how just about any type of content, fiction or nonfiction, can be self-published and transformed into a paperback or hardcover book. You also find out the specific skills you need to become a self-published author.

Don't get too excited just yet! Self-publishing does offer an amazing opportunity for just about anyone to have their book professionally published. However, compared to having your book published by a major publishing company, self-publishing has some drawbacks as well (covered in Chapter 2).

Gathering the Right Publishing Tools

Before you sit down to write your potential bestseller, gather the proper writing and publishing tools. Chapter 3 focuses on what you need to write a book with success. Some prewriting tasks you need to accomplish include

✔ Creating a comfortable writing environment

✔ Identifying and minimizing distractions when you're writing

✔ Putting together the perfect writer's toolbox

As an author, you need certain tools to make the writing process easier and to be able to maximize your productivity. A desktop or laptop computer that's equipped with a powerful word processor (such as Microsoft Word) and that has access to the Internet and a printer can be your most important tools, unless you plan to write the first draft of your book freehand, using a pad and pen. (If you do this, expect to wind up with a very tired hand!)

Putting Together a Winning Manuscript

The beauty of self-publishing is that almost any type of content can be transformed into a professionally published book. Depending on the type of book you're writing, a full-length manuscript may be anywhere from 50,000 to 100,000 words (or longer). There are plenty of exceptions, however. A children's book may contain 500 or fewer words, but a compilation of poems or short stories or a photo book or a cookbook containing recipes may all follow different formats altogether.

The trick to writing a successful book is carefully defining your book's audience and then making sure that the content of your book (and later all the marketing for it) targets that same specific audience. I explain how to determine your target audience in Chapter 4.

Coming up with the perfect book idea — something that's unique or that offers a new twist on something that's been written about before — is an important step in the book writing and publishing process. Equally important is researching your information and making sure that you have enough interesting and informative content to fill a book. The information then needs to be properly organized so it makes sense and is useful to the reader.

Most authors begin the writing process by creating a detailed outline for their book before they actually start researching, writing, and adding visual elements like photos and illustrations. Chapter 4 focuses on how to prepare an outline, research the content for your book, and decide what elements you want to incorporate into your manuscript.

Editing Your Work Effectively

After writing the book, it's time to edit. This process includes correcting spelling and grammatical mistakes, ensuring that the content is well organized and comprehensive, and doing some fine-tuning to ensure that the book properly targets its audience. At this stage in the publishing process, you may want to hire a freelance editor to review your manuscript. Even best-selling authors use professional editors to fine-tune their work before it's published.

The editing process requires several steps. It's an excellent strategy to begin by editing your own work and then hiring a professional editor to fine-tune the manuscript. In Chapter 5, find out what a professional editor does and how to hire someone who's highly skilled. Editing requires a very different skill set than writing, and people train for years to learn how to edit well.

Dealing with Administration and Design

Depending on what your goals are for your book, some self-published authors establish their own small publishing company (a formal business entity), especially if they plan to directly sell and distribute their book. Discover in Chapter 6 why forming a company can be beneficial.

Even without establishing your own publishing company, as a self-published author, some administrative tasks need to be completed before your book goes to press. For example, all books need an ISBN, a Library of Congress Card Number, and a copyright notice. Chapter 7 outlines many of these tasks.

Many companies that offer comprehensive publishing solutions for self-published authors, including Print-On-Demand (POD) publishers (described in Chapter 11), can handle some or all these administrative tasks on your behalf. Using one of these comprehensive publishing solutions is helpful to first-time authors because the service makes the whole process easier and saves you considerable time and money.

In addition to the many administrative tasks that must be completed before a book gets published, the manuscript must be laid out and designed, and the book's front and back cover need to be created. These steps you can handle yourself, using desktop publishing and graphic design software, or you can hire a professional graphic designer to do this design work for you.

Graphic design is a skill that takes tremendous creativity, artistic flair, and training and experience. For your book to look as professional as possible, consider hiring an experienced graphic designer to handle your book's interior layout and design and to design your book's front and back cover.

Chapter 8 focuses on how to design and lay out the interior of your book, using desktop publishing software, such as InDesign CS2, QuarkXPress, or Microsoft Publisher. Chapter 9 provides the information you need to create the most impressive and high-impact front and back cover possible.

Checking Out Your Printing Options

Published books come in all shapes and sizes. You have a handful of options when it comes to actually printing your book:

- *Traditional printing* options involve using offset printing technology to publish a large quantity of books at one time. This process is used by major publishing houses and offers many advantages but also a few drawbacks for self-published authors. See Chapter 10 for more details.

- *Print-On-Demand* (POD) has become the most viable publishing option for the majority of self-published authors (despite some small drawbacks). POD requires a relatively low initial financial investment and requires the author to maintain little or no inventory. For all the benefits and drawbacks of PODs, see Chapter 11.

- *eBooks* are another popular form of published material. Chapter 12 delves into how and why you may want to publish your book as an eBook and how you can potentially use a local print shop to photocopy and bind your book for small print runs.

Before choosing which printing and publishing option is right for you, consider your goals, your distribution plan, and your budget of your book. (Keep in mind that marketing, advertising, and promoting your book also requires a significant investment.)

No matter which printing and publishing option you choose, you should develop a good rapport with the company you work with. Chapter 13 focuses on how to develop a good rapport with any printer.

Delving into Distribution

As a self-published author, one of your biggest challenges (besides writing the book) is to get it into the hands of readers. You can sell your book in many ways; the trick is to find distribution methods that work best for your book and allow you to achieve your sales goals. Here are some methods:

- **Online booksellers:** In Chapter 14, you find out about distribution through online booksellers, like Amazon.com and Barnes & Noble.com, which for many self-published authors is the most viable and inexpensive way of making a book available to the general public.

- **Retail distribution:** Chapter 15 focuses on traditional distribution through retail booksellers and other specialty retailers. You find out about working with wholesalers and distributors, independent bookstores, specialty retail stores, direct mail, and professional organizations.

When you try to distribute your book through major retailers, you may be competing head-on with the major publishing companies that are supported by teams of professional salespeople who've well-developed connections to key buyers at the various retailers. You may be at a disadvantage in this situation, but as you can see in Chapter 15, your book can find its way onto the shelves of major bookstore chains and mass-market retailers.

If you plan to sell your own book to distributors, wholesalers, retailers, booksellers, or individual consumers, you need to deal with warehousing, order fulfillment, and shipping. Chapter 16 provides an overview of what's required when it comes to distributing your book.

After achieving some level of success as a self-published author, many people team up with a major publishing house to obtain nationwide distribution through the major bookstore chains and other retailers. For some self-published authors, approaching a major publishing house is a viable option. The benefits of working with a major publisher are explored in Chapter 17.

Getting the Word Out with Publicity and Marketing

Your book may not sell no matter how good it is unless you develop a comprehensive, effective, and well-timed marketing, publicity, and advertising campaign to reach and convince your intended audience. The following elements are a few successful publicity and marketing campaigns:

- ✔ Generating free publicity in all forms of media (radio, television, newspapers, magazines, newsletters, and the Internet) is one of the most powerful and cost-effective ways for self-publishers to generate awareness of their book. If handled correctly, public awareness can be transformed directly into book sales.

  In Chapter 18, I cover how to develop the publicity materials you need to promote your book properly. I cover items such as the press kit folder, press release, author bio, author photo, and pitch letter. Chapter 19 focuses on how to use those materials to generate media reviews, articles, and features about your book.

- ✔ Another way to educate potential readers about your book is through paid advertising. Advertising allows you to distribute your exact marketing message through appropriate media outlets. Chapter 20 covers how to create effective ads to promote and sell your book.

✓ The Internet offers you the opportunity to utilize cost-effective niche marketing techniques to easily target your book's intended audience. Tapping the incredible power of the Internet to promote your book is the focus of Chapter 21.

Whether your book sells for $9.95 or $29.95, your profit potential is ultimately limited because the book itself is a low-priced item compared to most other products with higher profit margins. Self-published authors need to use the recognition and credibility they receive as a published author and repackage their book's content into other, higher-priced items, such as DVDs and audio books. Many self-published authors also generate additional revenues by lecturing and hosting seminars or training programs relating to their book's topic. How to generate additional revenue streams from the content of your book is covered in Chapter 22.

Surveying a Brief Self-Publishing Timeline

Self-publishing your book isn't a fast and easy project. Plan on investing considerable time into each step of the process, especially when it comes to actually writing the manuscript.

Unfortunately, determining how long it takes you to sit down and write the full-length manuscript for your book is impossible until you actually begin writing and understanding more about your personal work habits as a writer. For some people, the researching and writing process takes weeks. For others, it takes months or years. After you've completed your manuscript, you can more accurately calculate a production timeline for your book, based on the printing and publishing decisions you make.

Here is a rough timeline of tasks to handle after you finish writing the manuscript:

❑ Establish your publishing company (if applicable).

❑ Have the manuscript edited.

❑ Choose a self-publishing option, such as offset printing or POD, and then hire a printer and/or publisher.

❑ Apply for an ISBN, copyright, and other book-specific information, if necessary (this step may be handled for you, depending on the publishing process you choose and the company you work with).

❑ Set the cover price for your book.

❑ Select a publication date.

❑ Have the manuscript's interior pages designed and laid out.

❑ Hire a graphic designer and create your book's front and back covers.

❑ Develop press materials for your book.

❑ Plan and implement a comprehensive marketing, public relations, and advertising campaign.

❑ Develop a Web site to promote your book.

❑ Begin pre-selling your book (pre-selling includes putting together and sending out press materials, promoting the book to distributors, lining up booksellers to sell the book, taking out ads, and so on).

❑ Have your book listed with online retailers.

❑ Publish the book and ship it to consumers, booksellers, retailers, and distributors (as appropriate).

❑ Continue promoting and marketing your book as you take orders.

As you develop your timeline, allocate ample time for each step of the publishing process to wind up with the best possible finished product. For example, a professional editor may take several weeks to edit your manuscript. It can then take a professional graphic designer at least a week or two to create a professional front and back cover (potentially longer), and additional time may be needed to do the layout and design work necessary for your book's interior.

As you read each chapter of this book, consider how long each step in the process may take you, based on your unique lifestyle, responsibilities, and personal situation. Make sure that the timeline and deadlines you set for yourself are realistic, using the time estimates you read about in each chapter. Stay focused on your goals and deadlines, and work hard to achieve them!

After the manuscript is complete, with proper planning, you can potentially have it professionally published in as little as two to three months. Just think, in 60 to 90 days, you can be a published author!

Chapter 2

Understanding the Pros and Cons of Self-Publishing

In This Chapter

▶ Considering self-publishing as an option for your book

▶ Looking at the benefits and potential drawbacks

▶ Surveying the skills that self-published authors need

▶ Wondering whether becoming a full-time self-published writer is right for you

So, you've decided to write a book. You have a great idea for content, you know your topic, and you've pinpointed your targeted audience. Or perhaps you've already written the manuscript that you believe has the potential to sell well. Now, you need to make a big decision. Are you going to approach major publishing houses in hopes of getting them to publish, distribute, and market your book, or do you plan to self-publish?

Thanks to a variety of recent technological developments in printing and distribution, self-publishing has become a more viable and cost-effective option than ever before. This chapter explores the pros and cons of self-publishing and helps you decide if publishing your own book is the right decision for you.

Why Should You Even Consider Self-Publishing?

Pursuing a traditional route for getting your book published may not be possible. It doesn't mean that you can't or shouldn't pursue your goal of getting your book written, published, and distributed, but self-publishing offers you — the author — a variety of benefits and significantly greater creative control over your project. Check out the additional reasons why you should consider self-publishing:

✔ **Competition in the traditional book publishing industry has become extremely fierce.** Tens of thousands of books are published every year and distributed through major retail stores, but only a small fraction of those books actually become bestsellers and earn a significant profit for the publishers and authors.

✔ **Getting the attention of a major publishing house is hard.** Even if writers develop a well-written proposal and are represented by a well-known literary agent, the chances of publication are still slim.

Unfortunately, it's likely that many potential bestsellers get passed over by the publishing houses, either because a proposal was one of thousands received that didn't get the proper attention, or because the publisher didn't have the resources to take the gamble involved with publishing a book by an unknown author.

✔ **You have 100-percent control over your publishing project.** This control even includes what content goes in your book. You don't have to answer to editors, a publisher, a publishing company's sales or marketing department, or anyone else when developing your book's content.

✔ **You can set your own schedule.** Decide when you want to write, edit, publish, market, and sell your own book. You can fast-track the project and make it available to the public within a few short weeks or months, or you can take your time and handle each step of the publishing process at your leisure. You aren't tied to deadlines imposed by a major publishing house.

Is self-publishing right for you? Maybe you need a checklist of sorts to see if you fall under the criteria for becoming a self-published author. Well, I've provided a list below. How convenient! Self-publishing your book may be the ideal solution for you, if the following criteria apply:

✔ You're a first-time author looking to publish, market, and distribute your book, but you can't get the attention of a major publisher.

✔ You're a business professional or expert in your field and want to use a published book as a marketing tool to enhance your professional credibility and reputation.

✔ You're an established author who wants 100-percent creative control over your next book project, and you want to make more money per copy sold than you would working with a major publisher.

✔ You want to put information in book form, such as your autobiography or family genealogy, and distribute it to a small group of friends and family.

✔ You represent a company that needs to develop book-length publications or manuals in-house.

✔ You work with a group or association and need to create a fundraising item, such as a cookbook or yearbook, that's sold to raise money and/or is distributed to members.

✔ You own the rights to republish a currently out-of-print book that you believe still has a viable market.

Before making the decision to pursue self-publishing, though, make sure that you review the potential drawbacks, which are outlined later in this chapter. For the author, self-publishing requires a much greater time commitment (above and beyond just writing the book's manuscript), a lot more work, and a financial investment.

What Are the Benefits of Self-Publishing?

Some of the biggest benefits of self-publishing include

✔ Having the ability to publish any type of content

✔ Maintaining total control over your entire project, including all creative control over the manuscript, cover design, and marketing of your book

✔ Saving time because the time it takes to self-publish a book can be significantly faster than working with a major publishing house

✔ Earning significantly highly royalties per copy of your book sold

✔ Keeping money in your pocket because you don't have to hire a literary agent to help you market your book

You may decide that approaching the major publishing houses, after finding out about the benefits of self-publishing in the following sections, isn't something that you want to do. You don't want to risk potential rejection and have to give up a lot of control over your project in order to get your manuscript published, so the self-publishing option may be more worth it for you.

After you decide that self-publishing is the right direction to go with your book project, you need to determine the most cost-effective and viable printing option that's based on your needs, goals, and budget. Part III of this book focuses on actually printing and publishing your manuscript using traditional printing methods, Print-On-Demand (POD) technology, eBook publishing, and local print shops.

Self-publish any type of content

No matter what type of book or the content of your book that you're looking to write and get published, chances are self-publishing is your answer. Thanks to the U.S. Constitution and the Amendments, the United States has freedom of speech and freedom of the press. If there's a topic that may be considered too controversial or edgy for a major publishing house, through self-publishing you have total control over the content of your book.

Although your book may not be controversial, its target audience may be too narrow for a major publishing house to consider sales worthy. Yet, if you know exactly how to market your book to your intended audience, publishing your book can become a profitable endeavor. (Check out Part V for the full scoop on publicity and marketing.)

Through self-publishing, you can publish any type of content. The possibilities are truly endless. Here are some of the common topics or genres authors have had success with through self-publishing:

- Autobiographies or biographies
- Children's books (fiction or nonfiction)
- Collection of artwork, drawings, or paintings
- Collection of poems or essays
- Cookbooks or a collection of recipes
- How-to books
- Reference books or textbooks
- Training manuals or guidebooks
- Works of fiction, such as a full-length novel or collection of short stories in any genre (horror, sci-fi, romance, comedy, adventure, erotica, and so on)

Self-publishing gives virtually anyone the ability to become a published author to share ideas, knowledge, experience, or creativity in a variety of formats. These books can then be distributed through almost any type of distribution channel including bookstores, retail stores, mail orders, and online (see Part IV for more about book distribution). And not only does self-publishing allow you to publish any type of content, but also it allows you to cost-effectively publish any number of copies of your book.

Maintain control over the entire process

When you publish your own book, you wear both the author and the publisher hats. You're ultimately responsible for handling *all* the work that a major publishing house typically handles on behalf of authors:

- ✔ Getting the manuscript edited
- ✔ Creating page layouts and design
- ✔ Crafting a front and back cover
- ✔ Getting the book printed
- ✔ Distributing your the book
- ✔ Managing marketing, advertising, and promotion

(What, you're not an expert in all these areas? Well, you're in luck once again. Every step is covered in this book!)

Authors who work with a major publishing house must give up a lot of creative control over their book project. It's the author's job to write the manuscript. The publisher typically handles everything else, often without consulting the author on creative decisions. Authors who have their book published by a major publishing house don't typically get a say on cover design or how their book is marketed or promoted.

By self-publishing your book, you're the boss. You can hire freelancers and consultants to help you edit, design, publish, distribute, and market your book, but ultimately, you're responsible for making all the creative and business decisions. So, if you're emotionally close to your book and don't want anyone taking away your ability to make creative decisions, self-publishing offers you a great opportunity to get your book published on your terms.

Taking on total control of your entire book project requires you to make a wide range of business decisions that impact the sales success and profitability of your book. You're responsible for the financial investment needed to print, distribute, advertise, market, and promote your book. See "What Are Self-Publishing's Drawbacks?" later in this chapter.

Quickly get your book into the hands of readers

Bringing a book to print yourself can happen significantly faster than if you were working with a major publisher. By self-publishing your book, you have the flexibility to set your own schedule and deadlines, without having to cater to the needs or demands of a major publishing company. You can dedicate the time and effort needed to write, edit, and publish your book in a few weeks or months, or you can take your time and complete each step of the publishing process at your own convenience. You set your own schedule, based on other personal and professional demands on your life.

When you work with a major publisher, bringing your book to print can take up to two years. Using many self-publishing techniques, such as POD or eBook (see Chapters 11 and 12), the process (after the manuscript is fully written) can take just a few weeks.

Achieve your career-related goals

Some people write books because they want to pursue writing as a career. (Check out "Can Self-Publishing Be a Full-Time Gig?" later in this chapter for more about this career option.) Others, however, use their work to promote other aspects of their established career.

After you become a published author, you instantly become a credible "expert" on whatever topic you wrote about. People respect authors and the knowledge they share. Therefore, being a published author can help you

  ✔ Land a new job in your area of expertise

  ✔ Earn a raise or promotion with your current employer

  ✔ Launch or expand your own business and earn the respect of customers

  ✔ Become a consultant or freelancer in your area of expertise

  ✔ Earn extra money lecturing or teaching seminars on your book's topic

  ✔ Be the media's go-to person whenever a news story breaks about your topic

  ✔ Pursue writing as a full-time career, assuming you're able to sell enough books or write enough articles for newspapers and magazines to earn a living

In addition, after your book publishes, it can be used as a powerful marketing tool for yourself and/or your company. The book serves as a resume or business card for promoting yourself as an expert in your field and helps you pursue your professional goals.

Depending on how you utilize your book as a marketing tool, the profits you generate from actual book sales can be insignificant compared to the boost in income from generated new business because potential clients and customers were able to find you as a result of reading your book or being exposed to publicity about your book.

Many self-published authors use their book as a promotional or marketing tool and give away free copies of their book to potential and existing clients. Wouldn't you consider giving away a book that costs between $5 and $10 per copy if you could generate hundreds or thousands of dollars in new revenue?

Published authors who have a proven track record can earn a significantly higher income and become a recognized expert in their field (compared to other in their professions who haven't written a book). The recognition and respect you receive as a published author can be extremely valuable.

Earn more royalties

Major publishers typically pay authors a recoupable advance, plus a pre-determined royalty on book sales as compensation. Writers who self-publish their books, however, must cover all their project's development, printing, distribution, and marketing costs out-of-pocket. The profit potential, how-ever, can be significantly greater.

Instead of receiving a 25-cent, 50-cent, or even a dollar royalty for each copy of your book sold, a self-published author can earn 40 to 60 percent of the book's cover price and sometimes even more. So, if your book sells for $15 per copy and you sell just 1,000 copies, the profit is between $6,000 and $9,000.

Conversely, if you're an author whose book is published by a major publish-ing house, you earn only a 25-cent royalty per book. If that book only sells 1,000 copies, your earnings are a mere $250. As initial sales are generated from your book, you potentially have to repay your outstanding advance to the publisher. (If the book doesn't sell, however, the advance doesn't need to be repaid.) Even if that's been done, your literary agent often takes between 15 and 20 percent of your earnings as his commission (see the following sec-tion, "Save money without a literary agent"). If the major publishing house sells tens of thousands of copies of your book, as the author, you stand to earn a decent income. This, however, doesn't always happen.

Another benefit to self-publishing is that you don't have to wait three to six months to receive royalty checks from the publisher. Authors who have their book published by a major publishing house often have to wait for the money they've earned, but self-published authors tend to be paid a lot faster, espe-cially on copies of the book they sell directly to customers. Self-published authors also aren't subject to a withholding of royalties as a reserve against returns for up to six additional months.

As a self-publisher you stand to earn more money per copy of your book sold, but it's also considerably harder, but not impossible, for self-publishers to get distribution in major bookstores. So you need to develop innovative ways to market and sell your book. Part V helps you kick start your public relations, marketing, and advertising efforts.

Save money without a literary agent

A literary agent is compensated by the author and typically receives a commission of between 15 to 20 percent of the author's revenues. As a self-published author, you don't need to work with a literary agent, which saves you money and gives you greater control over your entire book project.

The job of a literary agent is to help an author sell his book idea to a publisher, negotiate publishing contracts, and ensure that the author receives timely royalty payments from the publishing house. Not having proper representation by a literary agent keeps many authors from being noticed by major publishers.

Keep in mind that if you want to sell your self-published book to a major publisher down the road, you may benefit from hiring an agent. Also, most of the major publishing houses now require their authors to be represented by an established literary agent. But the choice is up to you. See Chapter 17 for details on selling your book the major publishers.

What Are Self-Publishing's Drawbacks?

Although many reasons exist for wanting to self-publish your book (see the previous section), a few drawbacks exist, too, when committing yourself to this type of publishing venture. These cons include large time and cost considerations, specific distribution issues, and finding professionals to help you produce the best book possible. I discuss them in the following sections.

Recognizing the time and costs involved

Having total control of the publishing process can be a double-edged sword, but from a creative standpoint, it can be liberating. Practically speaking, the time and financial commitment may be too much for you.

✔ **Time commitment:** Although all authors have to invest the time and energy to actually write the manuscript for their book, self-published authors also have to invest the time needed to edit, layout and design, print, market, advertise, promote, sell, and distribute their book. Each of these steps is vitally important in the success of a book, and each requires a time commitment on your part. If you're willing to write a self-published book but not prepared to invest the time necessary to promote and sell it, nobody will know that your book exists, and your sales may be minimal. The more time and energy you invest in marketing, advertising, promotions, and sales, the better your chances are of selling large quantities of books and generating high profits.

✔ **Financial considerations:** From a financial standpoint, all the costs associated with the publishing process become your responsibility as a self-published author. Depending on the approach you take, this expense can be anywhere from a few hundred dollars to thousands of dollars. The goal, however, is to invest money in marketing and advertising that generates higher sales for your book and results in higher profits. If all goes well, the investment you make offers a high return.

After you make the decision to self-publish, you must develop a plan to handle each major task or responsibility as both the author and the publisher. If you have the time, resources, and finances to handle all aspects of the self-publishing process, you're in excellent shape. However, if you're not equipped to handle even one aspect and you don't have the financial resources to hire experienced professionals to assist you (and save some of your own time), your potential for achieving success can diminish dramatically. See "Hiring all the help you want and need" later in this chapter for more information on hiring help.

Some of the popular ready-to-use self-publishing solutions, especially those that offer POD services (described in Chapter 11), can help you organize your publishing process. These services handle

✔ Basic layout and design

✔ Cover design

✔ ISBN number registration

✔ Hiring a professional editor to review your manuscript

In Chapter 6, you also see many of the business-related expenses in the budget as you set up your publishing company and begin making plans to write, publish, promote, distribute, and sell your book. Having your own company can have significant tax advantages and ultimately save you a lot of money and give you and your book additional credibility.

Encountering specific distribution snags

If you compare a self-published book with a trade paperback book published by a major publishing house, you may find many similarities in your book and any other book you'd see displayed on a bookstore's shelf (that's if you follow the advice offered in this book and create a professional looking book). In fact, you'd probably have a difficult time differentiating between the two products if you saw them side-by-side. Both a self-published book and a book published by a major publishing house follow the same basic format, including overall layout and design, front and back cover, how the title, price, barcode, and other information is conveyed, and the publishing materials used, such as the cover and internal paper stock.

But a difference does exist: The big difference between a self-published book and a book published by the major publishing house is the resources available for distribution, marketing, advertising, and promotion. The major publishers have fully-staffed and experienced people handling all these areas. They also have established distribution with the major bookstore chains. As a self-publisher, you may not have these resources at your disposal.

As a self-published author, you *can* have your book listed with Amazon.com or Barnes & Noble.com's Web site to sell your books. Chapter 14 explains how to work with these online distributors and retailers.

Realistically, getting traditional bookstore distribution for a self-published book, especially a book from a first-time author, however, is extremely difficult and often almost impossible. Major bookstore chains have buyers that deal primarily with the major publishing houses. Unless you work with a distributor or sales representative with experience getting your books into mainstream distribution, don't count on bookstore or mass-market retail distribution for your book.

Realistically, although you could sell your book through independent bookstores and specialty retailers, your sales, distribution, and marketing plan for your book should include alternate distribution options. These options include online sales, direct mail, and direct selling through your clients and people who attend your lectures or author appearances. Part IV focuses on how to distribute your self-published book effectively.

Make sure that your distribution expectations are realistic. You may have trouble obtaining national or international bookstore distribution for your self-published book. Some of the most successful self-published authors have a pre-existing way to reach their target audience. Plan on grassroots marketing to sell your book. This marketing plan includes

- ✔ Direct mail
- ✔ Existing customers or clients

✔ Extensive PR campaigning

✔ Online marketing

✔ Students

Hiring all the help you want and need

As you read *Self-Publishing For Dummies,* you discover the responsibilities of a self-published author. To maximize your success in creating, publishing, distributing, and selling your book, seriously consider hiring experienced professionals in the book publishing industry.

Although the publisher or printing company you use to self-publish your book offers a variety of services to you (see Part III for details on printing services), consider hiring the following types of freelance professionals to help you with various aspects of the self-publishing process:

✔ **Ghostwriter:** This person helps you actually write your manuscript (see Chapter 4).

✔ **Photographer, illustrator, artist, or graphic designer:** The job of this person is to help you create and incorporate graphics and other visual elements within your book (see Chapter 4).

✔ **Editor:** Your editor proofreads your manuscript and final page layouts (see Chapter 5). Depending on your deal with the editor you hire, he or she may only edit your book's raw manuscript. You may also need to hire a separate proofreader to review the final page layouts of your book. Handle this negotiation when you hire an editor. See Chapter 13 for more info on proofreaders.

✔ **Graphic designer:** This professional assists with your book's internal page layout and design, as well as the front and back cover design (see Chapters 8 and 9).

✔ **Sales representative:** A sales rep helps you obtain distribution of your book through retail stores, catalogs, and distributors (see Chapter 15).

✔ **Public relations, advertising, and marketing consultant:** This person creates, launches, and manages all aspects of publicity, advertising, and marketing (see Chapters 18 and 19).

✔ **Web site designer:** Make a presence on the Internet and hire a person to develop your Web site, so you can have a professional mass-marketed presence for your book (see Chapter 21).

Determine your needs and budget before negotiating with any type of freelancer. Most freelance professionals expect to be paid on a per-project basis, or they may bill by the hour. Make sure that you hire people with experience doing whatever it is you need them to do. Also review resumes and portfolios of work, as appropriate and ask for references from satisfied clients before hiring your team.

With the help of this book, you can handle most, if not all, of the tasks associated with self-publishing yourself, which saves you money and allows you to discover all aspects of the publishing business. Ultimately, you need to decide how involved you want to get with the process, keeping in mind that none of the major steps can be skipped if you want your book to be successful.

Do You Have the Skills that All Self-Published Authors Need?

An author who writes a book for a major publishing house is responsible mainly for the completion of the book's manuscript in a timely manner. As a self-published author, you're responsible for a lot more. The following sections help you determine if you have what it takes to become a successful self-published author or if you should focus first on fine-tuning your core skills.

Being willing to work hard

Writing the manuscript for your book can be a time-consuming project. After the manuscript is complete, more of the business aspect of the work really begins. Before embarking on a self-publishing project, ask yourself, "Am I really willing to work hard and dedicate the time and energy needed to do this project right?" Are you prepared to master new skills and focus your energies, as their needed, on each aspect of the book publishing process?

Each person is totally different. There's no way to predict what type of time commitment is required when writing your book. Everyone writes at a different speed and is willing to invest a different amount of time on each step of the process. Every project is totally different. So don't compare yourself to other authors, and use your time wisely to finish your book to the best of *your* ability.

Catering to your audience with the right writing style

Chances are you've decided to write a book because you have knowledge, experience, or an idea that you want to share with others. Like composing music or creating a sculpture or painting, writing is an art form. As an expert in your field, you need to be able to communicate your thoughts and ideas using the written word.

No matter what type of book you're writing, it's vital that you thoroughly understand the book's intended audience (see Chapter 4 for more about targeting certain readers). The vocabulary, sentence structure, and information within your book should all cater specifically to your book's target audience. The words you use, your sentence structure, and your use of punctuation and grammar make your book easy or difficult to understand.

For example, writing a children's book that's targeted to a 6-year-old and writing a how-to book written for college educated professionals differ greatly. The vocabulary you use should be easy for the reader to understand, and you never want to insult the reader's intelligence either. Good author know how to write specifically for the audience they're trying to reach.

Hire a ghostwriter to help you complete your manuscript if you're having trouble writing (see "Hiring all the help you want and need" earlier in this chapter). Or participate in a few writing classes to help craft your writing skills. Writing classes and workshops are offered at many community colleges, through local adult education programs, and through professional writers' and authors' associations. Refer to recent issues of *The Writer* or *Writer's Digest* magazines (available at most newsstands) for ads on writer's conferences, classes, and workshops that are held throughout the country.

It's your responsibility, as the writer, to create a manuscript that is well-researched and written and that appeals to your intended audience. If you hire an editor (see Chapter 5 about hiring an editor), it's the editor's job to fine-tune your manuscript and correct any errors; it's not his job to rewrite your manuscript completely so it adheres to basic rules of English style and punctuation. Never rely on your editor to take a poorly written manuscript and transform it into what could become a bestseller.

Injecting creativity and personality into your work

Having a great idea for a book is one thing, but being able to write a manuscript that's fun, engaging to read, informative, and well-written is something else altogether. If you're writing a how-to book, for example, what sets your book apart from the countless others that are published by the major publishing houses? What makes people want to read your book? After they decide to read it, what about your book keeps their attention?

Make sure that you develop your own voice as a writer and discover how to incorporate not just your knowledge and experience but your personality into your book in order to make it more appealing to readers. For some writers, creativity comes naturally. They've been given a gift that makes them good storytellers and excellent written communicators. Others need to work on developing their creativity skills and incorporating imagination into their writing. Check out the following ways to inspire your creativity:

- ✔ Take writing classes
- ✔ Attend adult education programs
- ✔ Enroll at the local community college
- ✔ Join a professional writer's association
- ✔ Read magazines that cater to writers
- ✔ Participate in a writer's workshop or special interest group
- ✔ Check the reference section of any bookstore for books on how to write fiction, nonfiction, children's books, poetry, or other types of literature

Becoming a good writer takes practice and is something that's acquired over time. Therefore, be prepared to write several drafts of your manuscript and have it undergo significant editing before it's ready for publication. If you're not sure you've managed to inject your own voice into your work, seek out constructive criticism from professional editors or other people you trust.

A bestselling book (by traditional standards) must appeal to the masses, not just a small niche audience, but if your book does target a narrowly defined audience, the way you convey your information still needs to cater to your readers and be easy to understand. If you're writing a novel or work of fiction, creativity is even more crucial. For example, your plot and characters need to capture the reader's imagination and take them on a journey. Keep in mind that a niche-oriented book can also have extremely strong sales potential over the long term. Your book may not make it onto a bestseller list, but it could sell a ton of copies and make you rich.

Honing your organizational skills

From the time you start working on your manuscript through the launch of your published book, taking a well-organized and deadline-oriented approach to each and every task associated with the publishing project helps keep you on track and within your budget.

This process has many steps and involves countless details, none of which can be allowed to fall through the cracks. If you get distracted easily or have trouble dealing with time management issues, check out these tips to help you get back on track:

- ✔ Keep detailed to-do lists of what you need to accomplish
- ✔ Set deadlines for yourself
- ✔ Stay focused on the big picture
- ✔ Micromanage the entire book publishing process
- ✔ Use an organization tool, such as a day planner or PDA

Don't allow yourself to become overwhelmed. The *divide and conquer* strategy works in almost every situation you encounter when it comes to handling the major tasks involved with self-publishing your book. When trying to complete a large task under a tight deadline, divide that task up into smaller, more manageable tasks. For example, instead of focusing on writing an entire 100,000-plus word manuscript, focus on completing each 5,000- to 8,000-word chapter. By focusing on and completing one chapter at a time, before you know it, your book is done. Chapter 1 has a brief self-publishing timeline that you can use to help you see the big picture.

Being self-motivated

One of the perks and drawbacks to self-publishing your book is that you are your own boss; therefore, no one breathes down your neck if you lose focus, fall behind in writing your manuscript, or miss an important deadline. For some people, getting overwhelmed when they're faced with having to accomplish tasks that they're not comfortable with is normal. If you're one of these people, determine in advance how you deal with difficult problems or situations. For example, if you have trouble sitting in front of your computer to write your book's manuscript because you keep getting distracted by the phone ringing, the dog barking, or your baby crying, you need to take active steps to eliminate those distractions. If you don't have a clue about marketing and advertising, consider hiring someone as a freelance consultant with this expertise to help you.

Stay motivated! As a writer and publisher, discover what motivates you, and do what's necessary to ensure that throughout the entire self-publishing process you accomplish each task in a professional and timely way. Your overall objective is to produce the best book for your readers. Ponder these motivations:

- ✔ Why are you writing the book and what do you hope to accomplish with it?
- ✔ Are you writing the book to establish yourself as an expert in your field and generate higher revenues as a paid consultant?

- ✔ Are you looking to communicate specific knowledge you possess to a group of interested readers?

- ✔ What do you hope to gain from the experience and investment of your time, effort, and money?

Don't be afraid to reward yourself for achieving specific daily, weekly, or monthly goals, and make a point to keep reviewing your progress to ensure that you're staying on track throughout the entire publishing process. Rewards can include time out of your schedule such as a night out with friends, a one-hour break to watch TV, or a run to Starbucks.

Can Self-Publishing Be a Full-Time Gig?

Being a professional, full-time, published writer can be a fun and rewarding occupation, but it's definitely not for everyone. Just because you've written one book-length manuscript doesn't mean that you have what it takes to quit your day job and become a full-time professional writer and self-publisher. Becoming a full-time writer means spending countless hours each day sitting in front of a computer typing, researching, and having minimal interaction with others. After all, for most people, writing isn't a team activity. If you're not writing, you're not being productive. If you're not being productive, you're not earning a living.

A full-time writer must possess the following abilities in order to earn a living:

- ✔ Disciplined hard worker

- ✔ Deadline-oriented

- ✔ Focus and organization

- ✔ Extreme creativity

- ✔ Cater to your audience

- ✔ Ability to sell your work to editors

- ✔ Financial means to market and promote yourself and your books

If you find writing to be enjoyable and rewarding, consider writing additional books as well as contributing articles to newspapers and magazines. You can do this on a freelance basis and still hold down a full-time job (in order to earn a living). And depending on how well your book sells, you might find that by supplementing book sales with paid author appearances, lecturing, and freelance article writing, that you can earn a full-time living.

Just as there are many bestselling authors out there, there are many, many more writers and authors who don't achieve success for a wide variety of reasons. If you don't have the skills that I discuss in the previous section, you may not be ready to become a full-time self-published author. Here are a few reasons why many authors fail to achieve success:

- **Lack of knowledge about the topic they're writing about:** If you don't have the knowledge and experience you need to be an expert on any given topic, doing the necessary research is critical before you actually begin writing. Check out Chapter 4 for more about research.

- **The inability to cope with writer's block:** At one time or another, all writers are faced with staring at a blank computer screen or sheet of paper and not being able to decide what to write or how to best put their ideas into words. That lack of ideas is called *writer's block.* The easiest thing to do is walk away and give up, but the best thing to do to battle writer's block is to ensure that you're chock-full of ideas about what you want to write about ahead of time and that you've done plenty of research and you're investing the time to fully develop your idea before sitting down to write.

- **The failure to hire out specialized tasks, particularly book design, to qualified professionals:** Too many self-published books look obviously amateurish because the author/publishers have decided that they can handle design themselves, even when they have no experience. The result is an unattractive cover and nearly unreadable type. The failure to hire editors as needed can make books difficult to read and eliminate the book's word-of-mouth potential with satisfied readers.

- **Poor marketing and promotional skills:** The ability to self-promote is one of the most important skills a writer should possess, especially if you plan to self-publish your work. If you don't properly promote your work, people may not know it exists, and they may never read it. Part V is full of helpful information on promoting your writing.

If you're interested in pursuing writing (and self-publishing) as a career, consider starting out part time, perhaps as a hobby. Write your first book or get a handful of newspaper and/or magazine articles published. Determine what area of writing you want to specialize in and begin fine-tuning your writing skills. Build up your experience, but don't give up your day job until you've established yourself as a writer with enough earning potential to support yourself.

Chapter 3

Equipping Yourself with the Write Stuff

....

....

*B*usiness executives work from offices (and golf courses); artists and musicians work in studios; and scientists work in laboratories. Each of these professions, along with countless others, requires that the person work within a special environment that's equipped with the tools they need to successfully complete their professional responsibilities. Because writing is both an art form and a job, most writers prefer to do their work in a specialized environment, which allows them to tap their true creativity, focus exclusively on their writing, and avoid common distractions.

This chapter focuses on how to create the ideal writing environment for yourself and how to gather the right combination of tools, equipment, and resources to ensure that your writing efforts are as productive and successful as possible.

Some of the tools in this chapter are also helpful in setting up and running your own self-publishing business. For details on additional self-publishing business supplies, see Chapter 6.

Fix It Up: Creating Your Ideal Writing Environment

Writing takes an incredible amount of focus, concentration, creativity, and, at times, research. Whether you're writing an essay, newspaper or magazine article, poem, short story, or the manuscript for a full-length book, as a writer, you need to focus not just on what you're trying to say but also on how you want to say it. Writing doesn't have a formula or easy, predefined steps you can follow to ensure that your finished product is a masterpiece.

As a writer, you need to follow established rules for grammar, punctuation, and spelling. Plus, if you want your writing to be understood, you need to use words that can be found in the dictionary. However, writing also involves creativity, organization, structure, and the ability to communicate with your readers by using only the written word (as opposed to spoken language, combined with body language and verbal intonations). Every word and sentence that you write need to convey meaning and emotion, and help the readers form a visual in their mind's eye.

To successfully write a well-written book and to be able to focus your talents on writing as an art form, most writers and authors find it extremely helpful to create a work environment for themselves that allows them to maximize their concentration, creativity, and writing skills. With the help of the following sections, you can create a writing environment virtually anywhere, as long as it's someplace where you're comfortable, able to think clearly, and relatively free from distractions.

Deciding where to work

The first step to creating the ideal work environment is to decide where you want to work: home, office, library, the park, an airplane, a train, or hotel room. As you choose your location, consider your needs. Ask yourself the following questions:

- ✔ Do I have ample space to work without feeling confined or claustrophobic?

- ✔ Is the lighting and climate appropriate where I want to work? Can I open windows, turn on lights, and adjust the temperature as needed?

- ✔ Is the environment clean and well organized?

- ✔ What distractions may I encounter? Does the phone constantly ring? Do my children scream in the background? Do people constantly drop by unannounced?

- ✔ What uncontrollable noise might I deal with? Does that noise bother me?

- ✔ What resources and equipment do I need at my disposal? Do I have the tools needed to conduct research such as access to the Internet? Is everything I need available and within reach? (See "Throw Away the Hammer: Assembling the Writer's Toolbox" later in this chapter for more about necessary tools.)

The writing space where you work needs to be a place that's comfortable for you and allows you to focus on writing (without distractions). This space may be a separate room or office in your home, an area of a room where you can spread out your writing tools and work effectively or even at a Starbucks or local coffee shop. Ideally, you don't want to feel confined or be distracted by outside stimuli when you're focused on writing. Every person has unique requirements for what constitutes an ideal writing environment. Do your best to define what works for you and then create that environment for yourself.

If you've created the ideal work space, you know it because you're able to be productive, work comfortably, and be free of distractions as you're working. The proof is in the pudding. If you're able to write and be proud of the work you're creating in the time you've dedicated to working, you're in good shape. If your work suffers or you're unproductive, consider modifying your workspace and environment.

Controlling your environment for maximum comfort and productivity

After you've established where you want to write the most, take control of your environment and make it fit your personal taste and needs by making the space most conducive to your personal work habits.

As you create your work environment, figure out exactly what work-related tasks you're going to do and make sure that you have the tools, resources, and equipment you need at your disposal. For example, if you're conducting phone interviews and doing research, having a telephone and recording equipment, along with access to the Internet and your reference books and paper-based files is critical. If you're setting up your computer system and related peripherals, such as a printer, you need ample electrical outlets and desk space for this equipment and someplace to store your supplies. (See "Throw Away the Hammer: Assembling the Writer's Toolbox" later in this chapter for more about writing tools.)

The perfect work environment should allow you to feel comfortable, relaxed, and focused on the task at hand. The furniture, décor, lighting, temperature, and ambiance should all be to your liking. Because you're going to be spending many hours at a time working in this environment, pay attention to ergonomics, especially in terms of your desk, chair, and computer keyboard. The environment should also be clean, clutter free, and well organized to help boost your creativity and productivity.

Sitting incorrectly for long periods of time, or having your hands at a bad angle when you're typing can cause back, neck, arm, and wrist pain, which can lead to other injuries. Not having proper lighting may strain your eyes and cause fatigue or headaches. If you're too warm or too cold in your workspace or uncomfortable where you're sitting, these factors can decrease your productivity, too.

Many office supply superstores (such as OfficeMax, Office Depot, or Staples) along with mail order catalogs, such as Levenger (www.levenger.com) and Relax The Back (www.relaxtheback.com), offer furniture specifically for designed home offices.

In addition to ensuring your physical comfort when working, focus on what helps you concentrate and bring about your creativity. Do you work well with music or TV playing in the background? Do you enjoy having a cup of coffee or a cold drink on your desk that you can sip throughout the day? Does using a particular aromatic candle or incense help you relax and focus? Every aspect of your environment can impact your comfort and creativity.

Even the smallest things can impact how productive and comfortable you are in your work environment. For instance, many writers use their computer to write. If this is the case for you, is your monitor large enough? Is there a glare from a nearby window that's distracting? Do you like your keyboard or is the clicking noise it makes too loud? If you're using a laptop, is the slightly smaller keyboard too small for you to use for extended periods?

Minimizing distractions and drains on your time

When you're trying to concentrate and be productive, there's nothing worse than being distracted. Multitasking is hard enough as a writer with trying to maintain focus, meet deadlines, be creative, and be productive at the same time. Constant distractions can greatly hinder your ability to work.

Pinpoint what distractions you're most apt to encounter while you're trying to work. Determine, in advance, how you control or minimize them. Also, consider how you're spending your time. Answering the telephone, responding to e-mails, interacting with people via instant messaging (IM), or taking too many breaks can all waste your time and keep you from your writing. The most common distractions are covered in the following sections.

An uncomfortable work environment

Make sure that you set yourself up with a comfortable desk and chair, ample lighting, and proper room temperature (or adjustable temperature). See the previous section for details on setting up a workspace that enhances productivity. Don't forget — even what you're wearing can affect your mood. Be comfy!

An impractical workspace layout

When you're working, you want to have a space that's organized and helps the flow of work and doesn't take up extra time to get things done. Here are some poor examples:

✔ If your printer is located across the room and you have to stand up and walk ten feet to pick up your printouts, that's poor planning.

✔ If you need to move around a lot to answer the phone or access your most important papers, you need to rearrange your workspace so it's better organized.

✔ Don't clutter your desk or work area with tools or items you don't use often.

Figure out what tools and equipment you need close by and then choose a desk and related furniture that allows you to have what you need where you need it. Office supply superstores and furniture stores offer a wide range of home office desks and furniture that allow you to maximize available space.

Unavailable resources

Before you sit down to start writing, make sure that you have everything you need within arm's reach. If you need specific research materials that aren't at your fingertips, you may have to stop what you're doing, find the necessary materials, and then go back to work. This interruption may even include a trip to the local library or searching through your files for something. I cover research materials in more detail later in this chapter.

An obsession with checking your e-mail or surfing the Internet

Everyday, people receive e-mails (many of which are spam or unsolicited junk). Reading and responding takes time. Plus, surfing the Internet can be a huge time waster. Being a writer takes discipline. Unless you're doing research that pertains directly to your work, perhaps you should disconnect your computer from the Internet while you're writing.

Aside from Web surfing, one of the worst distractions involving the Internet is IM. You don't want to get caught up in meaningless conversations with your Internet buddies while you're trying to write. For the most part, people use IM conversations to talk about gossip, pass along jokes, discuss the weather, or engage in unimportant chit-chat. To avoid being constantly distracted, disconnect from your favorite IM services when you're trying to concentrate on your writing. You can also put up an away message, so people know that you're working, if you must have the IM on.

Loud noises

Uncontrollable noise can be caused by a number of things: nearby traffic, airplanes flying overhead, construction, or obnoxious neighbors, children, and dogs. Try to find a work environment that's free from these distractions or find a way to deal with them. Here a few suggestions:

✔ If you have children or household pets, make sure that your space includes a door that you can shut and lock if necessary (make sure someone else is watching your kid, though!)

✔ Consider using noise reduction headsets while you're working. You can find these headsets at consumer electronics stores such as Best Buy or Circuit City.

✔ Playing music or the TV to drown out other noises can be an option for some people; however, this practice can be more distracting if you're not careful. If you're singing along with a song on the radio or trying to follow the plot of a TV show, chances are you're not focused on your work.

Constant incoming telephone calls

Telemarketers, friends, coworkers, relatives, and other people may call you throughout the day. These calls can be extremely inconvenient when you're trying to concentrate on your work. The easiest fix for this problem is to set up your answering machine or voice mail to answer calls automatically, so you don't even hear the ring. Then, take a break to check your messages every few hours, and set aside a time of day to call people back.

Unannounced visitors

If you're working in an office or even at home while others are present, set ground rules for when you're working. For example, block out several hours per day when you don't allow any intrusions whatsoever, unless it's an emergency. Consider placing a *Do Not Disturb* sign on the door, so people know not to bother you.

Worries about deadlines and other time-management considerations

Because writing is an art form, the process can't be rushed. The more you write, the more comfortable you become with your work habits. Your habits hopefully lead to meeting deadlines and making appointments and allow you to best maximize your use of time.

One way to avoid worrying about meeting a deadline is to ensure that when you start writing, you've already done all your research, so you know exactly what you plan to write. It's also extremely helpful for most writers to create a detailed outline for themselves, before they actually start writing. (See Chapter 4 for more information on outlines.) This preparedness gives you more confidence in your abilities with each writing session.

Proper time management also plays an important role in your ability to meet deadlines. Be realistic. Don't expect to write a 30-page chapter for a book in two or three hours. Allocate the necessary time in your schedule to accomplish your daily or weekly writing goals.

If you're thinking about everything else you need to accomplish, including other personal and professional responsibilities, you may never be able to focus on the task at hand — writing. The best way to deal with this situation is to block out a specific amount of time every day to write, knowing that you have the rest of the day to deal with your other obligations. For some people, this procedure may mean establishing a detailed work schedule. Some people block out entire weekends to do their writing and free themselves up during the week to manage their other responsibilities. Other writers prefer to work late at night to avoid common distractions. If you do this, make sure that you wind up getting enough sleep.

As you plan your writing schedule, take breaks throughout the day. Breaks can include the following:

- ✔ **5 to 15 minute breaks:** Reward yourself for reaching specific objectives or deadlines by taking 5 to 15 minute breaks.

- ✔ **Eating:** You also need to set aside time to eat a healthy meal and not just a granola bar and a soda as you work.

- ✔ **Stretching:** Your muscles get tense, especially if you've been sitting in front of your computer for several hours straight. Make sure that you take a break to stretch your muscles. Consider taking a walk around the block (and bring your dog, if you have one).

Throw Away the Hammer: Assembling the Writer's Toolbox

Every job enlists certain tools of the trade to complete the project. Writing is no different. Just as carpenters rely on hammers, doctors on scalpels, and painters on brushes, good writers need their own set of tools to help them maximize their productivity, organization, and creativity. The following sections help you gather what you need in your writer's toolbox.

The office equipment you need

Creating the right environment to do your writing is important. Equipping your workspace with the right tools is equally crucial for achieving success. In terms of office equipment and related technology, the following sections summarize what you need to get the job done right.

A desktop or laptop computer with appropriate software

Your computer can be your primary tool for writing, page layout and design, and cover design, as well as generating advertising, publicity, and marketing materials for your book. Depending on your work habits, using a desktop or laptop computer with a PC or Macintosh base is a personal decision. What's important is that you determine, in advance, how the computer is going to be used and then make sure that you invest in equipment capable of running all the software and peripherals you need. Here are some computer considerations:

- ✔ Almost any new PC or Mac-based computer on the market today can easily run word processing software, like Microsoft Word, plus be used to surf the Internet (see the next section). Microsoft Word, which is part of the Microsoft Office suite of applications, is the most commonly used word-processing software in the world. If you use other word-processing software, make sure that the files you create are Word compatible, so any editor or printer can access your files.

- ✔ If you use Print-On-Demand (POD) technology to publish your book, the company handles the necessary page layout and design for you. If, however, you're using a traditional printer to publish your book, you need to handle your own page layout and design. For this process, check out specialized software such as Adobe InDesign CS2.

See Chapter 8 for more about page layout software, Chapter 10 for details on traditional printers, and Chapter 11 for the scoop on POD technology.

An investment of under $1,000 (slightly more for a laptop computer) can buy you a well-equipped computer system. If you plan on running more complex page layout software, a computer with a larger capacity hard drive, faster processor, and more internal memory may be needed.

Computers are complex machines that occasionally break down. Therefore, always maintain a current backup on disk or flash drive of your important data, including your manuscript files. It's also worthwhile to invest in the extended service plan offered by most computer manufacturers and computer retailers. If you accidentally spill coffee on your keyboard, you have to pay for the repair unless you purchased the extended service agreement.

Before purchasing any computer, determine the manufacturer's repair policies and procedures for warranty and non-warranty issues. Some of the larger and more well-known computer manufacturers offer the worst customer service, technical support, and repair services in the industry. If you're relying on your computer and need it repaired quickly, make sure that the manufacturer will be there to help you. An alternative is to find a local computer repair shop with qualified technicians.

Internet access

As an author, in addition to sending and receiving e-mail, you may rely on the Internet to conduct a lot of your research, and if you're using a freelance editor or a printer who's not in your geographic area, you need to send and receive large manuscript files electronically.

Equipping your computer with Internet access has never been easier or cheaper. Obtaining a high-speed Internet connection, via DSL or Broadband cable, is a good investment. The cost of a high-speed Internet connection costs between $19.95 and $49.95 per month, depending on the provider and type of connection.

If your computer bites

Are you still a bit wary of computers? Other options for creating a manuscript include writing longhand (using a traditional pen and paper), using an old-fashioned typewriter (if you can find one that still works), or dictating your manuscript into a cassette recorder and later having it transcribed. But keep in mind that because most self-publishing relies on the creation of an electronic document (created using a word processor or page layout and design software) that ultimately goes to a printer, write out your manuscript in longhand or using a typewriter isn't too practical, but it can be done. You may be adding extra steps to the publishing process in order to prepare the manuscript appropriately. These steps also add to your costs.

Instead of investing in a traditional fax machine, a computer that's connected to the Internet can also be used to send and receive faxes. A service, like eFax.com (www.efax.com), makes easy work of sending and receiving faxes electronically from anywhere. For about $13 per month, eFax provides you with a unique fax phone number in your local area code. All of your incoming faxes arrive as e-mail messages in whatever e-mail account you specify. You can then view and print your faxes as PDF files, using your computer. If you have a laptop computer, you can send and receive faxes from anywhere that has an Internet connection.

A printer with handy features

For a writer producing a full-length manuscript, a good investment is a laser printer capable of printing at least 8 to 15 pages per minute. Having this capability is important because when you need to print chapters of your book or the entire manuscript to edit and review, printing doesn't take too long. A good laser printer costs between $300 and $500.

For some other handy features, you may want to invest in a wide-format color or laser printer that can handle 11-x-17-inch sheets of paper so you can easily view double-page spreads and view each page in its actual size (if you're creating and reviewing final page layout at home).

If you want to save space in a home office environment, consider investing in a laser printer that's also a scanner, fax machine, and photocopier. This combination printer is an excellent idea for a writer because it gives you a variety of tools right at your fingertips, especially if you're dealing with research materials that need to be organized, copied, received via fax, or scanned into a database for your document.

Telephone service

Whether you're conducting interviews, working with your editor over the phone, or discussing your book printing needs with a handful of publishers, you need access to a telephone.

If you want to establish your own publishing business (see Chapter 6 for details), invest in a company telephone line so your personal and business calls can be kept totally separate. Keep these tips in mind:

- ✔ Your telephone should be able to handle at least two phone lines and have a hold feature.

- ✔ Make sure that your phone service has the features you need, such as voice mail, call waiting, three-way calling, caller ID, call answering, and call forwarding.

- ✔ To facilitate order-taking, you may also want to arrange to have a toll-free phone number added to your existing phone service. See Chapter 16 for details on how to do this.

Chances are that you already have traditional home telephone service, but here are two other service options to consider:

- ✔ **Voice-Over-IP:** This service uses your high-speed Internet connection to give you local and long distance calling capabilities along with virtually all the calling features and services offered by traditional phone companies. Many Voice-Over-IP services are priced at a flat monthly fee, which varies depending on the provider. Check out Vonage at www.vonage.com as one service that you can use.

- ✔ **Cellular phones:** A cell phone has become an indispensable business tool; it's important to be able to reach people when you need them and to be readily accessible to the people and companies you work with. If you don't yet have a cell phone, service and equipment is available from a wide range of providers:

  - • **Sprint/NEXTEL:** Phone (800) 480-4727; Web site www.sprint.com
  - • **Cingular:** Phone (800) 331-0500; Web site www.cingular.com
  - • **T-Mobile:** Phone (866) 464-8662; Web site www.tmobile.com
  - • **Verizon Wireless:** Phone (800) 922-0204; Web site www.verizonwireless.com

When shopping for cell phone service, determine your needs and potential usage, then find the best deal available with the shortest contract commitment possible. Look for a plan with a high number of anytime minutes, unlimited nights and weekends, and no roaming or long distance charges.

Tools to enhance your creativity

A variety of tools exist that many writers can use to keep track of ideas, brainstorm, and stay organized. The tools in the following sections can be useful to writers.

Notebooks and pens

Have you ever woken up in the middle of the night with a great idea and not written it down and then forgotten it the next morning? You want to kick yourself, don't you? You never know when a brilliant idea may pop into your head, so have a small notebook with a reliable pen handy for whenever creativity strikes. Tuck away small notebooks near your bed and in your briefcase, desk, pocket, purse, or car (but don't write while driving).

Many journalists and reporters use 4-x-8½-inch reporter's notebooks, which can be ordered in quantity online or from your favorite office supply superstore. A more upscale version of the traditional reporter's notebook is manufactured by Moleskineus (www.moleskineus.com/moleskine-reporter-notebook.html). Their version, the 3½-x-5½-inch, 129-page-bound notebook, has a hardcover design and can last for years.

A tape or digital recorder

Some writers first prefer to dictate their ideas into a tape recorder before they start writing. Other writers record all their in-person and phone interviews to ensure accuracy. (A separate device for connecting any recorder to a telephone line in order to record interviews and conversations has to be purchased). Having a tape recorder in your car allows you to record ideas while you're driving instead of trying to write down your thoughts while you're sailing down the busy freeway!

When you're shopping for a recorder, you may want to look into microcassette recorders because they're portable, which offers added convenience. (Traditional cassette tape recorders can be a bit bulky and awkward, especially when you try to fit it in your pocket!)

In recent years, digital voice recorders have hit the market, allowing for hours of voice recordings to be made without a cassette tape. The digital audio files can then be quickly transferred to a computer (via a USB cable) for storage, playback, or editing. Start researching prices for your purchase, but I recommend Olympus. This company offers a full line of professional dictating equipment, digital voice recorders, and microcassette recorders, which fit in the palm of your hand. These units can be purchased at popular consumer electronics and office supply superstores, starting at under $50. Or visit www.olympusamerica.com.

A camera

Depending on the type of writing you do and whether you incorporate photographs in your self-published book (see Chapter 4 for more about using photos), you may consider investing in a high-end digital camera or traditional 35mm camera.

The benefits of a digital camera, over a traditional 35mm camera include

- Editing the pictures on your computer before incorporating them into your book
- Being able to quickly take pictures and then comparing many potential images before choosing the perfect one
- Saving time and money on film developing costs

Digital cameras range in price from around $100 to several thousand dollars. If you want to use photographs in your book, invest in a digital camera that offers at least 5,000,000 to 8,000,000 mega-pixel resolution. The quality of the pictures you take using a digital camera is determined by the resolution (the number of pixels or tiny dots that make up the image) the picture is taken in. A camera that can take photographs using 8,000,000 mega-pixel resolution means that 8,000,000 colored pixels are used to create it. The more pixels, the more detailed the image.

Many writers take photographs for their own purposes to help jog their memory of people they interview, places they've been, or events they've experienced. These photos may never actually get published, but they provide writers with additional documentation they can use when writing.

Research materials

Depending on the topic you're writing about, most authors rely on their research materials. These materials may include

- Audio tapes
- Books
- Company press kits
- Computer print outs
- Internet files
- Journals
- Magazines
- Newsletters
- Photographs
- Video tapes

No matter what type of research materials you rely on, when you're writing, it's important to have these materials within reach and to keep them organized in desktop files or filing cabinets so you can find the information you need quickly. See Chapter 4 for the full scoop on researching.

A dictionary, a thesaurus, and other writing reference books

As a writer or author, you rely on words to communicate. Having a dictionary and thesaurus on-hand when you're writing is a valuable tool, especially if you get into the habit of using them. In addition to helping you better communicate with your readers, a dictionary and thesaurus can help you build your vocabulary.

These references are readily available in a variety of traditional book formats, but if you rely on the Internet for many things (as several people do), access electronic formats on the Internet through `www.dictionary.com` or `www.thesaurus.com`. Or add an optional software application to your personal digital assistants (PDA) if you have one (see the next section).

Two additional and very useful reference books for writers are *The Associated Press Stylebook* and *The Associated Press Guide to Punctuation*. Both are published by Basic Books and available through bookstores. These reference guides quickly answer common questions about writing style, formatting, punctuation, and the use of common words or terms.

A personal planner or a personal digital assistant

A personal planner or a personal digital assistant (PDA) can be the ultimate time management and organizational tool that every author should own to help meet deadlines, plan schedules, keep track of to-do lists, and organize information (including a personal address book).

A *personal planner* is a printed notebook that comes in a wide range of sizes and formats. A personal planner can be purchased from an office supply store for between $10 and $100. A *PDA* is a palm-sized computer that's equipped with specialized software. PDAs are priced between $100 and $600.

Either of these tools can also be used to jot down notes and other pieces of information wherever you happen to be. Find a PDA or personal planner that you're comfortable carrying with you when you're on the go or keeping on your desk when you're working from home or the office.

Chapter 4

Creating a Winning Manuscript

· ·

In This Chapter

▶ Considering your audience's needs and wants

▶ Preparing an outline and researching your book's content

▶ Incorporating visual elements into your text

▶ Adding sections to your manuscript's beginning and end

▶ Securing the right releases and steering clear of plagiarism

· ·

*W*hen you first sit down at your computer, stare at a blank screen, and know you need to come up with hundreds of pages worth of interesting, informative, entertaining, and well-written text, it's enough to give anyone second thoughts about becoming an author. Well, don't panic! If you take an organized and disciplined approach to your writing, you discover that putting together a book-length manuscript is a manageable task.

As you develop your manuscript, which ultimately becomes your published book, you have a variety of things to consider. Assuming you already know your topic, this chapter provides you with strategies for considering the needs of your audience and creating the most well-organized, informative, and entertaining manuscript possible. I also explain how to effectively research your topic, incorporate visual elements and special sections into your manuscript, obtain permissions, and avoid plagiarism.

It's Not Always About You! Considering Your Audience Upfront

You may have already determined the audience to which you're writing toward. These people are your readers. Most books, whether they're fiction or nonfiction, cater to a specific audience or demographic. After you specify your target readers, you also need to make sure that the content you're giving them is appropriate for their wants and needs. In the following sections, I show you how to identify your book's target audience and choose the right content for them.

Targeting certain readers

No matter what type of book you're planning to write the first thing you need to do, before you start writing your manuscript, is determine exactly who your book targets. Who is most apt to purchase and read your book and why? What information does the reader want or expect to obtain by reading your book?

The target audience for your book may be somewhat broad. Or, your book may be targeted to a niche audience, comprising people with a very specific interest. Whatever the case, as the author, not only do you have to understand exactly who you're writing your book for, but also you must understand what the reader hopes to get out of your book. You need to ensure that you provide that information to your readers in the most enjoyable way possible.

After you pinpoint your target audience, get to know your potential reader. Ask yourself the following questions:

- ✔ Is my book's average reader a male or female?
- ✔ What age range do my readers fall into?
- ✔ How educated is my average reader?

Also consider why the reader may be interested in your book.

- ✔ What new information do I offer?
- ✔ How do I convey this new information?
- ✔ How much does the reader already know about the topic I'm writing about?
- ✔ Is my topic too simplistic or complex for the intended reader?
- ✔ If I'm writing fiction, what elements of the storyline do readers best relate to?
- ✔ Am I developing my characters so they appeal to my target audience?
- ✔ Does the audience understand, relate to, and appreciate the storyline, characters, and subplot(s) based on their knowledge, education, and background?

Doing research to understand exactly who your audience is helps you create a book that's of interest to readers. The book provides value to the readers, educates them, and/or entertains them in an appropriate manner based on age, education, interests, and intelligence.

Choosing appropriate content

To ensure that your book targets the appropriate audience, provides information of interest, and stays on target in terms of the content, ask yourself these questions:

- ✔ Specifically, what am I trying to teach the reader?
- ✔ Am I writing something that my target audience may be interested in?
- ✔ Do my readers find the information useful and/or entertaining?
- ✔ Am I taking into account the information or knowledge the reader already has and then building on it?
- ✔ How does my target audience use the information?
- ✔ Is the information informative, well written, and entertaining?
- ✔ Have I explained key concepts in a way my readers can understand?
- ✔ Do the examples, artwork, charts, or graphics I plan to incorporate into the book help convey the information? (See "What Meets the Eye: Adding Visual Interest to Your Manuscript," later in this chapter for details on graphic elements.)
- ✔ If I'm writing fiction, does my reader relate to the characters, plot, and subplots?
- ✔ Does my story tap into the reader's imagination and entertainment them?

After you become familiar with your audience, you're in a much better position to choose what content is most appropriate.

When it comes to choosing content for your book, consider what the reader may already know, and then slowly build on that knowledge. As necessary, provide the background information your readers need to understand fully whatever it is you're writing about, even if it's a novel.

Writing a full-length book is a process. Most writers create multiple drafts of their manuscript prior to getting it published. As you review each draft, follow these tips:

- ✔ Rewrite sections as needed.
- ✔ Delete unnecessary information.
- ✔ Fine-tune your approach to cover information.
- ✔ Carefully analyze each chapter to ensure that the entire manuscript flows smoothly and achieves its objectives.

Who you gonna call? Ghostwriters!

If you're a recognized expert in your field but not a writer, seriously consider hiring a professional ghostwriter who works closely with you to create your book's manuscript based on information you provide. Any literary agent can provide referrals for experienced and previously published ghostwriters. When you see a book written by a big-name celebrity, business executive, or athlete, more times than not, a professional writer was the ghostwriter on that book. Check out or Elance (www.elance.com) or the American Society of Journalists and Authors (www.asja.org) for info on finding a ghostwriter.

When working with a ghostwriter, remember the following information:

✔ Work closely with the person; don't just to provide exact information and content you want in your book.

✔ Ensure that the writer you hire communicates the information in your voice and that the ghostwriter understands the target audience.

✔ While a talented ghostwriter is able to write on any topic, hire someone with some previous experience writing about topics related to your book.

✔ Hiring a skilled and experienced ghostwriter may not be cheap, but the results can dramatically improve the overall quality of your book and improve its chances for achieving success.

Being an expert in your field and performing research to develop the content of your book is important. You may have to write several drafts of your manuscript before you're confident that you've successfully found the best way to communicate the information that's in your head.

Don't Be Sketchy: Creating an Outline

Writers can easily get lost in their manuscript of several hundred pages and lose focus on their true objectives. A lack of focus can lead to disorganization of information, repetition, deletion of key content, and ultimately production of a manuscript that's difficult to read, understand, and enjoy. The information you're writing about may be crystal clear in your head, but your goal as an author is to ensure that whatever you're writing is understandable in terms of how it's communicated on the printed page.

The easiest way to ensure that your manuscript is organized, flows nicely, and makes sense to the reader is to create a detailed outline *before* you actually begin writing. Also, if you've already started writing your book but find that you're having a hard time staying focused and organized, coming up with an outline may help you get back on track.

An outline for a book-length manuscript can be anywhere from 1 to 20 pages in length, depending on the level of detail you get into. This phase of the writing process is so important that most major publishing houses require even their most experienced authors to submit a detailed outline for each book before they begin writing.

In the following sections, I explain the importance of having an outline as you write and show you how to format and flesh out your outline with solid info.

Understanding an outline's importance

An outline provides a detailed overview of your book's content in just a few pages. The information gets divided up into sections and subsections, which ultimately expands into the individual chapters or sections of your book.

Working from a detailed outline forces you to consider every topic you plan to write about within your book. An outline should be created for any type of book, whether it's fiction or nonfiction:

✔ For a work of fiction, the outline helps ensure that the timeline of your plot makes sense and that plot twists, subplots, or aspects of each character's development happen at the appropriate time in the story.

✔ For nonfiction, an outline ensures that you first build a foundation of knowledge for your readers and then with each subsequent chapter, you appropriately build on that knowledge one concept at a time in an organized way without jumping ahead or repeating ideas from earlier chapters.

Creating an outline organizes your thoughts, research, and content, but it also helps with the following items:

✔ Assists you in deciding what information to include within your book

✔ Ensures that the information is placed in appropriate chapters and flows smoothly from the beginning of the book to the end

✔ Helps you avoid repetition

✔ Ensures that you don't forget to include key content

✔ Forces you to consider your book's page count and how much space you dedicate to each topic within each chapter or section

✔ Makes sure that you stay focused and take an organized approach to writing your manuscript

Working from your detailed outline can help you tackle the daunting task of writing, and it may even help eliminate that dreaded writer's block.

Ordering your topics

Before you begin writing an outline, consider putting together a detailed list of topics and subtopics to include in your book, and then follow these steps:

1. **Write each idea, topic, or subtopic on a separate index card.**

   By keeping each idea or concept separate, you can reorganize them or build on them with ease as you're planning your book's content.

2. **Spread out your collection of index cards on a table and begin moving them around.**

   With each idea on a separate card, you can pinpoint essential information and cluster cards that contain supporting ideas, concepts, or information.

3. **Place each card in an order that makes sense in your book.**

   As you do this, notice that the content for each chapter or section within your book begins to take shape. Be willing to tinker with your outline extensively by adding and removing topics and then moving content around, until you've developed a true template for your book.

4. **Arrange your chapters into a logical order.**

   This step ensures that your book is easy to understand. The chapters should nicely flow from one topic to the next and build on the knowledge the reader has already gained.

Creating an outline is easy if you're writing a how-to book, for example, but you can also create an outline for a novel. Consider how the story progresses from one chapter to the next. Describe plots, subplots, plot twists, characters to be introduced, timelines, settings, and so on.

After your index cards are properly grouped together, create a detailed written outline for your book (see the next section).

Formatting and polishing your outline

The level of detail you include in your outline depends on your knowledge of and comfort with the topic. The more detailed your outline, however, the easier it is to keep your manuscript well organized and ensure that you don't accidentally leave out important details, concepts, ideas, or content. In the following sections, I show you how to format and polish your outline.

Looking at different formats

Outlines typically are divided into A, B, C, D, and even E headings. An A heading might be a chapter title. Under each chapter title is a handful of topics included within that chapter (referred to as B headings). Under each B heading are key pieces of information or content that relates directly to that subheading or section. These can be C, D, and E headings, as appropriate.

Depending on the topic of your book and your personal work habits, choose an outline format that helps you best organize your manuscript and that supports your style of writing:

- ✔ Using a traditional outline helps you create a detailed template for your book and divides information based on chapters with headings, subheadings, and sidebars.
- ✔ Using a bulleted outline can help you better organize general ideas and decide where they go within your manuscript.

Figure 4-1 is a traditional outline format. Notice that it uses Roman numerals, letters, and numbers.

Instead of using Roman numerals to list heads and subheads within an outline, some writers prefer to use bullets, as shown in Figure 4-2.

An outline in either format can be created using a pen and paper or a word processor (Microsoft Word has a built-in outlining feature). An outline also can be written in sentence fragments as opposed to complete sentences; as long as the content makes sense to you, the outline should be functional. The goal is to organize your ideas as concisely as possible. The more topics and subtopics you include, the more detailed your outline becomes.

If you're writing fiction, you can also use a detailed outline to help you keep track of your overall storyline, plot twists, subplots, and characters. When writing a novel, keeping track of details about characters and storylines can become challenging. Because continuity and a clear timeline are important, an outline can help you keep the details straight.

Including the fine details

Writing a full-length manuscript is like taking a cross-country road trip. You can get lost with one wrong turn and then need to backtrack. To avoid unnecessary delays as you're writing, rely on your outline as your road map and refer to it constantly.

I.   Main topic, such as a chapter title ("A" heading)

A. Sub-topic ("B" heading)
1. Supporting information or content ("C" heading)
2. Additional supporting information or content ("C" heading)
   a. Sub-sub topic ("D" heading)
      1. Supporting information ("E" heading)
      2. Supporting information ("E" heading)
   b. Sub-sub topic ("D" heading)
   c. Sub-sub topic ("D" heading)
3. Additional supporting information or content ("C" heading)
   a. Sub-sub topic ("D" heading)
   b. Sub-sub topic ("D" heading)

B. Sub-topic ("B" Heading)
1. Supporting information or content ("C" heading)
2. Additional supporting information or content ("C" heading)
   a. Sub-sub topic ("D" heading)
   b. Sub-sub topic ("D" heading)
   c. Sub-sub topic ("D" heading)
3. Additional supporting information or content ("C" heading)
   a. Sub-sub topic ("D" heading)
   b. Sub-sub topic ("D" heading)

II.   Main topic, such as a chapter title ("A" heading)

A. Sub-topic ("B" heading)
1. Supporting information or content ("C" heading)
2. Additional supporting information or content ("C" heading)
   a. Sub-sub topic ("D" heading)
   b. Sub-sub topic ("D" heading)
   c. Sub-sub topic ("D" heading)
3. Additional supporting information or content ("C" heading)

B. Sub-topic ("B" heading)
1. Supporting information or content ("C" heading)
2. Additional supporting information or content ("C" heading)
   a. Sub-sub topic ("D" heading)
   b. Sub-sub topic ("D" heading)
   c. Sub-sub topic ("D" heading)
3. Additional supporting information or content ("C" heading)
   a. Sub-sub topic ("D" heading)
   b. Sub-sub topic ("D" heading)

Figure 4-1:
A traditional outline format features Roman numerals.

- Main topic, such as a chapter title ("A" Heading)

  - Sub-topic ("B" heading)
    - Supporting information or content ("C" heading)
    - Additional supporting information or content ("C" heading)
      - Sub-sub topic ("D" heading)
        - Supporting information ("E" heading)
        - Supporting information ("E" heading)
      - Sub-sub topic ("D" heading)
      - Sub-sub topic ("D" heading)
    - Additional supporting information or content ("C" heading)
      - Sub-sub topic ("D" heading)
      - Sub-sub topic ("D" heading)

  - Sub-topic ("B" heading)
    - Supporting information or content ("C" heading)
    - Additional supporting information or content ("C" heading)
      - Sub-sub topic ("D" heading)
      - Sub-sub topic ("D" heading)
      - Sub-sub topic ("D" heading)
    - Additional supporting information or content ("C" heading)
      - Sub-sub topic ("D" heading)
      - Sub-sub topic ("D" heading)

- Main topic, such as a chapter title ("A" heading)

  - Sub-topic ("B" heading)
    - Supporting information or content ("C" heading)
    - Additional supporting information or content ("C" heading)
      - Sub-sub topic ("D" heading)
      - Sub-sub topic ("D" heading)
      - Sub-sub topic ("D" heading)
    - Additional supporting information or content ("C" heading)

  - Sub-topic ("B" heading)
    - Supporting information or content ("C" heading)
    - Additional supporting information or content ("C" heading)
      - Sub-sub topic ("D" heading)
      - Sub-sub topic ("D" heading)
      - Sub-sub topic ("D" heading)

Figure 4-2:
This outline uses bulleted items to organize information.

Invest significant time developing your outline and fine-tuning it. Don't be afraid to move portions of your outline around and add or delete sections until you've created a document that can be used as a foundation for writing the actual manuscript. Here are some other tips to help you polish your outline:

- ✔ Consider adding actual chapter titles and section headings and subheadings to help you create a more comprehensive overview.

- ✔ List specifically where elements of your manuscript go, such as sidebars, interviews (quotes), photographs, examples, references, statistics, illustrations, graphs, charts, and checklists.

- ✔ Think about how many pages of your book you want dedicated to each chapter, topic, or section, keeping in mind the total number of pages your manuscript needs to be when complete.

- ✔ Try to keep your manuscript well balanced. All your chapters should be equal in length. This rule isn't steadfast but helps with the book's flow. This concept applies to fiction as well, although with fiction, it's more important that your story flow smoothly and engage the reader.

- ✔ If you're writing fiction, list what happens in each chapter, what plot twists you introduce, and the relevant details about characters.

Find a handful of people who are also knowledgeable about what you write and have them review your outline and provide feedback. Obtaining someone else's perspective may help you develop a more thorough outline. The more work you do now in terms of organizing and choosing the content for your book, the easier the actual manuscript writing process is.

As you're writing your manuscript, place a checkmark on your outline next to completed sections. During the actual writing phase, you may determine that a change to your outline is appropriate. Unlike the Ten Commandments, your outline isn't etched in stone. You're free to make changes as you go.

Dig for Facts: Doing Research

Even if you're the world's most renowned expert in your field, filling a book with interesting, informative, and accurate information can be a huge challenge. Either prior to writing your book or as you're writing, you may need to conduct research and combine that information with your own knowledge and experience in order to create the best possible book.

If you're writing anything that's technical in nature, you especially want to convey accurate information. Even when writing fiction, research helps your story be more believable. Bestselling authors, such as Tom Clancy, Dan Brown, and John Grisham often credit a handful of experts in their book's respective acknowledgments. These authors rely on experts to provide some of the technical details that allow their fictional stories to be more realistic.

The four primary methods for doing research include

- ✔ Surfing the Internet
- ✔ Visiting the library and reading books, magazines, newspapers, and newsletters
- ✔ Buying books and magazines from a bookstore that relate to your topic
- ✔ Interviewing experts

Avoid embarrassing errors in your text. No matter what type of research you do, make sure that the various sources you use are timely, reliable, and accurate. Here are some tips:

- ✔ Research each source.
- ✔ Try to confirm the facts and figures with other sources.
- ✔ Make sure that your information isn't outdated.
- ✔ Keep detailed notes about where information comes from.
- ✔ Include a bibliography section at the end of your book (I cover bibliographies later in this chapter), because you need to accurately cite all your sources.

It's useful to keep one master list of all your reference materials and resources. For each source you use, gather the following information:

- ✔ Title of the article or chapter
- ✔ Title of the book, publication, or source
- ✔ Name of the author(s) or people interviewed
- ✔ Contact information for each person you've interviewed or used as a source
- ✔ Copyright or publication date
- ✔ Specific page numbers, Web site URLs, or location of the information
- ✔ Written permission to use the information in your book, if applicable (see "Keep It Legal: Obtaining Permission to Use Other People's Materials," later in this chapter)

When using the Internet as a reference tool, print out the information you use and keep a file of those printouts. Make sure that the Web site address and date is printed on the various pages.

If you're looking to include the most timely and cutting-edge information possible, your best bet is to track down a handful of recognized experts on the topic you're writing about and interview those people. When conducting an interview for your book, make sure that you gather the following information:

- ✔ The interviewee's name (including the correct spelling)

- ✔ How the interviewee wants to be credited within your book, including their company's name and exact job title (if applicable)

- ✔ The source of any statistics or research data, for example, the interviewee provides during the interview

- ✔ A signed release stating that you have the interviewee's permission to include excerpts from the interview within your book

Whether you're an accomplished journalist or a first-time author, record all your interviews. Before doing this, however, make sure that it's okay with the interviewee. Having a recording to refer to while you're writing helps ensure proper quotes in your book and accurate context of the conversation.

What Meets the Eye: Adding Visual Interest to Your Manuscript

As soon as you begin creating the outline for your manuscript, decide what graphic elements to include for visual appeal. Graphics can also be acquired and placed within the manuscript as you're writing or during the final page layout and design process. After the pages are laid out, however, adding or deleting large amounts of text or graphics requires major layout and design changes, which can be time consuming and costly.

Use specific elements in your book to help organize information for your readers. Depending on your topic, approach, and applicability, consider using the following elements in your book (these don't apply in a novel, however):

- ✔ **Sidebars:** A sidebar is a subsection of a chapter that allows you to go off on a tangent without interrupting the reader's train of thought. Sidebars are used in nonfiction books to provide examples, short anecdotes, short interviews, or other information that doesn't directly flow with the main body of the manuscript. But the sidebar does relate to the topic at hand and tends to be short — between a quarter of a page and one full page.

✔ **Lists:** A list, like the one you're reading right now, can be in bulleted form. It's an easy way to communicate information to the reader. Items in a list can be short and concise and communicated in full sentences or sentence fragments. Lists can be numbered if they must be followed in a specific order, or you can use bullets to emphasize key pieces of information that can be followed in any order.

✔ **Checklists:** A checklist, like a list, can be used as a tool to help readers follow a list of steps without forgetting anything. Reader can check off boxes as they complete steps to ensure that nothing is forgotten.

✔ **Charts and graphs:** If you're trying to communicate a lot of numbers or statistics, a chart or a graph provides a visual, easier way to showcase the data. You can create a wide range of charts and graphics using a spreadsheet program, such as Microsoft Excel, depending on your needs. You can also hire a professional graphic artist to create visual elements for your book.

✔ **Graphics:** Graphics such as illustrations or drawings can be used to communicate information or simply add visual appeal. As you consider incorporating graphics, refrain from making your final laid out book pages look too cluttered. Illustrations and drawings should be created by a professional artist, unless you have strong artistic skills. The graphics should look professional and help communicate important information.

✔ **Graphic icons:** Throughout this book you find graphic icons called Remember, Tip, and Warning. Graphic icons can be used within your book, if applicable, to draw the reader's attention to something specific. A graphic artist can help you design these visual elements for your book.

✔ **Photographs:** Often, the easiest way to convey information is through the use of a photograph. Depending on the type of book you're writing, you can often include black and white images within the main body of your book. Some self-publishing options allow for full-color photographs to be used as well. You can take photographs yourself, purchase images from a stock photo agency, or hire a professional photographer to create customized photos for you (each option depends on your budget).

If you're on a tight budget, consider using photographic images from a stock photo library. To find a library of stock photography, use any Internet search engine and enter the search phrase *stock photo library*.

The following list includes three examples of stock photo libraries:

- PhotoObjects.net (www.photoobjects.net)

- Photos.com (www.photos.com)

- ShutterStock (www.shutterstock.com)

If you want to incorporate photographs, charts, or graphics in your book and refer to those elements within the main body of your text, use figure numbers and captions to identify each graphic or image. Figure numbers typically begin with the chapter number, followed by a dash or period and are in chronological order. The first image in Chapter 3, for example, is labeled Figure 3-1 or Figure 3.1. The second is Figure 3-2 or Figure 3.2 and so on. Below each image, include a one-sentence (or shorter) caption, identifying what the reader's looking at.

Put the Pieces Together: Examining Other Book Elements

If you look at any book — fiction or nonfiction — it typically contains special sections. Many of these sections are standard. Which elements you include within your book depends on your personal preferences and the type of book you're writing. I cover all these elements, in order of their appearance in a book, in the following sections.

Copyright page

The copyright page lists all the legal information pertaining to the publication of the book, including details about its copyright, publisher, ISBN, Library of Congress Control Number, and trademarks used in the book. The copyright page usually appears on a left-handed page, directly after the inside title page.

Author acknowledgments

This section of your book thanks anyone and everyone who helped you write and publish the book. It's also where the author can thank loved ones, friends, coworkers, and even her dog if she wants. This section can be a few sentences or up to one page long, but one to two paragraphs is standard. Don't forget to thank the reader for buying your book (not required, but a nice touch!).

Table of contents

A table of contents is simply a list of the chapters and major sections within your book and their respective page numbers in a directory-like listing. A table of contents makes it easy for readers to find what they're looking for and skip directly to that section or chapter.

Your table of contents can list just your chapters and related page numbers, like the Contents at a Glance section at the front of this book does, or it can include subtopics to provide a more comprehensive listing about what's in your book. Check out the table of contents in the beginning of this book.

Foreword and/or Preface

A *foreword* is typically written as an introduction to your book, but it's written by someone other than the main author, such as a famous person, another author, or a well-known expert. In terms of length, a foreword can be one to five pages, and contains information about what's included within the book, and it describes some of the reasons why the book may be of interest to the reader. When you have someone write your foreword, obtain written permission from the foreword writer (see "Keep It Legal: Obtaining Permission to Use Other People's Materials," later in this chapter).

A *preface* contains much of the same information as a foreword does, except that it's typically written by the book's author. The preface sets the tone of the book and tells the reader what to expect. A book, whether it's fiction or nonfiction, can have both a preface and a foreword; however, this practice isn't too common. If you have a foreword in your book, you can add any messages for your reader within the acknowledgements or introduction sections without using the preface, too.

Introduction

An introduction introduces the content in your book. It can be written in first person, so you, the author, can communicate directly with the reader. Don't confuse the introduction with the preface; the intro is typically longer and more detailed than a preface. The length typically runs one page, but it can be as long as the other chapters in your book if you want.

Here's what to include in your intro for different types of books:

- ✔ **Nonfiction:** Your introduction precedes Chapter 1 and provides the reader with a general overview of what the book is about, who's reading it, and what it contains. The intro can also include a summary of core knowledge that readers need prior to reading your book.

- ✔ **Fiction:** The introduction can be used to set the stage and provide readers with background stories, character information, or plot details they need before the actual story begins.

Appendixes

Found at the end of a book, an appendix can be a list of resources or the equivalent of a short chapter offering information that relates to your book's topic but that didn't easily fit into the main body of the book. The appendixes can also summarize important information and provide worksheets or additional checklists for the reader.

Appendixes are typically found in nonfiction books. If you plan to incorporate appendixes into your book, plan on having at least three to five of them (although this isn't a steadfast rule). Keep each appendix short (no longer than two or three pages). They're typically titled Appendix A, Appendix B, Appendix C, and so on, although each can also have a short title.

Bibliography

If you've relied on many sources of information for your book, include a detailed listing of your sources at the end of the book in the form of a formatted bibliography. Follow traditional formatting based on the type of source you've quoted, excerpted, or paraphrased as a reference.

The Chicago Manual of Style (University of Chicago Press) offers guidelines that are commonly used within the publishing industry for formatting bibliographies. Visit www.chicagomanualofstyle.org for more information.

Glossary

Found at the end of some nonfiction books, a glossary is a list of terms and their definitions. The length of a glossary varies, based on the number of terms you wish to explain. This section is a good quick reference for readers, so try to keep your definitions short.

A glossary is handy if your book contains a lot of technical terms the reader needs to know to better understand and use the content in your book. Italicize the words that appear in the glossary to indicate to the reader that the term is defined elsewhere.

Index

An index is a detailed listing of keywords and topics featured within a nonfiction book. Each keyword also has a specific page reference where more information can be found in the book. An index is far more detailed than a table of contents (covered earlier in this chapter). Putting together an index is time consuming, but it can be a valuable resource for your readers to find specifics quickly within your book.

Most companies that offer self-publishing services, including Print-On-Demand (POD) publishers (see Chapter 11 for details on these companies), provide an indexing service for an additional fee.

"About the Author"

Some fiction and nonfiction authors like to dedicate a page (either in the beginning or end of the book) with detailed information about themselves such as a picture, background, education, company or employer, credentials, or other personal details. Within this section, you may choose to also promote your Web site or disclose a mailing or e-mail address so your readers can contact you.

The "About the Author" section of your book provides more detail than the short paragraph you include about yourself on your book's back cover. (See Chapter 9 for details about creating your book's front and back covers.) If you're publishing a hardcover book, the "About the Author" section can be placed on the book's jacket.

Keep It Legal: Obtaining Permission to Use Other People's Materials

Anytime you incorporate someone else's words, writing, artwork, photographs, or original ideas into your writing not only do you need to give proper credit where credit is due, but also you must obtain the necessary permission, in writing, from the copyright owner of that material.

The written permission you obtain can be in the form of a standard release (a legal document any lawyer can create for you) or a simple letter stating that you have permission to use the material in your book. The letter you obtain should be signed and dated by all parties involved and should spell out exactly how and when the material is used.

Consult a lawyer who specializes in copyright laws for guidelines about what specifically you need to do to protect yourself from legal problems after your book is published. Generally, you want to obtain permission for anything that is copyrighted, trademarked, or patented that you plan to use in your book.

Interviews

Information from interviews can add valuable text to your book. Include the name of the person you interviewed and likeness (if applicable) within your book. Check out "Dig for Facts: Doing Research," earlier in this chapter for more details on interviews.

Foreword

If you've asked someone else to write the foreword for your book, make sure to obtain written permission from the writer to use the name and words within your book. Simply draw up a basic release or a letter stating that you have permission to use their words and name in your book, and then have the foreword writer sign the agreement.

Photographs

Depending on the situation, using photographs within a book can be a bit tricky from a legal standpoint unless you've taken the photographs yourself and have a signed release from the person (or people) featured within each photograph. If you use someone else's photos, you need the photographer's permission, as well as permission from the people in the photo. If the photo depicts someone's private property, make sure to secure permission from the property owner to use the photograph, even if you took the actual picture.

If you use stock photos (see "What Meets the Eye: Adding Visual Interest to Your Manuscript" earlier in the chapter), for a low flat fee, you can use images with no formal releases or fear of copyright infringements.

Aside from photographs, you also need permission to use any type of copyrighted artwork within your book. This includes drawings, graphics, logos, charts, illustrations, or icons that were created by someone else.

The concept of fair use

Depending on what type of material you wish to use within your book, if you provide the appropriate credit, you may be able to use copyrighted content without obtaining written permission. This concept is called *fair use* and applies when you use a small portion of another source (no more than 300 words). You're also allowed, from a legal standpoint, to quote information from press releases issued by companies or individuals.

To find out more about fair use, check out these resources:

- www.pma-online.org/scripts/shownews.cfm?id=403
- www.copyright.gov/fls/fl102.html

You're Not a Copier: Avoiding Plagiarism

Plagiarism occurs when you steal someone else's words, ideas, or materials and call them your own without giving the person you stole the material from proper credit. In the publishing world, this offense is a major no-no and can lead to costly lawsuits and also destroy your professional reputation.

You need to properly document your source(s) whenever you refer to or make use of any of the following information within your book:

- Quoting from another book, a newspaper or magazine article, TV or radio show, lyrics from a song, a blog, Web page, advertisement, or someone's words from any other published or electronic medium
- Quoting someone you've interviewed either in person or on the phone
- Quoting someone after attending a press conference, lecture, or speech
- Reproducing any type of artwork or graphic image

It is *not* considered plagiarism when you're writing about your own ideas, observations, experiences, and knowledge or when forming your own conclusions about a subject matter or topic. You're also allowed to make full use of what is considered common knowledge or generally accepted facts.

Check out these Web sites about plagiarism and copyright issues:

- **www.plagiarism.org/faq.html:** For useful information about what plagiarism is and how to avoid it
- **www.copyright.gov:** For details on how to protect your own work by copyrighting it or to find out more about how to avoid violating other peoples' copyrights

More information about copyrighting your manuscript is offered in Chapter 7.

Chapter 5

Fine-Tuning Your Work with Careful Editing

*W*ut wood you due if you purchased a book that wuz full of errors? Wood you still respect wut the author had to say? Probably not!

A good writer not only strings together the right combination of words, sentences, and paragraphs, but also they adhere to proper grammatical, spelling and punctuation rules in their work. While writers should edit their own work carefully before the book goes to press, they should also have the text professionally edited, especially with first-time authors looking to make the best possible impression with their self-published books.

This chapter discusses why good editing is important, provides an overview of the author's and editor's roles in the editing process, and explains how to hire a freelance professional editor for your book project.

A Bird's-Eye View of the Editing Process

When you hire a freelance editor, make sure that the editor is willing and capable of editing both the original manuscript you provide and the laid out pages before they go to press. At a major publishing house, two different people perform these functions. The editor edits the original manuscript and then a proofreader reviews the final pages before publication. To save money, hire someone who handles both of these important jobs for you.

A poorly edited manuscript can destroy a reader's appreciation and enjoyment of your work and take away from the overall professionalism of the publication. For a book to achieve its objectives, it should be written by a talented writer and reviewed by an equally talented editor. Authors and editors bring together unique skills and often work as a close-knit team.

Just as writing is a skill so is editing. Editing requires strong knowledge of grammar and punctuation rules and a command of the English language. It also requires extreme attention to detail as every line of the manuscript is reviewed. Without this proper editing pass, a book can easily contain a wide range of errors. As you review your manuscript, some of the more common errors you, as well as your editor, should look out for include

- ✔ Factual errors
- ✔ Grammatical errors
- ✔ Improper page numbering
- ✔ Improper use of punctuation
- ✔ Incorrect names, phone numbers, addresses, or Web site URLs
- ✔ Mismatched figures and captions
- ✔ Mistakes in chapter titles or subtitles
- ✔ Page layout and design errors, such as the wrong font, typestyle, type size, or paragraph formatting
- ✔ Incorrect references to specific page numbers, figures, or chapters
- ✔ Spelling mistakes
- ✔ The accidental deletion of content
- ✔ Typos, such as using a wrong word that the spelling checker didn't catch like *they're* instead of *their*
- ✔ Writing style mistakes, such as constantly switching between past and present tense or first and third person
- ✔ Inconsistencies in fiction storylines when it comes to characters, plots, and subplots
- ✔ Long sentences and paragraphs that can be broken up in order to make your book more straightforward, objective, and easy to understand

In the following sections, I give you the lowdown on your role as the author in editing and the tasks specifically performed by a professional editor.

Editing your own work first

As an author, you have a responsibility to review your manuscript several times before turning it over to a professional editor. During one read through, focus on content and make sure that the text flows smoothly. When you read it the second and third times, focus more on the quality of the writing; on the wording you've used; and on correcting spelling, grammatical, and punctuation mistakes.

Follow these steps to focus your editing efforts:

1. **Create a double-spaced print out of each chapter.**

   It's often much easier to edit a hard copy of your work than it is to review it on a computer screen. The double-spaced format allows room for marking your corrections.

2. **Grab a red pen (or any other contrasting color from your print out color) to make corrections and start reading.**

   As you go back to make the corrections in your Word file, you want to easily be able to spot them on the edited hard copy pages.

3. **Focus on one chapter or section of the book at a time.**

   Editing takes time and requires your total focus. If you find your mind wandering or you're getting tired, take breaks in between chapters and continue the editing process later. Never attempt to edit your entire book in one sitting.

4. **After you've reviewed your manuscript and have marked up the pages with your edits, corrections, and changes, incorporate them into the document using your word processor.**

   As you enter each correction or edit, review it and make sure that it works in the context of the manuscript. Doing this provides you with an additional opportunity to improve the overall quality of your work.

5. **Create a fresh printout and review it again.**

   Each time you review your work, you may think of potential improvements you can make to the content or flow of the manuscript. Perhaps you can think of additional examples to include or realize that a specific section doesn't really belong in the book after all.

Never rely exclusively on your editor to fix all the mistakes in your manuscript, especially those relating to the accuracy of information. Most editors focus primarily on spelling, punctuation, grammatical and formatting mistakes, and structural and organizational issues, as opposed to actual content-related issues.

Understanding an editor's responsibilities

The editor focuses on the minute and technical details of a manuscript but also maintains perspective for the bigger picture. Even experienced writers sometimes make different types of mistakes and lose a sense of their book's overall structure, which is where a good editor can step in and take over.

Editors aren't hired for their knowledge of the topic but for their knowledge of written language and how to best use it. The editor should understand the publishing process and what's required for a manuscript to be transformed into a professionally published book. Therefore, it's not necessary for the editor to be an expert on the subject matter of the book (that's your job) — although a basic knowledge is often useful. You're the expert in terms of the content and information being conveyed, but look to your editor as an expert at making sure the information is presented correctly.

Here are a few editor responsibilities:

- ✔ Reviewing your manuscript sentence-by-sentence
- ✔ Fixing the common spelling, punctuation, and grammatical mistakes
- ✔ Ensuring that the structure and organization of the entire manuscript have a nice flow and rhythm
- ✔ Making sure that your manuscript is easy to understand and that the writing style is straightforward
- ✔ Being objective and assisting the writer in fixing problem areas of the manuscript before it goes to press
- ✔ Certifying that the finished product is truly welcoming for the reader because a good book should draw the reader in to its subject, and to reach that goal, the writer and editor both need to be aware of the audience
- ✔ Checking the continuity in terms of the information, whether you're writing fiction or nonfiction

One important aspect of an editor's job is to make sure that all information is provided in a logical sequence, so the reader can understand it. Even if a book is easy to read, it doesn't mean that the subject matter has to be simple. A well-written and edited book can take extremely complex or technical information and clearly state it for the reader.

All authors and editors have their own style for how they work. So before you begin working with the editor you hire, decide if you want to supply a hard copy printout of the manuscript or a Word (electronic) document, and then develop a plan for how the work is edited. After that, answer the following questions:

- ✔ Do you provide the entire manuscript at once or supply the editor with several batches of chapters at different times?
- ✔ Do you plan to have the editor review and edit your work multiple times?
- ✔ Does the editor also take responsibility for proofreading the final pages before your book goes to press?

When a professional editor corrects your manuscript, she often uses special symbols and terms associated with publishing. The following Web site, published by the University of Colorado, offers a listing of popular editing terms and symbols: `www.colorado.edu/Publications/styleguide/symbols.html`. Make sure that you understand the editor's comments and corrections before deciding whether to implement them.

When using a word processor, an editor can utilize the Track Changes feature of the program to make collaborating on the same document easier. The editor's comments and edits, for example, can be color coded for your review. If your editor uses these Word features, make sure that you understand how to use the commands available to you under the Track Changes pulldown menu.

After your editor reviews your manuscript for the first time, don't be surprised if he comes back with many proposed changes. You're probably extremely attached to your work, but you need to trust the editor enough to allow him to improve your text. These suggestions aren't a personal attack on your writing skills. The editor is simply doing his job: transforming your manuscript into the most professionally written book possible.

The Nitty-Gritty of Hiring an Editor

Hiring your book's editor and proofreader (who can ultimately be the same person) are important steps in the publishing process. A highly skilled editor can dramatically improve the quality of your book, especially if you're a first-time author. The following sections help you hire the perfect editor for your book and develop a strong and productive working relationship with that person.

When should you hire an editor, and how long should the editing take?

Depending on your level of writing experience, hire your editor early in the writing process and submit individual chapters to the editor as you write them. Trickling the chapters to your editor allows more time for feedback and helps you keep your manuscript organized and properly structured.

If you're a first time author or your writing skills don't meet professional standards, trickling chapters is extremely important because it allows you to get some feedback. By receiving feedback from your editor as you're writing, you can cut down on the edits and rewrites that may be required in later chapters and before the book goes to press.

If you're confident in your writing ability, and you have other people (such as friends, family members, coworkers, and professional colleagues) who can review your manuscript as you're writing to provide impartial and objective feedback, hold off on hiring an editor until your manuscript is complete.

After the manuscript is finished, allow several weeks for your editor to properly review the entire project and complete the editing process. Depending on how busy the editor is, the length of your manuscript and the quality of your writing, allocate three to five weeks in your overall publishing timeline for proper editing of the manuscript to be done.

To ensure that you find the best editor possible and are able to give that person ample time to properly do her job, line up your editor as far in advance as possible. When you begin writing your manuscript, or at least several weeks before you need the editor to start working, begin your search to hire the appropriate person.

Avoid waiting to the last minute to hire your editor, or you can wind up having difficulty finding someone who has time to take on your project or who winds up having to rush to get your manuscript edited. If an editor tells you that he can edit your entire manuscript in a few days or over a weekend, run in the opposite direction as fast as you can. Find someone else. The editing process takes time and careful attention to detail. This step isn't something that you want to rush or cut corners on.

How much should hiring an editor cost?

As with any professional service, when you hire an experienced editor, you're paying for time, skills, experience, and knowledge. Plan on spending anywhere from $1,500 to $5,000 to have your book-length manuscript professionally edited. A book-length manuscript can be anywhere from 50,000 to 100,000 or more words, depending on the type of book. A children's book, cookbook, or poetry book may be significantly shorter.

Some editors charge a flat rate for a project, while others charge an hourly fee for their time, or they charge by the word for their editing services. (A price of two cents to five cents per word for a 50,000- to 100,000-word manuscript is common.) The price you pay for editing services depends on many factors:

- The length of your manuscript
- How much work the editor anticipates having to do on the manuscript
- How closely you work with the editor during the writing process
- The editor's current workload
- How quickly you need the editing work done

After the manuscript is fully edited, have the editor review the galleys (the laid out pages) of your book again right before the book goes to press. This extra check helps you catch any typos or formatting mistakes made by whoever handled the page layout and design of your book. Be sure to check all chapter titles and subtitles for accuracy, and make sure that all figures and captions are correctly matched up and placed within the book.

Where can you find an experienced editor?

When it comes time to finding a professional editor to work with you on your project, you have a multitude of choices, but the best way to find someone is through a referral from someone working in the publishing industry. If you don't know anyone firsthand, consider the following options:

- ✔ Call the editor of your local newspaper
- ✔ Contact members of a local writer's group
- ✔ Use an online service
  - • Elance (www.elance.com)
  - • Freelance Work Exchange (www.freelanceworkexchange.com)
  - • Manuscript Editing (www.manuscriptediting.com)
- ✔ Respond to classified ads in special-interest magazines for writers
  - • *The Writer Magazine* (www.writermag.com/wrt)
  - • *Writer's Digest* (www.writersdigest.com)
  - • *Publisher's Weekly* (www.publishersweekly.com)

Even when you work with a self-publishing company that offers a complete solution for publishing your book (such as Trafford, iUniverse, or Wheatmark as described in Chapter 11), editing isn't provided with the basic services offered. These companies, however, can refer you to a professional editor for an additional fee. Make sure that you also allocate funds in your publishing budget to hire an editor (see Chapter 6 for details about budgets).

Choose the person you hire carefully. Find an editor who's experienced, well educated, and one you're able to work well with. Your editor should never try to force his ideas, vision, writing style, or voice into your work. Find someone who's able to embrace your vision and who understands exactly what you're trying to accomplish with your book. The best way to find this person is to set up a phone or in-person meeting with the editor and to discuss credentials, approach to editing, and your concept for the book. Of course, you also want to discuss fees and scheduling early on.

Editing is a technical skill. Ideally, you want to hire an editor who's studied editing and/or journalism at an undergraduate or graduate level and who has experience editing full-length manuscripts for the general trade book market. Most professional freelance editors have no trouble providing you with their credentials and a list of published books they've worked on in the past.

Thanks to technology, like e-mail, fax, and the telephone, along with overnight mail services, it's not necessary for the editor you hire to be located near you. Most editors are extremely comfortable working with authors by exchanging e-mails and phone calls.

Do you also need a technical editor?

When hiring a technical editor, find someone who's extremely familiar with the topic or subject matter of your book and who's able to focus on the accuracy of information. This suggestion is particularly important if the copy editor you're using isn't too familiar with the subject matter of your book.

A technical editor's job can be time consuming and requires careful attention to the content-related details within your book. The focus is less on the accuracy spelling, punctuation, grammar, and writing style. A technical editor is someone who does the following:

✔ Fact checks the book's information

- Phone numbers

- Addresses

- Web site URLs

- Names

✔ Ensures complete content

- Facts

- Figures

- Statistics

- Research materials

- Cited works

Hiring a technical editor does come with its cons: It adds to the budget, and you get a more technically detailed or complex manuscript than you were hoping for, therefore developing creative differences.

Meet a professional editor

For over 20 years, Beth Adelman has been working as a freelance professional editor. She's edited hundreds of books published by major publishing houses and many other books written by self-published authors. She has a journalism degree and began her career working as a writer for newspapers and magazines. She quickly determined, however, that her interests lied in the publishing process as a whole and found editing to be far more rewarding. "An editor is a coach and mentor for writers, not just someone who fixes spelling mistakes and punctuation," she explains.

Adelman works from a home office and edits books on a wide range of subjects. She adds, "My job as an editor is to make sure that the writer ultimately puts his or her name on the best possible work that it can be. I very often begin working with writers before their manuscript is finished, so I am able to be an active resource for the writer to bounce ideas off of. When a manuscript is finished, it's my job to read it and to work with the author to make sure that the finished product is written clearly and presented in a way that makes sense."

As an editor, Adelman must always work using the voice of the writer. "The hand of a good editor is always invisible to the reader," she explains. "Generally, I rewrite paragraphs that don't make sense, but if there are large sections of the book that require major revisions, I go back to the author and provide them with extremely detailed feedback on what needs to be done. As a writer, I have my own very distinctive writing style. As an editor, I need to perfectly match the author's writing style. In essence, when I am editing someone else's book, I need to pretend I am the author and communicate using his or her voice and style. This process becomes more challenging, however, when an author has no unique voice or style."

The most common mistake Adelman sees when authors attempt to edit their own work is a lack of perspective. "When writers review their own work, they always think it's perfect. They love their own work. The problem is, nobody writes perfectly, but if you love your work, it's impossible to see the flaws. Authors and writers get overly attached to their work and lose perspective. Plus, when authors write something, in their head, they understand what they meant. Thus, it's much harder for them to look at just the words on the page and determine if their ideas are being communicated properly. This reason is why a professional editor should be used," she says.

Just about everyone working in the book publishing business agrees that every book should be edited by a professional before it goes to press. If, for whatever reason, you choose not to follow this advice and you decide to edit your own manuscript, Adelman strongly suggests putting the manuscript in a drawer for a week or two after it's complete before beginning the editing process.

"Putting the manuscript away for a while helps you regain your perspective before you begin editing. If you don't hire a professional editor, make sure that you have at least several people read the manuscript before it goes to press. Some writers belong to a writer's group where the members provide feedback to each other. If you pursue this route, don't get overly caught up in trying to include the advice offered by each member of the group. If you have six different opinions and try to incorporate all of them into your book, the manuscript begins to lack coherence. Take the advice you're offered into account, but in the end, make sure that you stay true to your vision."

When it comes time for an author to work with an editor, Adelman adamantly states that the relationship has to be based on mutual respect and trust for the collaboration to work. A good author working with a good editor is a formula for success.

The cost of a technical editor is considerably less than what it costs to hire a copy editor. Plan on spending anywhere from a few hundred dollars to $2,500, depending on the length of your manuscript and the type of work involved.

When trying to find a technical editor, check out these resources:

- ✔ The same Web sites or resources you used to find your editor and/or proofreader (see "Where can you find an experienced editor?" earlier in this chapter)
- ✔ Someone who's also an expert on the topic you're writing about
- ✔ Industry trade magazines

When interviewing a potential technical editor, focus on their knowledge of the topic and their willingness to fact check and do any research necessary to ensure that the information in your book is accurate.

Part II
Pulling Together the Details: Administration and Design

The 5th Wave   By Rich Tennant

"I self-published it myself, and the beauty is I saved money by using Word instead of desktop publishing software to set the text."

In this part . . .

In conjunction with the publication of your book, establishing your own small publishing company may make sense for many self-published authors. Starting a company offers a variety of benefits. This part helps you handle many book-specific tasks that are necessary before a book goes to press. It also helps you establish your company and assists you in making sure that your book's interior and cover look as professional as possible.

Chapter 6

Setting Up Your Self-Publishing Business

● ●

In This Chapter

▶ Looking at the pros of establishing your own company

▶ Forming your business from the ground up

▶ Watching costs carefully

▶ Getting help from business veterans

● ●

A s you begin to prepare your book for publication, depending on how you market, advertise, and sell it, and what involvement you have in those processes, you may find establishing your own publishing company very beneficial. This chapter focuses on the benefits of establishing your own business, offers basic advice on how actually to get started, advises you on watching your budget, and provides tips for finding expert help.

As a self-published author with only one book title, you may need to establish and operate your business only for the life of the book. Unless you plan to follow up with additional book titles, eventually, the sales from the original book title typically fizzle out.

Understanding the Benefits of Establishing a Publishing Company

Establishing a business offers a variety of tax advantages and potential legal protections. Your accountant and attorney are able to review these benefits with you, based on the state where you're establishing your business and based on your personal situation. Here are a few general benefits:

- ✔ **Credibility:** In terms of actually selling your book, obtaining publicity, buying advertising, and coordinating distribution, a legitimate company gives you credibility.

- ✔ **Loans:** You can qualify for small business loans or grants. In fact, it's also easier to obtain a small business loan if you actually operate a legitimate business.

- ✔ **Location:** Most self-publishing businesses can be operated from a home or apartment as opposed to an office or warehouse. Although it's necessary to legally establish your business and submit the appropriate forms to the state and federal government (see "Legally establishing the right type of business," later in this chapter), you don't need to rent office space, especially if you're running a one- or two-person operation. (But consider opening a post office box to keep your personal and business mail separate.)

- ✔ **Tax deductions:** By establishing a company, most or all of your legitimate business-related expenses are tax deductible.

Not all self-published authors need to create their own business. For example, if you're writing a book that's going to be published using Print-On-Demand (POD), establishing your own business may not be necessary. (Chapter 11 has details on POD publishing.) But, if you're a self-published author who wants to sell your own books, now may be a good time to establish your own business. (Part V has more information about publicity and marketing tactics.)

Prior to establishing any type of formal business, be sure to consult with an accountant and attorney who can review your situation and help you determine the best type of legal business entity to create.

Taking Official Steps to Create a Company

Starting an actual business doesn't have to be expensive or require a pile of paperwork, but you want to establish your business as early in the self-publishing process as possible, especially if you're ultimately selling your book directly to consumers. This section helps you take the necessary steps to establish your business.

Starting with a name and an image

Because you're about to launch a business to self-publish and sell your book, you already have an overall objective for your business (see the next section for developing a more detailed business plan). Now, you need to come up with a business name. Go ahead; think of something that's unique and catchy.

The name you choose helps establish your company's image. The name needs to sound professional, hold meaning (at least to you), and establish your credibility in the publishing field. The name can be either specific or general:

✔ If you know you're publishing only travel books, name your company something such as Acme Travel Adventure Publications.

✔ John Doe Enterprises, Inc. incorporates the owner's name yet doesn't reveal anything about what the company actually does.

If you're providing other services in addition to publishing books, you may want to reference this within the name of your company, or at least refrain from implying in the company's name that it's exclusively a publishing company. A name like Acme Publishing, Inc. implies the company is a publishing company. Acme Ventures, Inc., Acme Worldwide, Inc., or Acme Enterprises, Inc. is less specific.

After you've come up with a name, you want to do a few things to protect and promote your company:

✔ **Register the company name as a DBA (doing business as).** You need to ensure that no one else is already using your name. Contact your local County Clerk or Recorder's Office for details on how to complete this process. You need a DBA to establish a bank account or a P.O. Box.

✔ **Register your name as a Web site domain name.** Even if you don't have a site designed yet, reserve the name for your site, so no one else takes it from you. See Chapter 21 for more information on this process.

✔ **Develop a logo to promote your identity and image.** A *logo* is a graphic that accompanies your company name, and many people first identify your logo with your company. Any graphic artist can help you create a logo, which you can use on all your promotional materials. See Chapter 8 for details on finding a graphic designer.

Making your mark

If you're using a unique or original company name or if you've developed a company logo along with the name, be sure to trademark the name and logo with the United States Patent and Trademark Office (www.uspto.gov). Obtaining a trademark for your unique company name and logo gives you added legal protection and helps keep your competition from using a similar name or logo to confuse consumers.

Keep in mind, you can trademark any unique logo, but to trademark a company name, it has to include something special, such as a made-up word or unique spelling of a word. You can't trademark words that appear in the dictionary, for example. Consult with an attorney or the U.S. Patent and Trademark Office to find out more about what can and can't be trademarked.

Developing a business plan and securing financing

The company you establish most likely handles the book's marketing, advertising, distribution, order fulfillment, and other business-related matters. So, it's important to create a well-thought-out business plan for the company you're about to establish. In a nutshell, you need to develop a thorough understanding of what the business does. Does the company simply help you sell books? Or does the company serve to forward your own career?

The business plan

Before investing your time and money in your business and into the publishing of your book, create a detailed business plan that specifically defines your business, identifies its goals, and describes how the business operates. Be sure to include a balance sheet and cash flow analysis as part of the business plan. For more on business plans, check out *Business Plans For Dummies,* 2nd Edition (Wiley) by Paul Tiffany and Steven D. Peterson.

If you don't have a financial background, consider hiring (in advance) an accountant or bookkeeper — someone with the expertise to help you create a financial model for your company (which you may later need to secure a loan or pitch to investors) and help you set up the financial aspects of your business. The following people can help you with this process:

- ✔ An accountant
- ✔ A Certified Public Accountant (CPA)
- ✔ A financial planner
- ✔ A professional bookkeeper

The money

After you have your business plan and financial planning in place, you have to get some money to run that business of yours! The type of business you're forming and the purpose of the business determine how much money you need. Plan on spending at least several hundred dollars to complete and file the necessary paperwork to establish your business. Beyond that, the costs associated with writing, editing, printing, promoting, selling, and distributing your book need to be calculated into your budget.

Where do you get the money? Try getting a small business loan or borrowing money from family or friends. You can even look at private investors. Of course, if you have money in your savings, you can start there!

Obtaining cash advances on your credit cards to launch your business can be a costly choice. If the business fails and you can't pay at least your monthly credit card minimum payments, you can find yourself in serious financial trouble and having to pay extremely high interest rates and other fees.

Legally establishing the right type of business

When it comes to actually creating your business or company, you have a variety of options. Some common types of businesses include

- **Sole proprietorship:** A *sole proprietorship* means that you're the exclusive owner of the business. It's the most inexpensive way of creating a legal business entity, and it's the quickest and easiest way to start. As your business grows, you can transform the company into some type of corporation, for example. If you have a small publishing program and it only breaks even, it's easy to remain a one-person company indefinitely. But successful sales of a title (25,000 copies sold in one year) dictate that you either expand into a company with employees or sell off the successful property to a larger publisher.

  Be careful with this type of business because it offers fewer legal protections and benefits. When you operate a sole proprietorship, all profits and losses are included on your individual tax returns. If a customer sues your business, he may also be able to sue you personally, which makes your personal and business assets subject to those claims.

- **Partnership:** When two or more people work together as co-owners of a company, this business is referred to as a *partnership.* It's like a sole proprietorship, but multiple people are involved, which increases the complexity and the amount of required paperwork.

Keep in mind that partners in a business share unlimited liability: Each partner is usually responsible for the acts of the other. Also, if someone sues your business, he may also be able to sue you and your partner(s) personally, which makes your assets subject to those claims.

- **Corporation:** For the maximum amount of legal protection and potential tax benefits, establishing a corporation may be in your best interest. A *corporation* is a legal entity. All business-related liabilities are held by the corporation. This practice minimizes the personal liability of its owners. The corporation operates as a business and can be owned wholly or partially based on registered certificates, called *stock*. Some major steps required to set up a corporation include

    - Filing an application for a legal name

    - Paying a corporate franchise fee to the state in which you file

    - Appointing a board of directors and corporate officers

    - Keeping minutes of periodic meetings of the board

    Check your individual state's rules and regulations for setting up a corporation.

- **S corporation:** This type of corporation offers many of the same advantages as a regular corporation. But, unlike a corporation, it's treated for income tax purposes as a flow-through entity. This means that as a company, it pays no income taxes. Instead, all income and losses are reported individually by the owners or stockholders on their personal income tax returns. If your new business has fewer than 35 stockholders, consult with your accountant and attorney about this option.

- **Limited Liability Corporation (LLC):** When this type of corporation is created, income is distributed among partners, but the partners aren't usually personally liable for the corporation's debts. Therefore, the personal assets of the company's owners are generally protected. Only the money that's invested into the company by the owners can be lost.

There are many kits, books, and online services that allow you to form your own corporation in minutes for a flat fee. But you may want to seek the guidance of a lawyer to help you with this process to ensure that it's done correctly (especially completing and filing the correct paperwork) and that you've made the best decisions based on your personal situation. The paperwork that needs to be filed varies dramatically by state.

Organizing your office

After your business exists and is operational, you discover that whether you're operating from home or an office building, you need to make a financial investment in office supplies and equipment. The following sections provide a sampling of the equipment you need to get started.

Writers need a lot of the same tools that business operators need, long before they even consider starting a self-publishing company. The most important tools are the following:

- ✔ A computer with Internet access
- ✔ A combination printer/scanner/fax machine and their supplies
- ✔ A telephone with home service and/or cellular service

I cover these items in detail in Chapter 3.

The right computer software

Your computer may be your most important business tool. Figure out what types of applications you need to run on your computer, and then make sure that you purchase a PC or Mac-based machine powerful enough to handle those applications.

Having your computer connected to the Internet via a high-speed DSL or Broadband connection is a necessity. After you have the right software and capabilities, use your computer to perform your major tasks:

- ✔ Bookkeeping
- ✔ Handling your business's finances
- ✔ Inventory management
- ✔ Laying out and designing your book
- ✔ Managing a Web site
- ✔ Managing and editing electronic photography
- ✔ Research
- ✔ Sending/receiving e-mail
- ✔ Surfing the Web
- ✔ Writing

Chapter 8 has the scoop on design and photo software. Chapter 16 has details on software related to warehousing, order fulfillment, and shipping. Head to Chapter 21 for info on Web site design. For software suitable for running a small business, try QuickBooks Premier Edition (www.quickbooks.com).

Other tools and resources you need

To do your daily business operations, you need a wide range of basic office supplies. In addition to visiting your local office supply superstore, you often find low prices by shopping online for items such as toner cartridges for your printer and fax machine.

Some of the supplies you may want in your office include the following:

- Answering machine (if you don't have voicemail)
- Bookshelves
- Briefcase and pad/paper folio
- Business cards and stationery, including letterhead and business-size envelopes
- Calculator
- Cassette or microcassette recorder (or a digital recorder)
- CD-ROMs (blank)
- Copier and supplies
- Credit card processing equipment (if you sell directly to customers)
- Desk and chair(s)
- File cabinets and folders for organization and storage
- Label printer
- Paperclips
- Paper shredder
- Pencils, pens, and paper
- Postage machine, postage scale, and other shipping materials (envelopes, packing tape, labels, and so on)
- Power strips and extension cords
- Ruler/tape measure
- Scissors and tape
- Stapler and staples
- Wastepaper basket

Here are a few additional tips to consider as you finish setting up your office:

- **Set up accounts with shipping companies.** After your company is established, contact companies such as FedEx, UPS, DHL, and/or the U.S. Post Office. If you fulfill your own book orders, setting up in-house warehouse, inventory control, and shipping departments are essential. (See Chapter 16 for details on fulfillment, warehousing, and shipping.)

- **Subscribe to publishing trade magazines.** These publications keep you informed about news in the publishing industry and provide valuable how-to articles on a range of topics. Check out these Web sites:

  - www.bookmarketingupdate.com

- www.publishersweekly.com
- www.writersdigest.com

✔ **Acquire adequate insurance for yourself and your business.** If disaster strikes, not being adequately insured can quickly put you out of business and cause serious financial hardship. Protect your assets from theft, fire, lawsuits, and other disasters by obtaining homeowner's insurance (if your business is run from home) that covers all your equipment, inventory, and other business assets. In terms of your personal insurance, consider obtaining health insurance, life insurance, long-term disability insurance, and an umbrella insurance policy.

Consult with several insurance companies and independent insurance brokers to determine your needs and find the best deals for the most comprehensive coverage.

Keeping Costs Tracked and Under Control

The success of your business and publishing venture depends on your ability to manage your money and generate a profit. Allocate the money that you spend wisely. Focus on your company's objectives and how to best use your available funds to achieve those objectives. One of the biggest mistakes start-up company operators make is misallocating their money, so they run out of operating funds before their company is able to turn a profit.

Listing your expenses

Successfully launching and running your own business involves many start-up costs. Some of the initial business expenses you need to budget for include

✔ Accounting services

✔ Answering service

✔ Banking fees

✔ Business licenses and filing fees (including fees for incorporating)

✔ Insurance

✔ Internet service

- ✔ Legal services
- ✔ Merchant account establishment
- ✔ Office equipment and furniture, including computers and software
- ✔ Office supplies
- ✔ Phone service and equipment
- ✔ Postage meter rental
- ✔ Professional association membership fees and dues
- ✔ Subscriptions to publishing trade magazines
- ✔ Warehouse (storage) rental fees

In addition to these business costs, create a budget for your actual publishing project. Some of the upfront expenses you have that relate to the development and publication of your book include the following:

- ✔ Writing (hiring a ghost writer, if necessary; see Chapter 4)
- ✔ Editing (see Chapter 5)
- ✔ Obtaining the copyright, ISBN #, Library of Congress Card Number, and barcode for your book (see Chapter 7)
- ✔ Photography/artwork (see Chapter 4)
- ✔ Page layout and design (see Chapter 8)
- ✔ Front and back book cover design (see Chapter 9)
- ✔ Printing (see Part III)
- ✔ Order fulfillment/warehousing/shipping (see Chapter 16)
- ✔ Marketing and public relations (see Chapters 18 and 19)
- ✔ Advertising (see Chapter 20)
- ✔ Web site development and maintenance (see Chapter 21)

Formulating a budget

Figure 6-1 is an example of a budget worksheet to help you keep track of various costs. For each type of business expense, this worksheet allows you to calculate your monthly expenses (if applicable), as well as your total or annual costs. You can adjust the categories to fit your particular project.

Operational Expenses

Expense Type	Cost Per Month/Unit (Subtotal)	Total
Accounting Services		
Answering Service		
Association Membership(s)		
Computers		
Corporation/Company Establishment Fees		
Insurance		
Internet Service		
Legal Services		
Merchant Account Establishment and Monthly Fees (for Credit Card Processing)		
Office Equipment		
Office Furniture		
Office Supplies		
Order Fulfillment Services		
Postage Meter Rental		
Software		
Subscriptions		
Telephone Service		
Toll-Free Phone Service		
Warehousing/Storage Expenses		
Other		
Other		
Other		

Subtotal: $

Publishing Expenses

Expense Type	Cost Per Month/Unit (Subtotal)	Total
Barcode		
Copyright Filing		
Freelance Editor		
Freelance Illustrator, Artist, or Photographer		
Ghostwriter		
Graphic Designer for Book's Cover Design		
Graphic Designer for Book's Interior Design		

Figure 6-1a: Many costs figure into the budget of a self-publishing company.

Expense Type	Cost Per Month/Unit (Subtotal)	Total
ISBN Acquisition		
Printing Expenses		
Shipping Fees (Postage, Envelopes, Packing Supplies, and So On)		
Other		
Other		
Other		

Subtotal: $

Publicity, Advertising, and Marketing Expenses

Expense Type	Cost Per Month/Unit (Subtotal)	Total
Envelopes		
Freelance Public Relations Consultant or PR Firm		
Mailing Expenses		
Mailing List Rental or Purchase		
Paid Advertising Costs		
Postage		
Press Kit Folders		
Printing of Letterhead, Press Releases, Business Cards, and So On		
Promotional Material Design, Printing, and Distribution (Bookmarks, Postcards, and So On)		
Review Copy Expenses		
Trade Show Booth Space		
Travel Expenses		
Web Site Development		
Web Site Hosting		
Other		
Other		
Other		

Figure 6-1b:
Many costs figure into the budget of a self-publishing company.

Subtotal: $

Total: $

As you plan your business' operating budget for its first six months and then for one year of operation (it's best to complete a six-month budget and a one-year budget, which incorporates the 6-month budget), allow for unexpected expenses and have money available to deal with them.

Your accountant (get one if you don't have one) helps you properly budget for all your anticipated and potentially unexpected expenses. Ideally, you want to launch your business with enough money in the bank to operate for at least six months without generating any revenue. Update your budget as needed based on how the business grows and develops over time. It's an ongoing process.

Many costs are associated with successfully writing, editing, laying out, printing, distributing, marketing, advertising, and fulfilling orders for a self-published book. Establishing a proper budget like the one in Figure 6-1 and then carefully managing your finances help ensure your success:

- ✔ Have an adequate accounting and recordkeeping system in place (see "The right computer software" earlier in this chapter for some ideas).

- ✔ Maintain at least a monthly current balance sheet and income statement (a profit-and-loss statement) along with accurate banking records is important for keeping your business on track financially.

Finding Additional Expert Advice on Your Business Adventure

When you first came up with the idea to write and publish a book, you probably didn't realize that you can also be a small business operator. Well, in addition to becoming an author and figuring out how to publish a book successfully, if you plan to launch a business, you need to understand the fundamentals of business administration.

If you've absolutely no experience working in the business world, don't panic. First, focus on writing and publishing the very best book you can. Then, consider seeking the help of someone who can help you set up and potentially manage your business to compensate for your lack of experience. In addition to the folks and resources that I mention throughout the rest of this chapter, you can try the following sources:

- ✔ **Credit-card companies:** Both American Express (home.american express.com/home/open.shtml) and Visa (www.usa.visa.com/business) operate Web sites that cater to small business owners. These Web sites are chock-full of helpful articles, links to resources, and online-based tools.

✔ **Professional trade associations:** These organizations typically offer significant discounts on services and equipment, networking benefits, and informational resources. Consider joining the following publishing industry trade associations:

- **Small Publishers, Artists, and Writers Network (SPAWN):** SPAWN is a professional association offering resources, advice, and services to self-published authors. Visit the organization's Web site at www.spawn.org or call (818) 886-4281. Membership dues are $45 per year.

- **Independent Book Publishers Association (PMA):** With over 4,000 publishers represented, PMA (www.pma-online.org) is the largest, nonprofit trade association in the country, which represents small and independent publishers. This organization can help you establish your business, acquire a merchant account, and obtain discounts on book publishing and marketing services. Annual dues are about $110 per year.

- **The Small Publishers Association of North America (SPAN):** For self-published authors and small publishers, SPAN (www.spannet.org) is an organization that's well worth joining. Through publications, conferences, the Web site, and a wide range of other tools, SPAN is dedicated to advancing the interests and expertise of independent publishers through educational opportunities and discounted services. You can also reach SPAN by dialing (719) 475-1726. Dues are $105 per year.

✔ **Service Corps of Retired Executives (SCORE):** Although you can hire someone with experience as a partner or employee, a cheaper option is to take advantage of the free resources available to small business owners from SCORE. As a nonprofit association comprised of over 12,000 volunteers from across the country, SCORE is a division of the Small Business Administration (SBA) and is dedicated to aiding in the formation, growth, and success of small businesses nationwide. SCORE volunteers are trained to serve as counselors, advisors, and mentors to aspiring entrepreneurs and business owners.

SCORE volunteers in your area can be reached by calling (800) 634-0245 or by visiting the organization's Web site (www.score.org), which offers a variety of free resources to small business operators

Chapter 7

Tackling Book-Specific Tasks

*I*f you look at any commercially available book, the back cover lists the book's International Standard Book Number (ISBN) and barcode, along with the book's price. Within the front matter of your book (right after the title page inside your book), you typically find the copyright page, which lists legal information, including the book's copyright notice and the Library of Congress Control Number (LCCN).

This chapter focuses on how to obtain this information, which is exclusive to your book. I also show you how to select a proper publication date for your book and how to fill out Advance Book Information (ABI) forms.

Not all self-published authors have to handle these administrative tasks on their own. In many cases, your Print-On-Demand (POD) publisher or traditional book printer obtains the necessary ISBN, barcode, LCCN, and copyright, on your behalf. See Chapter 10 for more about traditional printers and Chapter 11 for details on POD publishing.

This chapter contains a bunch of legal stuff that may at first seem confusing. Don't despair! In addition to the information here, you may want to check out the Internet to for easy-to-understand resources. You can also seek help from an attorney or book printer that has experience in the areas covered in this chapter. Worst case scenario: You attend law school for three years and then self-publish your book (but chances are it won't come to that).

Obtaining an ISBN for Your Book

Any book that's sold anywhere in the world must have a unique ISBN. The following sections describe what an ISBN is, what the number signifies, why your book needs to have one, and how to obtain it.

An ISBN: What it is and why your book needs one

The ISBN system is an internationally recognized book identification system that's been in use since 1970. An ISBN is used for a variety of purposes, including inventory control; sales tracking; and order processing by booksellers, wholesalers, distributors, libraries, and universities. It's currently a 10-digit number, divided into four parts of variable length, with each part separated by a hyphen.

Some books have similar titles, or the same book may have multiple editions published over several years. To help keep track of every edition of every book that's published, each book is given a unique ISBN, which starting in January 2007 will be 13 digits long instead of 10 (see the nearby sidebar for details). The ISBN is displayed on the back cover and inside the book's interior on the copyright page (and sometimes on the inside front or back cover as well).

The five parts of an ISBN-13 offer the following information:

- **The new prefix:** This three-digit number (currently 978 or 979) identifies the book industry.

- **Group of country identifier:** This section indicates the country where the book was published.

- **Publisher identifier:** This part of the number is a unique code given to every individual publishing company (see the next section for more on this code).

- **Title identifier:** This part of the ISBN is unique to every book and identifies the particular title or edition of that title.

- **Check digit:** This single digit at the end of the ISBN validates the number. In some cases, this could be the capital letter 'X' (the Roman numeral for the number 10).

The ISBN undergoes a makeover

According to The ISBN Agency, the conversion from 10-digit ISBNs to 13-digit ISBNs is being done to accommodate the ever-expanding number of books published each year. In 2005, for example, more than 195,000 new titles and editions were published.

For books published prior to January 2007, each publisher needs to recalculate books' ISBNs to adhere to the new 13-digit numbering system. It's recommended that publishers print both the 10-digit and 13-digit ISBN on books published during the potentially long transition.

Books published after January 2007 should use the new ISBN-13 format exclusively. It looks something like this: "ISBN-13: 978-1-873671-00-9," as opposed to the old format, which looks like this: "ISBN-10: 1-873671-00-8." The look of the corresponding ISBN barcodes remains the same but contains the new 13-digit numbers. (See "Ordering a Barcode for Your Book," later in this chapter for more about barcodes.)

In addition, the new 13-digit numbers will be integrated with the European Article Number (EAN) system, which uniquely identifies every product available for retail sale. This new numbering system makes it easier to distribute books worldwide and makes books more compatible with inventory, sales tracking, and order systems that currently use the 13-digit EAN system.

The new ISBN-13 system replaces the Bookland EAN system, which has been in use since the 1980s. The Bookland EAN system was used by retail inventory, ordering, and sales tracking systems not equipped to understand or utilize the ISBN-10 system.

Publishers who want to find out more about implementing the new 13-digit ISBNs can check out the following two sources:

- ✔ Download the free guide *Guidelines for the Implementation of 13-Digit ISBNs* at `www.isbn-international.org/en/download/implementation-guidelines-04.pdf`. The guide is published by The International ISBN Agency.

- ✔ Download the free, 21-page eBook *ISBN-13 For Dummies,* Special Edition (Wiley) at `www.bisg.org/isbn-13/ISBN13_For_Dummies.pdf`.

Without a proper ISBN, most places that sell books won't be able to order or sell yours.

How and when to register for an ISBN

Throughout the world, there are 160 ISBN agencies; each is responsible for assigning unique ISBNs to new books published within a specific region. The

U.S. ISBN Agency (www.isbn.org) handles the United States, the U.S. Virgin Islands, Guam, and Puerto Rico.

It's important to understand that if you're using a POD publisher or a publisher that offers a turnkey self-publishing solution to authors, that the publisher/printer typically obtains an ISBN on your behalf. You only need to acquire your own ISBN if you plan to self-publish your book entirely by yourself and establish your own publishing company to do this.

Only established book publishers can acquire ISBNs for books they publish. If you're self-publishing a book without the help of a POD publisher or another type of turnkey publishing solution (as described in Chapter 11), you first need to establish a publishing company; see Chapter 6 for details on doing this task. As soon as you do that, contact the U.S. ISBN Agency.

Even if you represent a small publishing company planning to publish only one or two book titles, you still need to acquire an ISBN publishing prefix, along with a block of at least 10 ISBNs. This process takes approximately 15 business days; however, for an additional fee a Priority Processing (two-day) or an Express (one-day) service is available.

To acquire an ISBN publisher prefix and purchase a block of ISBNs, you must first complete and submit the appropriate form — Application for An ISBN Publisher Prefix — to The U.S. ISBN Agency. This process can be done in a couple of different ways:

✔ **Online application:** Visit www.isbn.org/standards/home/isbn/us/secureapp.asp and fill your forms out online and submit immediately. Online applications are free of charge.

✔ **Printed forms:** Visit www.isbn.org/standards/home/isbn/us/printable/isbn.asp to download the printable forms. After you've filled out the forms, send them via

 • **Mail:** R.R. Bowker, 630 Central Avenue, New Providence, NJ 07974

 • **Fax:** (908) 219-0188

 • **E-mail:** isbn-san@bowker.com

There is a one-time application submission fee of $20 for submitting paper forms.

Additional processing fees for either way of submission include a Publisher Registration Fee for each block of ISBNs purchased: 10 ISBNs–$29.95; 100 ISBNs–$64.95; 1000 ISBNs–$179.95; 10,000 ISBNs–$399.95.

All fees are nonrefundable and can be paid using a major credit card, check, or money order. In addition, ISBNs can't be transferred, sold, or reassigned because a portion of the 10- or 13-digit number represents the individual publishing company.

As of the printing of this book, the prices for obtaining a block of ISBNs from the U.S. ISBN Agency with regular processing are as follows:

> 10 ISBNs: $240
>
> 100 ISBNs: $850
>
> 1,000 ISBNs: $1,250
>
> 10,000 ISBNs: $3,050

The cost of acquiring a publishing prefix and at least 10 ISBNs, along with the fees associated with creating corresponding barcodes for each ISBN (see the next section), should be calculated into your overall budget. See Chapter 6 for details on creating a budget for your publishing company.

After you've submitted your application, you'll be asked for a wide range of information about your publishing company:

- ✔ The company/publisher name
- ✔ The company/publisher address, phone number, fax number, e-mail address, and Web site
- ✔ The name of the Rights and Permissions Contact within the company, the person's title, and phone number. (In most cases, this person is the self-published author.)
- ✔ The name of the ISBN Coordinator within the company, the title, and phone number. (In most cases, this person would be the self-published author.)
- ✔ The year the company was founded and started publishing
- ✔ The type of products produced by the company (books, videos, software, eBooks, spoken word cassettes/CDs)
- ✔ The company's primary focus in terms of subject areas covered
- ✔ Information about how your products are distributed (see Part IV for distribution details)

After you've obtained your ISBN publisher prefix and have assigned individual ISBNs to your upcoming books, each title can then be listed with *Bowker's Books In Print,* a comprehensive database and directory of all current and upcoming books. This directory is used by booksellers, libraries, schools, universities, and other institutions to search for and pre-order books and decide what books they want to carry in advance of the publication date. Check out the Web site at www.booksinprint.com.

Ordering a Barcode for Your Book

In conjunction with each ISBN issued for a book (see the previous section), you can order a corresponding barcode (which prints on the back cover of your book). The purpose of this barcode is primary for retail inventory control and sales. It's made up of several parts. The primary barcode recreates the book's ISBN, while a secondary barcode recreates the book's cover price. You can see a barcode for yourself on this book's back cover.

Obtain your barcode from Bowker Bar Code Service. The cost per barcode, when ordered at the same time, is as follows:

✓ $25 for one to five barcodes

✓ $23 per barcode for six to 10 barcodes

✓ $21 per barcode for 11 to 100 barcodes

Each barcode comes in hardcopy, camera-ready, or digital format in 2400 dpi, 99.26 percent magnification. You receive a vanilla bar code (white background and black text) with accompanying price add-on. Contact Bowker Bar Code Service (www.bowkerbarcode.com) for additional details.

The barcode that appears on your book follows a different format than a UPC symbol that appears on retail products. The book publishing business uses its own unique barcode system tied to each book's ISBN. Many publishers include the Price Code extension onto their barcode as well.

When designing your book's back cover, the barcode must be positioned near the bottom of the back cover and be accompanied by the book's ISBN printed in a readable font. The barcode should also appear on the inside front cover of strippable paperback books. (When retailers return the books for credit, they rip off the front cover of the book and send it back — hence the strippable cover.) Chapter 9 has additional details on incorporating a barcode into a back cover's design.

A group decision: Including BISAC Subject and Audience information

Created by The Book Industry Study Group, a professional trade association comprising companies and individuals working in the publishing industry, the BISAC Audience and BISAC Subject are industry-standard categories that your book should fit into. These classifications help booksellers display your book in the appropriate section, based on subject matter and target audience.

The BISAC Subject and/or BISAC Audience classifications for your book should be printed (in small type) on the back cover of your book, either near the barcode or in the upper-right or left corner of the back cover. You also need this information when submitting listings to online booksellers (see Chapter 15) and selling your book to distributors or wholesalers (see Chapter 15).

For a comprehensive list of BISAC Subjects and subcategories, point your Web browser to www.bisg.org/standards/bisac_ subject/major_subjects.html. In addition to choosing a Subject that's most appropriate for your book, you can further classify your book using a subcategory. For example, a book

about Yorkshire Terriers fits into the subject *Pets,* with the subcategory *Dogs.* Therefore, next to the barcode on the book's back cover, you see "Pets/Dogs" printed.

BISAC Audience refers to the intended reader for the book. Ideally, you should only use one audience code for your book .Two industry standards exist for classifying books by audience, including X.12 and Onix:

- ✔ Audience codes under the X.12 system include COL (College), JUV (Juvenile), PSP (Professional and Scholar), TRA (Trade), and YA (Young Adult).

- ✔ The Onix Code has the following categories: 01 (General/Trade), 02 (Children/Juvenile), 03 (Young Adult), 04 (Primary & Secondary/ Elementary & High School), 05 (College/ Higher Education), 06 (Professional and Scholarly), 07 (English as a Second Language), and 08 (Adult Education).

For more information about BISAC Subject and BISAC Audience classifications, visit www. bisg.org.

For more information about bar coding and incorporating the appropriate barcode information within your self-published book, check out www.bisg.org/pi/barcode_considerations.html.

Filling Out the Advance Book Information Form

After your book has its own ISBN, complete the Advance Book Information (ABI) Form so your title can be listed within *Bowker's Books In Print* directory. The appropriate forms for submitting your book title(s) are provided by R.R.

Bowker (www.bowker.com). If you're using a POD publishing service or another turnkey self-publishing solution, the company or service you use most likely obtains an ISBN on your behalf and completes the necessary ABI paperwork to get your book listed.

If you're handling ABI paperwork yourself, Bowker offers the online BowkerLink service that allows publishers to create and update listings in the company's databases. This is a free service for registered publishers that replaces ABI paper forms. To register for this service, click the *Books In Print* icon found on the main page of the BowkerLink Web site (www.bowker link.com), and then click *Register.* Only recognized publishing companies are granted access to this service. After you establish a publishing company (see Chapter 6 for details on doing this), complete the registration form and you're granted access to the service within three days.

After you're registered, select the *Add Item* icon to begin adding information about specific book titles. After completing the online form, the information is added to the *Bowker Books In Print* database within one to two business days. Details about books should be added to the *Books In Print* database 180 days prior to publication.

Information you need to provide about each book title to be listed in the *Books In Print* database includes

- Audience
- Binding
- BISAC subject
- Description (25 to 200 words)
- ISBN
- Language
- Page count
- Price
- Publication date
- Publisher
- Publisher imprint (if applicable)
- Ship date
- Title and subtitle
- Trim size

Publishers have the option of including additional details about their book titles, which the BowkerLink Web site prompts users to enter, if it's applicable. You can also include a cover image.

Securing a Library of Congress Control Number

The Library of Congress Control Number (LCCN) is a number assigned to your book that's used by libraries for numbering and cataloging books. The system was implemented in 1898. This number includes the year of publication and a unique serial number for each book title. Make sure to obtain your LCCN prior to the book's publication, and then the number should appear on the copyright page of your book.

There is no charge to obtain a LCCN. To get one, visit `pcn.loc.gov` and complete the necessary form and mail it to Library of Congress, Cataloging in Publication Division, 101 Independence Avenue, S.E., Washington, D.C. 20540-4320. Your book needs an ISBN to participate in this program.

Can I have it? Cataloging in Publication

Major publishing houses use a Cataloging in Publication (CIP) number, which serves the same purpose as a LCCN but follows a slightly different format. Books can have a CIP record filed with the Library of Congress. This bibliographic information consists of details about books that allow libraries to catalog them quickly. Information about a book's title, publisher, author, trim size, binding, copyright, and table of contents are included. The bibliographic information is compiled from the book or manuscript itself, not from forms submitted by the publisher.

Prior to a book's publication, the full text of the publication is electronically submitted to the Library of Congress, which then creates an original bibliographic record (CIP data). This data is then returned to the publisher so it can be included within the front matter of the book, usually right after the title page.

At the same time, information about the book is immediately available to each library that acquires the book, which ultimately saves librarians time and expense when it comes to cataloging the book within their collections. Librarians also use pre-publication data from the Library of Congress to order books.

Here's the kicker, though: Only U.S. publishers that publish titles most likely to be widely acquired by U.S. libraries are eligible to participate in the CIP program. Self-published authors need to utilize the Control Number program, which offers the same benefits in terms of making information about your book readily available to libraries across the country.

An alternate CIP is available to self-publishers called Publisher's Cataloguing in Publication (PCIP) and provided for a fee by Quality Books, Inc. Many independent publishers use PCIPs in lieu of the standard; the PCIP contains the same needed information to librarians. Librarians who happen to know the LOC cataloguing system can also write CIP data; it's worth checking with your local library to see if anyone knows cataloguing data and wants to pick up a freelance job! You aren't required by law to get CIP data only from the LOC.

Most POD and turnkey self-publishing solutions handle acquiring the LCCN. When researching which self-publishing solution to use (solutions covered in Part III of this book), inquire if this service is automatically offered. If not, you need to obtain a LCCN for your book.

It's Mine, All Mine! Copyrighting Your Work

When you write a book, it's an original literary work. You're so proud of the work that you've done, and you want to ensure that your work remains your own and isn't misused or stolen. Therefore, make sure to properly copyright your book. As an author, you can copyright any original work, including literary, dramatic, musical, artistic, and certain other intellectual works.

The most important reason to copyright your work is so no one else can steal or plagiarize it (calling it their own and publishing it under their own name). After a work is copyrighted, it's protected for the life of the author, plus 70 years. In some cases, the duration can be for 95 or even 120 years after the author's death. Contact the United States Copyright Office (`www.copyright.gov`) for details on which situation applies to your book.

In the following sections, I show you how to create a copyright notice and give you steps for registering your copyright.

Including a copyright notice in your book

All versions of your work should include a legal copyright notice. When your book is formally published, the book's copyright page typically goes right after the title page as part of the book's front matter; see Chapter 4 for more details about the makeup of a copyright page.

A legal copyright notice should contain these three main elements:

✔ The copyright symbol — the letter *c* in a circle ("©") or the word *Copyright*

✔ The year of first publication

✔ The name of the owner of the copyright

A one-line copyright notice reads: © 2007 Jason R. Rich.

For details about creating the appropriate legal wording for your book's copyright page, contact an attorney who specializes in copyright law and consult with your book printer, who may also be able to provide guidance.

Registering your copyright

The purpose of actually registering your copyright (as opposed to just printing a copyright notice in your book) is to create a public record of your book's existence and to announce your ownership of the copyright. It also establishes an official date when your ownership of the work began. To find out more about the protections offered by filing the appropriate copyright forms for your book, visit the Library of Congress Copyright Office's Web site at www.copyright.gov.

Registering the copyright for your book is a fast, inexpensive, and simple process. Simply mail the following three elements (in the same envelope) to The Library of Congress Copyright Office:

- ✔ A completed copyright application form. The appropriate form (which is "Form TX" for a literary work) can be obtained online (www.copyright.gov) or by calling (202) 707-3000. The form must be completed by the author or someone representing the author, such as the copyright claimant, the owner of exclusive rights to the manuscript, or a duly authorized agent of the author or copyright claimant.

- ✔ The nonrefundable fee of $30.

- ✔ A copy of your complete manuscript in hardcopy form. (This can be a photocopy of your book's manuscript.) If you wait until your book is actually published to file your copyright, be sure to send in a printed and bound copy of your book.

Mail your completed package to Library of Congress, Copyright Office, 101 Independence Avenue, S.E., Washington, DC 20559-6000. Your registration becomes effective on the day that the Copyright Office receives your application package. However, receiving a written notification that the copyright is in effect can take up to five months.

Send your copyright application package via U.S. Priority Mail with Signature Confirmation or via an overnight courier (such as FedEx or UPS). You want to be able to track the package and to prove it was received by the Copyright Office.

Increasing Profits by Setting the Right Cover Price

Prior to printing your book and officially announcing its publication, you need to set its cover price. This figure is the retail price of your book (the cost readers pay to purchase it, either from you or from a bookseller).

Setting your book's cover price is an important business decision that must be made based on accurate market research, knowledge of the publishing industry, and educated predictions for what you believe sales of your book will be. Handling this aspect of the publishing process correctly could mean the difference between generating a profit and losing money on your publishing venture. In the following sections, I explain several factors to consider as you choose a cover price.

If you're working with a POD publisher instead of a traditional printer, chances are that the company either helps you set your cover price or sets it for you. See Chapter 10 for the scoop on traditional printers and Chapter 11 for more about POD publishers.

Calculating your publication costs

The first step in your calculation of cost should be mathematical estimations and budgeting. Determine how much money you invested in your publishing project in order to write and publish your book. A wide range of costs and fees are involved in every aspect of the publishing process. The costs you specifically need to know to start figuring your cover price include

- ✓ Fixed expenses, such as writing, editing, and designing costs
- ✓ Printing costs, based on the print run (the number of copies) you order (see the next section for details on print runs and Part III for basics on printing)
- ✓ The costs of shipping, warehousing, advertising, marketing, and promoting your books
- ✓ Market comparisons — looking at published books already in bookstores that are similar to yours in size, format, and topic — to make sure that you aren't underpricing or overpricing your book for the current market

If you plan to sell most of your inventory at personal appearances, you may be able to price your book higher than the market average. If a substantial proportion of your books are headed for bookstores, however, it's important to be price-competitive. In some cases a self-published author's costs are much higher. A book from a major publisher may sell for $14.95; the self-published author might have to sell a similar book for $19.95 to make any money. This pricing depends on how the book is printed or published; however, using POD often requires a higher cover price, regardless of the competition.

Here are a couple of options to help you work with numbers:

✔ Use a spreadsheet program, such as Microsoft Excel, to create a detailed budget, track expenses, and help you calculate your break-even point as you begin to determine what the cover price of your book will be.

✔ Contact a consulting firm that specializes in the publishing industry. These firms offer spreadsheets designed to help small publishers calculate their costs, establish budgets, and set their book's cover price.

Gropen Associates, Inc. is one company that can help. For more information, visit the company's Web site at www.gropenassoc.com/Top LevelPages/DoItYourself.htm.

See Chapter 6 for more about keeping track of costs and creating a budget.

Predicting demand

Accurately anticipating the demand for your book helps you predict sales and calculate potential revenues. There's a huge difference between having anticipated sales of 1,000 copies of your book that targets a very niche audience and sales of 25,000 copies or more for a general interest book to the mass market.

✔ A *niche-oriented audience* limits sales potential, and you may want to have a higher cover price for your book sales to ensure profits.

✔ A *mass-market audience* requires an expansive marketing, advertising, and promotional campaign, which costs more money. If you plan to sell a lot of books, you can reduce the cover price somewhat to earn higher profits based on sales volume.

Doing proper market research, knowing the size of your audience, and having realistic expectations helps you anticipate demand for your book. Begin by researching the sales success of previously published books with similar topics and marketing campaigns. You need to market your book directly to readers and determine the best ways to reach them. Chapter 4 helps you better understand who your target readers are.

Considering wholesale and discounted pricing

Depending on how you plan to sell your book, you may need to calculate potential profits based on the wholesale or discounted price for which you plan to sell your book. (Also consider sales commissions and royalties you may need to pay for certain distribution opportunities.) For example, book-sellers, distributors, and wholesalers may purchase your book in large quantities but at a discount of 40 to 60 percent off the cover price.

Unless you're going to sell your book directly to readers, via your Web site or when you make appearances or do lectures, plan on selling it at a significantly discounted price. See Chapter 15 for details about distributing your book through traditional channels.

Determining your book's perceived value

How much are people really willing to pay for your book? Some nonfiction, special interest trade paperbacks have a retail price of $39.95 or higher because the information it contains is perceived to be valuable to the intended reader. Knowing your audience helps you evaluate how much they may be willing to purchase your book for at retail.

If you're providing information, facts, statistics, or other content that can only be found in your book, readers may perceive that to be extra valuable and they may pay a slight premium for their perceptions. Note that perceived value doesn't really apply to fiction. Why? Readers expect to pay under $10 for a fiction paperback. Even if the novel is a bestseller, readers won't pay a premium for it. This is why mass-market paperbacks (novels) typically have a relatively low cover price compared to nonfiction trade paperbacks.

After performing your own financial calculations and sales projections, take a look at competing book titles already in your market to determine what they're selling for and what the sales history is for those titles. Use this information to determine if your book's cover price is too high or too low, based on the competition. If a book is much cheaper than its competition, it can be perceived as possessing less valuable information. If the book is priced much higher than the competition, the potential reader may opt to purchase the less expensive book.

Putting everything together to come up with a magic number

After you know the total cost per book to have it printed, use this important piece of information to help you create your book's cover price.

Your cost per book is the total amount of money you need to spend to have each copy of your book printed. To determine your cost per book, simply add all your publication costs together and divide it by the number of copies you plan to have printed. There is no set formula to figure cover price based on cost per book. This is totally different for everyone, based on how the book is being printed and published, the distribution method, and target audience. Do consider, however, how you're going to be selling the book and what distribution methods you plan to use. Will you be earning the entire cover price of the book or just 40, 50, or 60 percent of the cover price?

If you're selling your book directly to consumers at its cover price, your profit can be calculated by subtracting the cost per book from the cover price. For example, if you want your book's cover price at $19.95 and your total cost per book is $6, your profit — if you sell your book directly to a customer for the cover price — is $13.95 per copy. If you sell your entire print run of 2,000 books directly to customers (through your own Web site or when you make appearances), your total profit is $27,900.

However, if you're selling your book through retailers, booksellers, wholesalers, or distributors, you're selling your book for 40 to 60 percent off the cover price. You also need to calculate any sales commissions you need to pay.

So, if you want your book's cover price to be $19.95 and the total cost per book is $6, but you're selling the book to a retailer at 40 percent off the cover price ($11.97), your per copy profit is $5.97. If you sell your entire print run of 2,000 books through booksellers and retailers, you earn $11,940.

Choosing the most competitive printer, negotiating your best deal, and accurately anticipating demand so you can determine the most appropriate size of your print run helps you keep your costs down and increase your book's profit potential based on your book's cover price. Factors like trim size, page count, paper type, cover stock, and binding all impact your printing costs. For example, you can cut costs by hiring a traditional printer to publish a trade paperback book (as opposed to hard cover) with a less expensive paper stock, a larger trim size, and fewer pages. (However, you don't want to jeopardize the professional look of your book.) It's important for the printer you hire to understand what your book is about, its intended audience, how you plan to distribute it, and your budget, so he can help you make appropriate printing decisions. See Part III for more about printing options.

If you're selling your book directly to consumers or retailers, for example, you may need to charge sales tax. Every state has different guidelines, so be sure to consult with your accountant to ensure that you collect the appropriate amount of sales tax on applicable sales. As for shipping charges, this doesn't need to be calculated into the cover price of your book. When people place an order for your book, from your Web site, for example, they expect to pay extra for shipping and handling.

The Right Time: Selecting Your Book's Publication Date

Part of taking a well-organized and well-thought-out approach to self-publishing is to determine the best time of year to release your book. Consider the time it takes to complete each stage of the publishing process (taking into account lead times and processing times needed by editors, layout people, graphic designers, proofreaders, printers, distributors, order fulfillment houses, and so on) and plan your release date accordingly.

Your *publication date* is the date your book goes to press. Your *street date* or *release date* is the day your book is available to the public.

If your book has seasonal interest or must be released in conjunction with a certain holiday or date, scheduling becomes that much more critical. Missing that date could cost you sales. You can find a holiday to tie into any kind of book with a specialty calendar like *Chase's Calendar of Events*. (Do an Internet search for *Chase's Calendar of Events* to get your copy.)

Based on your audience, the topic of your book and your writing, production, printing, distribution, advertising, public relations, and marketing schedules, choose a date to release your book that's achievable and that makes the most sense in terms of generating the highest possible sales. For example, if you're releasing a book about decorating your home for the Christmas holiday, a good time to release the book would be late Fall (two or three months before Christmas), not after the holiday season. Meanwhile, January or February is a great time to release a book about dating or romance, because you can tie in your promotional efforts with Valentine's Day. Check out Chapter 1 for a general timeline of the self-publishing process to help you decide.

Chapter 8

Coming Up with Creative Page Design and Layout

In This Chapter

▶ Beginning with the basics of designing your book

▶ Using popular desktop publishing software

▶ Creating a final digital file for the printer

▶ Finding a graphic designer for expert help

*W*hen readers open your book, they expect to see each page professionally designed. In addition to the content being free of spelling and grammatical mistakes (something a professional editor helps you with; see Chapter 5), from a visual standpoint, each page should look appealing and easy to read.

Making your book's interior look good involves laying out each page in a PDF or Postscript PRN file before it goes to press. The formatting and design you apply to your book's interior directly impacts how your book looks when it's ultimately printed. This chapter focuses on your manuscript's layout and design, so the book's interior looks professional and appealing.

Many companies that offer all-inclusive publishing solutions such as Print-On-Demand (POD) (see Chapter 11) include basic page layout and design services. If you're handling your self-publishing project entirely on your own and you're not proficient in using a popular desktop publishing software package, such as Adobe InDesign CS2 or QuarkXPress (described later in this chapter), seriously consider hiring a professional graphic designer to handle this aspect of the book publishing process for you. There's a big difference between mere legibility and effective page design, which takes experience to create. I cover strategies for hiring a graphic designer later in this chapter.

Delving into Do-It-Yourself Page Design

A book's interior pages must contain the proper information, displayed using headline and body text fonts that are easy to read. If your book includes pieces of artwork, they must be properly formatted and placed on the appropriate pages. A properly designed book also includes all the elements common to professionally published titles in the front and back matter. In the following sections, I guide you through setting your type in word-processed documents, deciding on a few upfront design considerations, and creating the body of your book.

For help creating the design and layout for your book, visit the Help Publish Web site at www.helppublish.com/layout.html.

Setting your type in a word processor

Most manuscripts are created using a word processor, such as Microsoft Word. Unless the person who does your page layout and design tells you differently, within your manuscript you can add basic formatting instructions, telling the layout and design person where headings, subheads, sidebars, photos, illustrations, and other elements go. (The actual text of your manuscript doesn't need any formatting instructions.)

For example, while you're writing, you can add the line *<BEGIN SIDEBAR>* and *<END SIDEBAR>* into your manuscript to tell the design person where a sidebar begins and ends. For a level-one heading (the biggest heading you use), you can use the code [H1] following by the heading. For a subheading smaller than a level-one heading, you could use the code [H2] or [H3] followed by the heading text as appropriate.

A level-one heading created in a word processor looks like this example:

[H1] This Is a Sample Level-One Heading

When the layout and designer starts doing his job, the heading would be transformed to look something like the heading of this section (although you can choose the font and type size; see "Choosing fonts" later in this chapter).

The more direction that you provide within the manuscript itself, the easier designing the book's internal layout to match your vision can be.

Making some upfront design decisions

As you embark on the page design process, focus on your book's target audience and on what's appropriate for the type of book you're publishing:

✔ **Font:** The font can make your book more visually appealing but can also set a tone. Using a font that's too small or difficult to read can make it much harder for the reader to appreciate and understand the content.

✔ **Too much content:** Putting too much content on each page can also make the overall book more challenging to read.

✔ **Layout and design:** Just as creating the content for your book was a creative and well-thought-out process, so is the layout and design of your book. The creativity you incorporate into this phase of the publishing process can determine how well your book sells and whether your readers enjoy looking at the pages as they're reading.

One of the first steps in developing your book's interior page design is choosing the trim size (dimensions) of your book. This step determines the dimensions of each page and helps you figure out how much actual content fits on each page. At this stage, don't aim for a certain page count for the total book; wait and see how long the book winds up to be before tweaking anything with the layout. Chapter 10 delves deeper into choosing trim size.

Next, you need to decide how much color, if any, will be used in the book. Many books use just black ink and black-and-white photos within the book's interior. You can, however, opt to include a second or third color or utilize full-color printing throughout your entire book, but remember that this decision increases your production costs dramatically (Chapter 6 covers publishing costs in more detail). The additional colors can be used to highlight headings or specific contents. The text in your book can be printed in one color, but the drawings, charts, or illustrations, for example, could be displayed in a different color to make them easier to read and stand out more.

Another important part of the design process involves knowing the specific order for major elements of your book, and then deciding how each element will look. The front matter and back matter of your book typically requires more formatting than the main body of your book. The front matter includes

✔ The book's title page

✔ Copyright page

✔ Acknowledgements and dedication

✔ Table of contents

✔ Foreword or preface

✔ Introduction

The back matter can include

✔ The appendixes

✔ Bibliography

> ✔ Glossary
>
> ✔ Index
>
> ✔ Author bio

Not all of these elements are necessarily appropriate or required for the type of book you're publishing. If you're using a POD printer or an offset printer that offers a turnkey publishing solution, the front matter and the back matter typically are compiled for you.

Building the body of your book

Based on the type of book you're publishing, your target audience, and your own sense of style, you need to make decisions about the overall look of your book's interior. These decisions should remain consistent from page to page and determine how your book ultimately looks when it's printed.

Coming up with the right page design means incorporating a bit of creativity into the process and focusing on each element of your book's interior. You need to select a headline font and a text font and determine font sizes to be used. You also need to decide on a master page design, so all the interior pages are consistent in terms of margins, layout, and overall appearance. I cover these topics in the following sections and provide some handy hints for creating chapter title pages and incorporating artwork into your book.

Choosing fonts

In the world of graphic design and typesetting, typed characters are measured in points. There are 72 points in one inch. This measurement means that the smaller the point size of the font, the smaller it appears on the printed page. If you make the text too small, your readers may be unable to read your words. If the text is too large, your book takes on the appearance of a children's book and may look amateurish.

For the main body text within your book, the size of the font should be between 10 and 12 points, unless your book is targeted to children or adults who are visually impaired (in which case a larger point size type could be used, such as 14- or 15-point type.) Chapter titles and headings should be larger than your body text and be displayed in a bold font. The font's point size depends on the overall look you're going for with your design decisions.

Figure 8-1 showcases how Garamond (a common text font) looks in several different point sizes: 9 points, 10 points, 11 points, 12 points, and 13 points. Also displayed in Figure 8-1 are several different sizes of the Georgia font, one of many fonts that can be used for headings.

This is a sample of Garamond displayed in a 9-point size. As you can see, it's a bit difficult to read.

This is a sample of Garamond displayed in a 10-point size. For certain types of books, when you're trying to make a lot of words fit on a page, this point size is appropriate.

This is a sample of Garamond displayed in an 11-point size. This point size is much easier to read and more pleasing to the human eye.

This is a sample of Garamond displayed in a 12-point size. Most people will have no trouble reading this size type. It's suitable for the body text of almost any type of book.

This is the Georgia font displayed in 17-point type. It's ideal for level-one headings.

This is the Georgia font displayed in a bold, 17-point type. It's also ideal for level-one headings.

This is the Georgia font displayed in a bold and italicized 17-point type. It's another way of displaying this font when using it for a level-one heading.

This is the Georgia font displayed in a bold, 15-point type. It's ideal for level-two headings.

This is the Georgia font displayed in a bold and italicized 10-point type. It's ideal for level-three headings.

Figure 8-1: Choose the fonts for your main text and headings from a variety of point sizes.

Decreasing the point size of your font, even by a small amount, decreases your book's page count dramatically (resulting in lower production costs) because more text fits on each page. But remember that a standard 10- to 12-point font is much easier on the eyes to read than a smaller 9-point font.

The font you choose for your book's main text should be easy-to-read and needs to be based on the look you're trying to achieve for your book and its intended audience. In the United States, serif-based fonts tend to be popular.

- ✓ A *serif font* uses short, lines, curves, or embellishments, called serifs, that project from the top or bottom of a letter's mainstroke. This style of font helps guide the reader's eyes in a straight line across the page.

- ✓ *Sans serif fonts* use less curves and embellishments. They're great for headings, but are a bit harder on the eye when used as a main text font.

See Figure 8-2 for a sampling of common text fonts. Visit the Adobe Type Library online (`www.studio.adobe.com/us/type/main.jsp`) to see a sampling of over 2,200 fonts — many of which are suitable for use in books.

Keep the following points in mind when you select fonts:

- ✓ Make sure the font is available in a variety of typefaces, including normal, **bold,** and *italics.* (Refer to Figure 8-2 for examples of fonts in all three styles.) This variety gives you the most flexibility when laying out your body text.

- ✓ Make sure the fonts you choose are compatible with the printing technology you use to print your book. Some POD publishers don't accept books that use Times New Roman or Arial fonts, due to incompatibility issues with the printing equipment.

Focusing on formatting

Formatting refers to how the text is formatted on the page — the page margins, page numbers, and running heads. A cluttered page is harder to read and potentially confusing. Learning to use white space effectively on each page helps make your book more visually appealing.

Follow these steps for formatting your text:

1. **Set the margins for each page.**

   All your margins must be consistent. The margins used are determined in part by the book's trim size, how long the manuscript is, and your desired page count. Your printing company or professional designer can help you choose appropriate margins, because there are no hard rules.

This is an example of Garamond, one of many popular body text fonts. It's displayed here using a normal 12-point font size. **This is what it looks like displayed in bold.** *This is the same Garamond 12-point font displayed in italics.*

This is an example of Times New Roman, one of many popular body text fonts. It's displayed here using a normal 12-point font size. **This is what it looks like displayed in bold.** *This is the same Times New Roman 12-point font displayed in italics.*

This is an example of Baskerville, one of many popular body text fonts. It's displayed here using a normal 12-point font size. **This is what it looks like displayed in bold.** *This is the same Baskerville 12-point font displayed in italics.*

Figure 8-2: Garamond, Times New Roman, Baskerville, Goudy, and Bookman Old Style are common serif-based fonts.

This is an example of Goudy, one of many popular body text fonts. It's displayed here using a normal 12-point font size. **This is what it looks like displayed in bold.** *This is the same Goudy 12-point font displayed in italics.*

This is an example of Bookman Old Style, one of many popular body text fonts. It's displayed here using a normal 12-point font size. **This is what it looks like displayed in bold.** *This is the same Bookman Old Style 12-point font displayed in italics.*

2. **Choose whether your book has a running head.**

   Your book's running head can consist of the book's title, chapter title, or the author's name appearing across the top of each page. If you study other books, you may see that some display the book's title on the left pages and the chapter title on the right pages. What's included within the running head is entirely up to you.

3. Decide where you want the page numbers to appear.

You have a number of choices: At the top of the page in the center, upper-right corner, or upper-left corner; at the bottom of the page in the center, lower-right corner, or lower-left corner.

See Figure 8-3 for a sample of what a basic page layout may look like for your self-published book. This page from my book *The Bachelor's Guide To Life,* (designed and published using POD technology) features standard body text, one level-one heading, and the running head at the top of the page.

42   The Bachelor's Guide To Life

Before looking for an internship program to participate in, determine what your goals are. Possible goals might be to get your foot in the door at a specific company, to learn about a specific industry, to obtain real world work experience doing something that interests you, to master skills that can only be learned on-the-job (as opposed to in a classroom), to earn college credit and/or to earn a pay-check.

Once you land an internship, consider it an audition for ultimately obtaining a full-time job. Always act professionally, ask questions, follow directions, display plenty of enthusiasm, volunteer to take on additional responsibilities, meet dead-lines, and work closely with your boss/supervisor. Upon graduating, make sure to highlight your internship work on your resume.

Are You Earning What You're Worth?

Are you like most people, working too hard, for too many hours per week, yet not getting paid what you believe you deserve? Due to ever increasing competi-tion, employers often push employees to work longer hours and take on more responsibilities, yet are offering less pay. Since salaries and compensation pack-ages are typically kept confidential within a company, it can be difficult to deter-mine if you're getting paid what you truly deserve based on your experience, skills, education and overall value to the company you work for.

Whether you're looking for a new job, hoping to earn a raise, or you're con-vinced you're not getting paid what you're worth in your current job, there are things you can do to discover your own true earning potential.

Many things contribute to someone's salary and overall compensation pack-age. Work experience, education, skills, the size of the company, the industry, the geographic location of the employer, demand, the number of hours you work, and your ability to negotiate the best possible salary/compensation package all help to determine what you get paid.

Once you know exactly what type of job you're looking to fill (or you cur-rently fill), by performing research you can determine what salary range someone holding a similar job title and responsibilities earns within your industry and/or geographic area. Using this information, you can then determine if you're cur-rently earning less than what you're worth and take the necessary steps to either pursue a higher paying job or a raise.

No matter what industry you work in, its possible to pinpoint average salaries paid by employers for specific jobs. One of the best resources for gathering cur-rent and accurate salary information (available online or in printed form) is *The*

Figure 8-3:
This basic page layout includes a running head and a page number at the top.

To help you develop design ideas, examine a handful of books that target a similar audience. Scrutinize the different design elements that have been incorporated. Pick and choose elements you like from those books, but be sure to add your own personal creativity when finalizing your book's design.

Crafting chapter title pages

Chapter title pages can be used on the first page of each new chapter. The title page displays the chapter number for a fiction or nonfiction book, but for nonfiction, you should also include the chapter title and perhaps some type of graphic and/or a short paragraph about what that chapter is about.

Depending on your creativity, you can jazz up your chapter title pages in several different ways:

- By using a different and larger font than your body text
- Altering the font and/or size of the first words or letters at the beginning of the first paragraph of each chapter
- Creating a special graphic that goes on each chapter title page

When creating chapter title pages, you're free to use your own creativity; however, all the chapter title pages in your book should be similar in their formatting to maintain continuity throughout the book.

Some publishers insist that all chapter title pages be on the right side and include a blank left-side page prior to it. This is a tradition that not all publishers adhere to, so ultimately it's your decision. Generally, running heads and page numbers don't appear on chapter title pages.

Figure 8-4 features a chapter title page from *The Bachelor's Guide To Life*. Notice that it's a right-handed page. While the page number is displayed in the bottom center, there's no running header on this page.

Incorporating artwork

Depending on the type of book you're publishing, artwork — in the form of photographs, graphs, charts, tables, figures, illustrations or clip art (see Chapter 4 for more about these formats) — adds visual appeal, impacts your book, and helps you better communicate information.

To enhance the impact of your artwork, make sure that each graphic element is sized and formatted properly and placed on the appropriate page in your book:

- **Sizing:** The size of images, charts, illustrations, and other graphics of your book should be easy to read. Depending on the trim size of your book, you may want to allocate at least a half-page per photograph, chart, or graphic. Some charts or graphs, however, may warrant a full page if they contain a lot of detailed information.

6

Dress Like A Fashion Icon

You're a guy. You're single. Chances are, you want to show yourself off to the world as the hottest stud possible, especially if you're always on the prowl for new dates. Part of making a positive first impression involves always looking your best. This chapter is all about how you dress, your wardrobe and how to accessorize your outfits to complete your personalized look. You'll discover what's appropriate to wear at work, plus how to be fashionable and comfortable at play, and how to always look your absolute best.

Simply buying designer clothes isn't enough to make you look like a fashion icon. In fact, you can dress extremely well without relying on expensive designer labels. The clothing you wear needs to fit properly (to compliment and showcase your body) and be properly cared for. After all, you can spend hundreds of dollars for a pair of designer slacks, for example, but if you don't have them properly dry cleaned or ironed before you wear them, you'll look like a wrinkled mess. When expanding your wardrobe, it's important to purchase articles of clothing that:

- Look good on you
- Fit properly
- Will last a while (with proper care)
- Are easy to care for
- Coordinate well with articles of clothing you already own

Especially if you're on a budget, it's important to round out your wardrobe with staple clothing items that look good, are fashionable and that won't quickly go out of style. It's also an excellent strategy to choose new articles of clothing that can be mixed and matched with other items you already own in order to create several different and well coordinated outfits. Thus, to develop an awesome wardrobe requires planning, not necessarily a large budget.

111

Figure 8-4:
A professional-looking chapter title page includes the chapter number and title.

✔ **Formatting:** When it comes to incorporating any type of artwork into your book, that artwork must first be translated into a digital format (if it's not in a digital format already), and then imported into the desktop publishing software used to lay out your book's interior pages (see "Surveying software packages" later in this chapter). It may be necessary to scan photographs or other images and/or use specialized software to edit or fine-tune the digital images to meet the resolution requirements and technical specifications provided by your printer.

Don't use low-resolution artwork into your book. If the photographs and artwork aren't created or scanned in high resolution, the printed version (versus the on-screen version) appears blurry or *pixilated* — the picture appears as a bunch of dots instead of one smooth image. This error can dramatically detract from the professional appearance of your book. Ideally, reproduced photos at 300 pixels-per-inch (ppi) resolution. Contact your printer for details about specific printing requirements.

✔ **Placement:** The artwork should be placed in the appropriate location, after its reference in the text. You can reference figure numbers within the text and display the corresponding figure numbers with the artwork to help readers understand where to look for the image that corresponds to the text they're reading (for example, in Chapter 1, the first figure would be labeled Figure 1-1. The second figure would be Figure 1-2 and so on). Also, don't cluster too much artwork together, because that can detract from the text and look messy.

To help you edit artwork and prepare each image for inclusion within your book, you can use many graphics programs:

✔ Adobe Photoshop or Photoshop Elements (www.adobe.com/products/photoshop)

✔ Corel Paint Shop Pro (www.corel.com/paintshop)

✔ LView Pro (www.lview.com)

✔ Microsoft Digital Image (www.microsoft.com/products/imaging)

These and other graphic editing software packages can be purchased online or from any software retailer.

Laying Out Your Book with Popular Desktop Publishing Software

If you handle your book's page layout and design yourself, you need to select a desktop publishing software package. In the following sections, I discuss the most popular package and give you a quick rundown on laying out your book with templates.

Surveying software packages

After your manuscript is created using Microsoft Word (or another popular word processor; see "Setting your type in a word processor" earlier in this chapter), import your text into a desktop publishing software package to be laid out. This step is called creating the *galleys* — exactly what the pages look like after they're printed in book form.

I suggest designing and laying out the pages of your book with some powerful desktop publishing software. Now, you have some choices when it comes to these programs, which I cover in the following sections, but you can use Microsoft Publisher, Adobe InDesign CS2 (formally PageMaker), or QuarkXPress (three of the most widely used programs). Be sure to check out the specific *For Dummies* books on these programs for more details on how to use them successfully.

Not sure which desktop publishing software to use? Check out the following software publishing company's Web sites for information (some companies even have free 30-day trial version of its desktop publishing programs):

- ✔ Microsoft Publisher (www.microsoft.com/office/publisher/prodinfo/default.mspx)
- ✔ Adobe InDesign CS2 (www.adobe.com/products/tryadobe/main.jsp#product=31)
- ✔ QuarkXPress (www.quark.com)

Microsoft Publisher 2003

Microsoft Publisher 2003 is desktop publishing software that's part of the Microsoft Office family of products. Priced at around $200, this software can be used for designing and laying out the interior of virtually any type of book.

The advantage to using this software is that it's very similar to all the other applications in the Microsoft Office suite of products. So, if you're already familiar with Word, Excel, or PowerPoint, the learning curve for mastering Publisher may be much shorter for you. But don't worry if it isn't. Publisher is still the easiest of the three programs that I recommend.

Publishers' functions are simpler and user friendly. Check out these tasks you can perform with Microsoft Publisher:

- ✔ Cut and paste text or graphics from one Office application to another.
- ✔ Download (from www.microsoft.com) free, professional-looking, pre-created layout and design templates.
- ✔ Use the *Design Checker* feature to ensure that each section of your book has consistent design elements.

Out of the three desktop publishing applications described in this chapter, Publisher is definitely the easiest to use, but it's not the most powerful, based on the functionality it offers.

Adobe InDesign CS2

InDesign CS2, Adobe's comprehensive desktop publishing solution, features all the tools and functionality you need to expertly design your book's interior layout and design. (This program replaces the company's popular PageMaker application and is priced at $699.) It's also compatible with a wide range of graphic development and editing programs, such as Adobe Photoshop CS2 (used for editing photographs and other graphics).

InDesign CS2 was created for professional graphic designers and relies on the user's working knowledge of graphic design to use it properly. If you're an inexperienced user, you can expect a steep learning curve, so you may want to use a pre-created template with the software to save you time (see "Utilizing templates for maximum layout ease," later in this chapter).

QuarkXPress

Ever since page layout and design went digital, QuarkXPress (priced at $749) has been on the cutting-edge when it comes to this aspect of publishing. This software is the leading choice for book and magazine publishers, as well as corporate America, to handle a wide range of desktop publishing needs.

QuarkXPress was created for use by professional graphic designers and offers a large assortment of tools and features for creating extremely complex page designs. The software is a comprehensive tool designed to handle all aspects of page layout and design. You begin by loading your basic text into this software, and then if used correctly, what you wind up with is a fully designed book ready to go to press.

The only con to this program is that it's difficult to figure out how to use, especially if you don't have a publishing background.

Using templates for maximum layout ease

Templates reduce the number of design-oriented decisions you need to make. They also help minimize design errors and ensure that your book's appearance is professional. Using a template can also save you a lot of time and effort. Check out these steps:

1. **Choose a professionally created design template that resembles how you want your book to look.**

2. **Cut and paste or import your text and artwork into the template.**

3. **Customize the template to better meet your own design needs.**

4. **Save each chapter of the book as a separate laid-out file because it's easier to manage smaller files (with each chapter kept separate until they're merged once the layout and design is complete).**

You can find plenty of resources to help you with templates:

- ✓ **www.ideabook.com:** *The InDesign Ideabook, The QuarkXPress Ideabook,* and *The PageMaker Ideabook* are three books priced at $59.95 each and that include a CD-ROM filled with dozens of pre-created templates for creating books and a wide range of other publications. You can also order any of these books by calling (804) 266-7996.

- ✓ **www.stocklayouts.com:** StockLayouts (www.stocklayouts.com) is another source of downloadable templates.

- ✓ **Publisher's Web site:** Be sure to visit the Web site operated by the publisher of the desktop publishing software you're using to find additional templates available for downloading.

- ✓ **A professional designer:** If you're dead set against using templates, hire a designer.

- ✓ **Create your own:** Create your own template using the design software. All templates can be fully customized, and they can make your book look totally unique, so nobody has to know that a template was used.

Converting Laid-Out Pages into Printer-Friendly Files

After the interior of your book is designed and laid out by using a desktop publishing software application (see the previous section), the next step is to convert that file into a file that your printer can read.

Portable Document Format (PDF) files

You can use Adobe Acrobat or a compatible program to create a PDF. The PDF file is the one that's handed over to the printer along with your cover design; see Chapter 9 for details on covers. The offset printer or POD publishing company you use provides the technical specifications the PDF must adhere to; see Chapters 10 and 11 for more about these printers.

The Adobe Acrobat 7.0 software ($299 or $449, depending on the standard or professional version) takes virtually any type of file, such as a document created using Microsoft Publisher, InDesign CS2, or QuarkXPress, and translates it into a digital PDF file. Find out more about this software at www.adobe. com/products/acrobat/main.html. You can also check out various *For Dummies* books on Adobe Acrobat, depending on the version you have.

After your book is in a PDF format, it basically contains the ready-to-publish galleys for your book. Each page appears exactly how it will look when printed. The entire book has to be in a PDF format to send to your printer.

Some programs, such as InDesign CS2, have the ability to create PDF files without using the Adobe Acrobat 7.0 software. If you're hiring a professional graphic designer to handle the layout and design of your book (see the next section) or using a POD publisher, chances are, they handle this phase of the publishing process for you.

PostScript PRN files

A PostScript PRN file is similar to a PDF file and is compatible with printing equipment used by book printers and publishers. Most desktop publishing software packages have the ability to export a file into the PostScript PRN format. Depending on the printer you hire, you need to supply your file when your book goes to press. Your printer provides specific guidelines on how to create this file to meet their needs.

Hiring a Professional Graphic Designer

If you're not comfortable with handling the design and layout of your book (and/or the cover design, which I explain in Chapter 9), consider hiring a professional graphic designer to help you out. This person has experience working with visuals and knows how to choose fonts, typestyles, color schedules, and graphic images and makes them all work together to help communicate your message in a visually appealing way.

Graphic designers are typically born with natural artistic ability, which they then supplement with several years of training by completing college-level courses. These people also know how to work with complicated software-based graphic design tools, such as InDesign and QuarkXPress, used in the publishing industry. Designers have experience creating images that are compatible with what your book printer needs to publish the most professional-looking book possible.

In the following sections, I give you guidance on finding a graphic designer and providing your designer with proper information on the layout you envision. For specific information on working with a graphic designer to create your book's cover, head to Chapter 9.

Finding the right expert

Hiring the right expert to help you layout and design your book is critical if you want your book to look professional and truly appeal to readers. Even if the content of your book is perfect, if the book doesn't look professional, you can lose credibility. Hiring the right designer means finding someone with experience in layout and design work for books (preferably the type of book you've written). Look for someone with top-notch design skills and creative, artistic abilities and an impressive portfolio of work.

Knowing where and when to find a designer

Finding a professional graphic designer can be easy. Ideally, you should find someone who comes highly recommended by someone you know. However, you can also find freelance graphic designers on the Internet:

- ✔ www.elance.com
- ✔ www.guru.com/category.cfm/207
- ✔ www.Project4Hire.com
- ✔ freelanceworkexchange.com
- ✔ hotgigs.com

 Also check out advertisements on Web sites operated by professional associations targeted to writers and small publishers. Or you can do a Yahoo! or Google search, using the phrase *graphic designer*.

 The process of finding a graphic designer to work with should start early in the self-publishing process. The process takes time from tracking down suitable candidates, evaluating their portfolios, communicating your needs, negotiating a price to being able to give the designer ample time to work on your book.

Plan on hiring a designer as early in the self-publishing process as possible — like as soon as you're finished writing and editing your manuscript. (Begin the design for your front and back cover as soon as you decide to write the book.) Here are some important considerations:

- Ask your designer about the time frame he's capable of working within to ensure it fits with your publishing schedule.

- Depending on the work load of the designer, laying out and designing your book properly can take anywhere from a few days to several weeks.

- Leave ample time to make corrections to the design after it's complete.

Evaluating designers' work

After you have a creative vision regarding how you want your book to look, interview a handful of graphic designers and review their portfolios of work. Find someone whose work resembles your vision or who's capable of taking your vision and transforming it into a professional-looking book.

As you interview designers and evaluate their portfolios, ask the following questions:

- How and where were you trained?

- How much experience have you had with book layout and design and/or creating book covers?

- Do you understand what my book is about and who it targets?

- Do you have experience doing book layout and/or creating book covers for my intended target audience?

- Do you know how to use popular software tools, to create laid-out pages and/or cover images that are compatible with the technical requirements of your printer?

- How willing are you to make multiple versions of the page design and/or cover and then make changes as I fine-tune the design?

- What are your rates and how do you bill?

- Can you complete the book's layout and/or front and back cover within the time frame I need?

- Can I see your portfolio of sample work?

Graphic designers are only as good as the work they create. Having an impressive educational background is useful, but having natural artistic ability and the skills to create high-impact designs are more important. Examine the designer's portfolio of work and use that as your main criteria when making a hiring decision.

Setting a fair price

The cost of hiring a graphic designer can be anywhere from $500 to several thousand dollars, depending on the designer's experience and how much time he or she invests in creating your book's layout and/or cover. This step is where your negotiating skills come into play. First, find a graphic designer whose work you really like and who you believe can do the job, and then negotiate a price. You often have much better luck negotiating a lower price with an individual designer or freelancer as opposed to someone who works for a graphic design firm that sets their prices for the company. You can often save money by negotiating a flat-rate for the project instead of an hourly rate.

Deciding how many graphic designers you need

Many graphic designers are capable of doing interior page layout and design as well as cover design. However, some designers specialize only in one area. If you're hiring designers with specific areas of expertise or you're under a very tight deadline, consider hiring a separate designer to handle each part of the book. Discuss your requirements with the initial designer you're interested in hiring and determine if she's capable and comfortable handling everything.

In some cases, if you use a turnkey POD solution, the publisher provides both interior design and cover design services (included in the price the author pays). In this situation, I recommend allowing the publisher to handle the internal design but still hiring a graphic designer (at an additional expense) for the cover. Having two people work on these elements of your book ensures that the cover looks its absolute best.

Supplying your layout preferences

Most graphic designers aren't going to sit down and read your book in its entirety. So, it's your job to properly educate the designer you hire about your book and its intended audience. Be prepared to supply the following info:

- ✓ Details on what you want the interior of your book to look like
- ✓ Guidance about fonts and typestyles you want used
- ✓ Details about how you want artwork, graphics, and other visual elements to be incorporated
- ✓ Your preferences about the content in the front and back matter

✔ Your preference in regard to the use of running heads

✔ Any other creative input you have in regard to page layout and design

Layout design is a highly creative process that involves plenty of tweaking and fine-tuning as you go. As the graphic designer begins to provide you with drafts of the layout, be open and honest with your thoughts and criticisms. Communicating your desires ensures that you wind up with a layout that you really like. Expect to go back and forth multiple times before you wind up with a final design. Remember — you're paying for this aspect of your book's creation too! Make sure that you leave ample time in your publishing schedule to give the designer time to go back and revise the book based on your comments and new ideas.

Chapter 9

Judging a Book by Its Cover

....

....

*Y*ou know that saying, "You can't judge a book by its cover"? Well, forget you've ever heard it! The truth is, intended readers of your book are your jury, and these people *will* judge your book by its cover and often make their buying decision based on how well it captures their attention. So, for a verdict in your favor — in this case, a sale — create the best front *and* back cover, plus brainstorm the best title and subtitle (if applicable) possible.

This chapter focuses on the importance of having an awesome title and subtitle, and I delve into how to create an attention-getting front cover and a back cover that does everything possible to help you sell books. You also discover that even the book's spine can be used as a powerful sales tool, especially when it comes to bookstore sales.

Having a Grade-A cover probably means you have to hire a freelance graphic designer with book cover creation experience. The additional investment in hiring a graphic designer is worth it because having an incredible cover that stands out translates into more sales and enhanced credibility. I discuss working with a professional graphic designer to craft an impressive book cover later in this chapter; Chapter 8 also has general information on hiring the best graphic designer for your needs.

Constructing a Catchy Title

What makes a catchy title? Some authors and publishers believe it's a clever play on words or something memorable. Others believe it's a short combination of words that communicates exactly what the book is about. The truth is there's only one rule when it comes to creating a title for your book: Capture the reader's attention.

For works of fiction, creativity is more important than communicating a clear message. However, for nonfiction, the title and subtitle should quickly educate the reader about the topic of the book and who it appeals to. Think of your book's title as the main headline of a breaking news story. If the person wants to discover more, instead of tuning in for the newscast at 11:00 p.m., he can flip the book over and read the back cover. Then, when he's ready to delve into the topic, he can purchase the book and read it in its entirety.

Generally, fictional books, such as novels, don't have subtitles. However, if your book is nonfiction, creating a catchy and informative subtitle definitely helps you sell books. There's plenty of room for creativity when deciding on your book's main title, but your subtitle (for works of nonfiction) should explain exactly what the book is about or offer a really compelling reason why someone should read it. In the following sections, I show you how to create a title that's clear, concise, and memorable.

Keeping your title short and clear

Long book titles are confusing. They don't usually look good on a book's cover, and they seldom help actual sales of the book. You want to make your main title short and sweet. The shorter, the better. The subtitle (if you choose to use one) can be a short explanatory sentence or phrase.

Ideally, you want your main title to be under five or six words. Keeping the number of words to a minimum allows the title to be displayed using a large font. The main title of your book should be displayed large enough on the book's front cover so it can be seen and easily read from up to six feet away. (See "Selecting the right font and placement for the title," later in this chapter for more about displaying your book's title effectively.)

As you develop your title, think about your intended audience (see Chapter 4 for more on targeting certain readers) and create a title that appeals to those people. Consider the following list when creating your title:

- ✔ Who does the book target and what does it take to get attention?
- ✔ Why would someone want to read your book?
- ✔ What does the book offer?

✔ What's unique about the book?

✔ What will someone discover from reading it?

✔ What problems can the book help solve?

The title of your book is a sales tool. When people hear or read the title, their attention should immediately be captured, and they should want to find out more about your book. By using a play on words in your title, this attention-getting device may often boost sales (make sure that your nonfiction book has a subtitle that clarifies what the book is about, though).

For fiction books, create a title that captures the reader's attention or that somehow relates to the storyline. For nonfiction books, the title should offer a clear benefit or solution, worded in a straightforward way that requires no interpretation or assumptions by the potential reader. Need inspiration? Take a trip to your local bookstore and check out the book titles for books that relate to yours in terms of audience or subject matter. Also, review the best-sellers lists. Of course, you don't want to copy a book title from another book, but you can get a good idea of what types of titles work well.

Making your title stand out

Your book may be competing at least with a few others for a reader's attention (that is unless your book covers a topic that's so targeted to a small niche market that it has absolutely no competition, which is very rare. Your book's title is its first line of defense against someone turning to the competition instead of reading your book.

Therefore, your title should stand out from the competition and make the potential reader immediately think, "Hey, I need to read that!" or "That book could really help me." Creativity is what sets your book apart from the thousands of others on the bookstore shelves or the potentially dozens of others that focus on the same topic. After you capture someone's attention with your title, the book's back cover copy and design should sell the potential reader on actually buying the book (see "Turning to Your Book's Back Cover," later in this chapter for details).

Here are a few tips to help you come up with an attention-grabbing title:

✔ **Create a title for your book *after* you've completed some or all of the manuscript.** As you delve deeper into your own manuscript, you have a better understanding of what it's about, the actual content it contains, and what readers may be interested in. Use this information to help you narrow down a good title. It's much easier to create a title based on a finished book than it is to create a manuscript around a pre-created title.

✔ **Ask others for help.** Write out a list of titles, and then slowly narrow down the list based on feedback you receive from others.

✔ **Incorporate action verbs and avoid clichés.** Many powerful words and specific phrases help sell.

- Choosing action verbs can add intensity or impact to the title and help the reader relate better to the subject matter. They can also be used to draw the reader in and demonstrate what the book is about.

- Using a cliché in your title takes away from its originality and detracts from the potential reader's perception of the overall content of your book. After all, if the title is unoriginal and uninspired, what does that say about the content of the entire book?

✔ **Purchase help aids.** The book *Words That Sell, Revised and Fully Updated Edition* (McGraw-Hill) by Richard Bayan is a thesaurus to help you promote your products, services, and ideas. This book can help you choose powerful and attention getting words and phrases to work into your book's title and subtitle as well as the back cover copy and promotional materials for your book.

✔ **Examine other book titles.** Visit any bookstore or check out the *New York Times* bestsellers list and carefully look at those book titles. Ask yourself what makes those titles work? Why did the authors and publishers choose them?

Keeping a Close Eye on the Front Cover

A lot goes into a book's cover and into creating a positive first impression on the prospective reader. Whether consciously or subconsciously, the reader focuses on the following when he or she first sees your book's cover:

✔ The wording of the title and subtitle (if applicable), its placement, size, color and overall appearance

✔ The author's name and credentials

✔ The cover's color scheme and image

✔ The cover's overall design

✔ The paper stock used for the book's cover

If you want to really bring your book's front cover together, you need a great title and subtitle (see the previous section) along with a superb cover designed by a skilled graphic designer (see "Working with a Design Expert to Create Your Cover," later in this chapter). Unless you're planning to use one or more photographs acquired from a stock photo agency, line up a professional photographer and/or illustrator to create your cover's main image(s). In the following sections, I give you tips on highlighting the book's title and the author's name; show you how to select a cover image and a color scheme; and explain how to pull an attractive cover design together.

Showcasing the front cover's text

Your book's cover should be used to attract the reader's attention by incorporating an eye-catching visual design, plus text that the potential reader quickly relates to and is inspired by. The actual text used on your front cover (the title, subtitle, and so on), is important. But equally important is how that text is displayed. The font, color scheme, size of the text, and its placement are all important cover design considerations.

Selecting the right font and placement for the title

Just as important as the actual title on the front cover is the font you use to create visual appeal. Here are a few considerations when thinking about font:

- **Font selection:** The font you choose can convey emotion, give meaning to the title, and add visual appeal to your book's cover design. To display your title, choose a font that's eye-catching, yet appropriate.

- **Font style:** After you select the actual font, decide if you need to enhance it by using **bold,** *italic,* or <u>underlined</u> text. Using bold or italics for one word in the title or the entire title can help draw the reader's attention. For example, if your book's title is *Stop Smoking Now! 20 Proven Ways To Quit,* you could use bold font to highlight the words ***Stop Smoking*** if doing so enhanced the appeal of your cover design.

- **Font size:** The size of the font determines how much space it takes up on the cover. In most cases, the title of your book should be displayed in a large size font and take up considerable space on the front cover. However, if you're also incorporating a relevant graphic on your cover, you need to adjust the font size so ensure that all the cover's elements fit nicely and don't look cluttered.

- **Font color:** Choosing the right color scheme goes a long way toward making your cover visually pleasing. Using a bright colored font, however, can make your title stand out. Make sure that the font color you choose works to enhance the overall design and appeal of your cover and doesn't clash with the other visual elements you've incorporated.

All the above elements should be displayed in a visually appealing color scheme. If you're using a graphic on your book's cover, chances are that image communicates a message, has meaning, or is relevant to your book's content. The font you choose to display your book's title and subtitle should complement that image, not compete with it. For example, a modern-looking photo should be paired with a modern-looking title font. The artwork shouldn't overpower your title, so the title gets lost in the cover design. Remember, your cover should be a powerful selling tool for your book. It's not an art project where abstract design is appreciated or rewarded.

Choosing the right font can add emotion and power to the title, just as music and sound effects add mood and ambiance to a scary movie. Based on the topic of your book, the title, and the intended audience, choose a font that grabs attention and makes a statement. There are literally thousands of fonts you can choose from. The font can then be customized by adjusting its look by displaying it in bold or italics, or changing the color, for example.

In Figure 9-1, author Jamise L. Dames originally designed this cover for her bestselling novel (well, it wasn't bestselling at the time). The graphic of a pregnant mother and father is powerful and directly relates to the storyline of the novel. The title itself is positioned prominently and complements the image from a visual standpoint. The wording of the title also forces the reader to consider its meaning. (The cover was later redesigned for bookstore distribution after selling over 25,000 copies as a self-published title.)

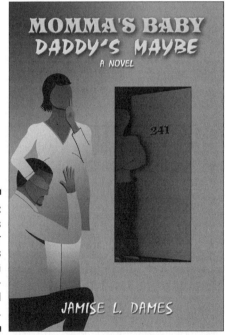

Figure 9-1:
The book's author created this cover for a self-published release.

Here are a few Web sites that you can check out to help you select a font:

✔ **www.1001fonts.com:** To see a selection of fonts available for use on your book's cover, check out 1001Fonts.com's Web site.

✔ **www.studio.adobe.com/us/type/main.jsp:** The Adobe Type Library offers over 2,200 different fonts and typestyles, which can be previewed and purchased online. You can enter a short phrase, such as your book's title, and see how it looks displayed in hundreds of different fonts.

✔ **www.groan-zone.net/delphi/font.html:** FontView is free software that allows you to type your book's title and see how it looks when it's published. The text displays in different fonts, styles, sizes, and colors.

✔ **www.styopkin.com:** Styopkin Software offers Advanced Font Viewer as a downloadable software application that serves the same purpose as FontView (see previous bullet).

Highlighting the author's name and credentials

Typically, the book's main title should be the most prominent thing displayed on the front cover. But, of course, there are exceptions to every rule. If you're well known and people are buying the book because you've written it, you want to showcase your name and even your photo, along with the book's title, because these tactics may help you sell books. For example, on the covers of many bestselling books, you often see the author's name displayed in a larger type than the title, because it's the author's name and reputation that sells the book. On the hardcover edition of Stephen King's novel *The Cell*, King's name is displayed much larger than the title is.

In addition, if you're an expert in your field or a well-known person, promote it on the front cover. For example, you can say, "From the bestselling author of [insert title] . . ." or "From the President or CEO of [insert company name] . . ." Depending on the author's credentials truly and how helpful those credentials are in selling books determine how large they're displayed on the book's cover. Typically, the author's credentials should be easily visible, but displayed in a smaller font size than the name on the book's front cover. This, however, is a creative decision and not a design rule that must be followed.

Using attractive images

The correct cover graphic has a huge impact on the appeal of your cover. So whether you choose one or more photographs, pieces of clip art or illustrations, or any combination of these graphic elements combined with a title that's displayed in an appropriate and eye-catching font, think about how readers may view your book.

There are no rules for choosing an image to display on your book's cover, but you should follow these guidelines:

- The image should be relevant to the book's topic.
- Your graphic should make a statement.
- The picture should help convey information about the book's content.
- The images should be visually appealing and attention getting.
- All graphics shouldn't distract the reader from the book's main title.

Whether you use a photograph, illustration, or some other type of graphic on your book's cover is entirely your creative decision. Your goal is to create a book that looks highly professional, though, and one or more photographs often convey a more professional look that other types of graphics.

The size and placement of the image(s) you use is also a creative decision. You want the image to be visible, but not contrast with or overpower the title.

In Figure 9-2, you can see how the cover images used to promote a fictional novel can be used to attract the reader's attention. For his self-published psychological suspense novel *Angel Falls,* author Oliver Dick uses a strong graphic image to capture the reader's imagination. In full color, you'd see deep reds, blacks, and yellows with the title displayed in white.

When it comes to acquiring artwork for your book's cover, you can take your own photograph(s), find relevant clip art, or incorporate an appropriate illustration. Depending on your budget, you can also have these graphic elements custom-created specifically for your book by hiring a professional photographer, artist, or illustrator in addition to a graphic designer (see "Working with a Design Expert to Create Your Cover," later in this chapter). You can also utilize stock clip art or photos that you license from an agency. Chapter 4 offers additional information on acquiring art for your book.

Choosing colors carefully

Although a cover printed using a four-color printing process is ideal, you can get away with a one- or two-color cover if your use of color and design is creative. Certain colors attract attention and create a certain mood or convey an emotion. Consider reading some introductory books about graphic design to discover how colors can be used to create a mood or emotion and what color combinations may appeal most to your readers.

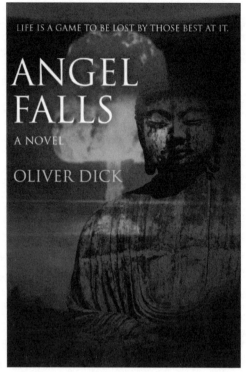

Figure 9-2:
This cover
features an
attention-
grabbing
image.

Oliver Dick

Pulling together the overall design

A cover's overall design refers to how all the cover's elements are put together to give it visual impact. This design includes the appearance of the title and subtitle; the appearance of the author's name (and credentials, if used); and the use of photographs, clip art, or illustrations. It also includes the use of a distinct color scheme.

The cover's design conveys a message. It can attract positive attention (which is what it's supposed to do), blend in (so the potential reader passes by your book and picks up a completing title), or get attention for a negative reason. You don't want someone noticing your cover and thinking to themselves, "Gee, that's ugly!," "What was that author thinking?," or "I have no clue what this book is about."

The front cover graphics should complement the title and be used to communicate information. Figure 9-3 is the cover of my self-published book *The*

Bachelor's Guide To Life: Answers To Common and Not-So-Common Questions Every Single Guy Often Asks. Every element of the cover, from the title and subtitle to the photographs and color scheme, helps explain what the book is about and who should read it:

- **The title:** The title of this book is pretty straightforward. From the main title, you immediately know who the book is targeted to and you get a pretty good idea of what it's about. The title is displayed in a large and easy-to-read font.

- **Subtitle:** The subtitle explains that the book is chock-full of answers that the intended audience needs.

- **Author's name:** Place the author's name in a readable font (not so small you need a magnifying glass to read it) in the lower-left corner.

- **Images:** The four photographs used on the cover also communicate the type of information within the book.

    - Clearly visible in the upper-left corner of the front cover is a young man shaving (a topic covered in the book).

    - Moving to the right, another young man is participating in sports (a popular pastime among single men).

    - Toward the bottom of the cover, potential readers see a guy on a romantic walk with his girlfriend because dating is another huge aspect of a single guy's life.

    - The last photo is of a man in a business suit, showcasing the professional/career aspect of his life.

- **Colors:** The cover design for *The Bachelor's Guide To Life* also utilizes a bright and cheerful, red, white, and blue color scheme. This subtly conveys a sense of patriotism and communicates the message that this book is for "All-American" guys.

Because you're so close to your own work, before choosing a final title and cover design, get some input about the design. Think of it as forming your own little focus group. Form the group from 10 to 20 people you don't know. Try getting feedback from total strangers or salespeople and managers at bookstores, as well as librarians. These participants need to fit your book's target audience. Ask them what they think about the book's title and cover design. After showing the book's title and cover design, ask your focus group specifically what they think the book is about and who they think it targets.

Their answers should be correct and intuitive. If you get responses like "I don't get it" or "What's this book about, anyway?" go back to the drawing board. If the intended audience for your book doesn't understand what you're trying to say with your cover, the title, and/or the design, your ideas aren't appropriate, and they need to be reworked before publication. (See Chapter 4 for more about determining your book's target audience.)

The thickness of the cover and whether it's finished with a glossy or matted look also impacts its appearance and showcases its quality. The most popular cover stocks are 10-point or a thicker 12-point, which is coated on one side in either a glossy or laminate finish. See Chapter 10 for more about cover stock.

Turning to Your Book's Back Cover

After your book has grabbed the reader's attention (by its title and design, of course) and said, "Look at me! Look at me!" the next job of your book's design is to convince your reader to flip the book over to read what's on the back cover. When someone has taken the time to make the flip and read the back cover, it's your chance to make a sale! You have to work fast, though; you may only have that person's attention for a few seconds.

The back cover of your book includes other important information. In the following sections, I describe all these elements and explain how to pull them together in the overall design of the back cover.

The elements of a back cover

If you plan to sell your book through bookstores or retailers or want it to look extremely professional, be sure to incorporate the elements in the following sections into your back cover design.

The book description

The back cover text must convey all the important information that a potential reader may want and need in order to decide whether to buy your book. Space on the back cover is limited, so every word and phrase must have meaning and communicate the importance of your book.

Your back cover text should be sales oriented, well written, up beat, easy-to-read, informative, and attention getting. Be concise and visually appealing in the way it's laid out (see "The overall look of a back cover" later in this chapter for more back cover layout). In one or two *short* paragraphs, the back cover needs to

- Explain exactly what the book is about
- Describe what the book offers and what makes it unique
- Inform the reader who the book is targeted to
- Establish credibility with the reader
- Create demand for the book and its content

To save space on the back cover, use a bulleted list when describing key features or content. If your book is fiction, use the description to offer a brief synopsis of the plot and main characters, without revealing too much. Obviously, never reveal the ending!

The description of your book that appears on the back cover should provide a summary of what your book is about and who it appeals to. This information can be adapted from the marketing materials (such as the press release) you've created for your book. Chapter 18 focuses on how to create a cohesive marketing message to promote your book.

The art of writing effective back cover copy involves taking the most marketable, appealing, or valuable aspects of what the book offers and describing these areas using the most sales-oriented and believable words possible. Never make statements or promises that you can't keep or create expectations that the content of your book doesn't live up to. If readers buy your book based on lies, promises, or intentional embellishments of the facts, they may feel ripped off, and you lose some credibility. You can also be sued. Assuming that your book is informative, well written, and well researched, you don't need to make false claims about what your book offers.

Information about the author and an author photo

An *About the Author* section on the back cover is optional, but it can be a powerful tool for establishing credibility with the reader through listing your primary qualifications, credentials, or educational background. This information helps portray you as knowledgeable about the topic you've written. The author's credentials are less important for fictional works. For works of fiction, write an *About the Author* section that readers relate to. It can contain more personal information about the author, such as hobbies, interests, and details about family and pets.

Within the author bio section, some authors opt to include a small publicity photograph (a head shot). Many readers appreciate seeing a photo of the author simply to satisfy their curiosity. Just like when you listen to the same radio show day after day, you wonder what the radio host actually looks like. It's also customary (although not a requirement) to include an author's photo on the back cover or within the *About the Author* section of the book.

Chapter 18 is full of information on writing an author bio that you can tailor for use on your book cover. You also find information on author photos.

If you have a Web site, be sure to list it within the About the Author section on the back cover. Even if potential readers decide not to buy your book on the spot, they may still visit your Web site later and order the book online. See Chapter 21 for more about creating your own Web site.

The barcode, ISBN, and price

At the bottom of every book's back cover, a barcode must be displayed in black ink with a white background (called a vanilla bar code). Within this area, the book's ISBN must also be displayed in a readable font. (The barcode and cover price for the book is also often printed within the inside front or back cover of the book.)

The cover price of your book can be worked into the barcode through the *price add-on.* This smaller barcode goes immediately to the right of the ISBN barcode. The price add on begins with the number 5, which represents that the price is stated in U.S. dollars, and is followed by the four digit price of the book. For example, a book that's priced at $18.95 would be listed as 51895 in the price add-on section of the book's barcode.

The cover price of the book should also be printed in a font that consumers can read. You can place the cover price in the upper-left or -right corner or in the lower-left or -right corner. If the book's cover price is $18.95, the price should be listed as U.S. $18.95 or $18.95 U.S.

To discover more about the technical specifications for reproducing your book's ISBN and related barcode on the back cover, visit the U.S. ISBN Agency's Web site (www.isbn.org). When you receive your barcode, the information is supplied in the following standard specifications: 2400 dpi,

99.36 percent magnification, vanilla bar code, and price add-on. The barcode can then be reduced slightly but should typically cover a total area of 1¾-x-1 inches and 2-x-1¼ inches.

See Chapter 7 for more information on securing your book's ISBN and barcode and establishing a cover price.

The Book Industry Standards and Communications (BISAC) Subject and Audience

As you find out in Chapter 7, selecting and choosing an appropriate BISAC Subject and Audience Code helps booksellers and libraries categorize and display a book in the appropriate section. For help choosing the appropriate BISAC Subject and Audience Code for your book, visit www.bisg.org.

The BISAC Subject and Audience categories are typically displayed in small type on the upper or lower left or right corner of the book's back cover. Some publishers opt to display this information near the barcode, while others avoid including it altogether. By not including this information, you run the risk of your book being displayed in the wrong area or section of a bookstore. This misplacement makes your book harder to find and may result in lost sales. Never assume that the title of your book is obvious enough that a bookseller or librarian can automatically display it in the right section. You'd be surprised how often mistakes are made because the book didn't display the appropriate BISAC Subject and Audience Code.

Publisher imprint information

The publisher of your book usually displays its name and logo somewhere on the book's back cover, typically in the lower right or left corner. In addition to its name and logo, some publishers also display a Web site and/or address on the back cover.

If you're book is being published by your own publishing company using traditional offset printing, you can display your publishing company's name and logo (see Chapter 6 for more about creating your own publishing company). If, however, you're using a Print-On-Demand (POD) service (see Chapter 11 for details), technically that company is your book's publisher and that's the company name that appears as the publisher.

Reviews and quotes

One or two excerpts of positive reviews of your book (from established media outlets) or endorsements in the form of quotes from other well-known experts, celebrities, business leaders, or trade associations are a powerful sales tool and should be proudly displayed on your book's back cover (if possible). These quotes quickly enhance your credibility and show the potential reader that your book has already received praise from others. See Chapter 19 for more about reviews.

The overall look of a back cover

Placement of your book's back cover elements is entirely up to you from a creative and design standpoint. But keep the following issues in mind as you settle on a design for your back cover:

- ✔ The description shouldn't look too cluttered or take up too much space on the back cover. The use of *white space* is important to ensure that the copy is inviting and visually appealing.

- ✔ The back cover must contain all the necessary elements, including the book's description, information about the author, the barcode, price, publisher information, and book category details.

- ✔ The design used for your book's front cover (in terms of color scheme and font selection) should carry over onto the book's back cover.

- ✔ Your back cover copy should be used as a powerful marketing tool. In 5 to 15 seconds, it should convince a potential reader (who's part of your target audience) to purchase and read your book. If it doesn't do this, the back cover isn't properly designed.

The back cover design used for *The Bachelor's Guide To Life* (see Figure 9-4) is rather basic, yet it includes all the key elements. Although plenty of information is displayed on the back cover, there's also plenty of white space, so the design doesn't look cluttered. Someone can pick up the book and quickly find out what it's about and who it appeals to.

Figure 9-4:
A book's back cover contains a description of the book, along with other important elements.

Hire an experienced graphic designer with a flair for creating visuals to put the title, text, and pieces of the front and back covers together into one visually appealing, professional-looking, and cohesive presentation. The graphic designer you hire to create your book's cover should have experience with this type of work. See "Working with a Design Expert to Create Your Cover," later in this chapter for more about working with a designer.

Remembering Your Book's Spine

The book's spine can be a highly effective marketing and sales tool, especially if your book is sold in bookstores or at retail. When you visit any bookstore, most of the books are displayed sideways in order to conserve shelf space, so all that's typically visible is a book's spine. Dozens of titles could be crammed onto a single shelf, with your book stuck in the middle. How is your reader going to find you?

If someone's looking for a book about a specific topic, he may browse a shelf in a bookstore that contains multiple titles. Most people glance at the title printed on the book's spine, and then they pull out only the few books that truly capture their attention, based on the title and/or how well the title was displayed and stood out on the spine. For more info on catchy titles, see "Constructing a Catchy Title," earlier in this chapter.

The most important thing to display on the book's spine, in the largest possible typestyle and font, is the book's main title. You should also display the author's name and the publishing company (but this can be printed in a much smaller type size). The font color and spine color should also stand out to capture the attention of a casual browser. Make sure that the spine design is cohesive with the design of the front and back covers.

Go to any bookstore, stand in front of the section where you believe your book would be displayed, and examine the spines of competing titles. Determine which books' spines stand out and capture your attention and why. Now, when designing your book's spine, do something that makes it stand out more than the competition.

Working with a Design Expert to Create Your Cover

Throughout this chapter, I stress how important it is to hire a professional graphic designer to create your book cover, even if the printer or publisher you choose to work with offers a basic cover design service as part of the publishing package you're already paying for.

Meet a book editor and cover designer

Susan Wenger is a professional book editor and cover designer who works for Wheatmark (www.wheatmark.com) — one of the leading POD publishers in the industry that caters to self-publishers and first-time authors. You can read more about Wheatmark in Chapter 11.

In seven years in the publishing industry, she's designed or contributed to over 100 book covers. Most of the covers she's done have been created using the popular Adobe Photoshop software (a powerful graphic design and photo editing tool).

When an author hires Wheatmark to publish their book using POD publishing, Wenger is one of the designers who provides the cover design services offered by the company. Her job involves working with authors to help them conceptualize their book's cover. Then, she takes those ideas and incorporates them into an actual cover design. She also often works closely with graphic designers hired separately by authors to ensure that the cover being created meets Wheatmark's technical specifications for printing.

Wenger recommends that before any work begins on designing the cover, one must determined the book's trim size (see Chapter 8 for more about trim sizes). That way the designer knows the exact measurements of the final design. Often, if a design is created and then it needs to be enlarged or reduced to accommodate a different trim size, it can distort the design or require additional time to modify.

"When I start working on a new book project, my first task is to have an in-depth discussion with the author to find out about the book and the vision for the cover. Some authors can provide very specific design ideas while others leave it entirely up to me," explained Wenger. "Authors who are willing to share their ideas, but give their graphic designer freedom to explore their own creative expression are more apt to end up with a book cover that's unique and professional looking. After I get an idea of what the cover should look like, I begin searching for the perfect cover image. This image might be a photograph or an illustration, depending on the type of book. Stock photo agencies are a great resource for finding perfect images for book covers, because you can quickly obtain a handful of images and then try several in your cover design before narrowing down your choice to one image."

After the image is selected, Wenger begins working with the specific text, such as the book's title and subtitle, that must be incorporated into the front or back cover. She looks at various fonts and styles and makes her decision based on how all the elements ultimately fit together. "The job of the graphic designer is to take a cover image, text, and other graphic assets and combine them so they work seamlessly together to create the book's cover," said Wenger. "Based on the topic of the book and the cover graphic to be used, it's usually easy to select an appropriate font or fonts to display the title, subtitle, and author's name. I use a program that allows me to see the title displayed in multiple fonts at once, which makes the decision process a bit faster and easier."

So what are a few cover issues that authors should keep a close eye on? Wenger has a few mistakes that should be avoided:

- ✔ **A long title:** The title should be short and catchy or it won't jump out at the potential reader.

- ✔ **Subtitles:** A subtitle for a work of fiction isn't necessary and usually shouldn't be used.

- ✔ **Poor images:** Digital photographs or artwork that was saved in a very low resolution makes the images look awful in print. Just because something looks okay on the computer screen, that doesn't mean looks fine when it's professionally printed.

When you simply utilize the cover design services of a POD company (see Chapter 11), your cover often is created by someone quickly, using a previously created template. In many cases, the person designing your cover may not even have professional graphic design experience.

Hiring your own graphic designer ensures that your book's cover is given the right amount of personalized attention and that your creative vision is adhered to. If you have no artistic flare or ideas about how you want your book's cover to look, professional graphic designers can also use their artistic skills and creative visions to create an appropriate cover, based on information about your book that you provide. I provide general information on hiring a graphic designer in Chapter 8.

Suppose that you find someone to create your cover — great! Now what? Start off by spending some time with your cover designer and describe your book in detail. Make sure that the designer understands what your book is about and specifically who your target audience is — your designer probably won't take the time to read your entire manuscript.

In order to supply your designer with this proper education, be prepared to supply the following:

- ✔ The book's title and subtitle
- ✔ A detailed description of the book and its audience
- ✔ The exact information you want on the book's front and back cover
- ✔ A rough sketch or description of what you want the front and back cover to look like with as many specifics as possible
- ✔ Any graphic assets you've already acquired, such as photographs, illustrations, or clip art that you want incorporated into the cover design

The fee you pay the graphic designer is for time worked and skill. If the designer needs to acquire artwork, such as photographs or illustrations, be prepared to pay separately for those graphic extras.

When you receive drafts of the cover design, share your like and dislikes with your designer. Open communication ensures that you end up with a product that you love. Do expect to go back and forth many times before you settle on a final design. Remember, you're paying the designer to help make your book shine, so don't be hesitant in saying what you like and don't like.

Part III
Start the Presses! Examining Printing Choices

The 5th Wave   By Rich Tennant

"No, it's great. I'm just saying 'The Gospel of St. Luke' is an ambitious title for a first-time self-publisher."

In this part . . .

*P*rinting and publishing your book actually involve several different methods and technologies. Which method you choose is based on your budget, goals, distribution plan, target audience, and the final look you're going for.

This part focuses on several different printing methods, including traditional offset printing, Print-On-Demand (POD) technology, eBooks, and local print shops. I also give you tips on working successfully with any printer.

Chapter 10

Trying Out Traditional Offset Printing

. . . .

In This Chapter

▶ Knowing the nuts and bolts of working with an offset printer

▶ Making important printing decisions

▶ Selecting the best printer

. . . .

*T*his chapter focuses on offset printing and is for self-publishers who plan to establish their own small publishing company (see Chapter 6 for details on this process) or who want to handle many of the tasks associated with publishing a book themselves, without using a turnkey publishing solutions (such as Print-on-Demand — POD). Offset printing, which has been around since 1875, is the most widely used method of commercial printing in the world. In this technique, an inked image is offset (transferred) from a plate to a rubber blanket and then to the printing surface (the paper).

If you're choosing a traditional offset printing option for your book, having your book printed and bound is one of the most costly aspects of the whole publishing project. You want your investment to result in the most professional looking and highest quality book possible, and poor printing and/or binding impacts the look of your book and dramatically takes away from your credibility. So going with a professional printer is your key to making your book look its best.

In this chapter, I cover the basics of working with an offset printer, features you can choose for your book, and tips for hiring a printer.

The Basics of Working with a Traditional Offset Printer

A professional offset printer capable of printing and binding books is very different from your local print shop that specializes in printing business cards and stationery. In the following sections, I explain the pros and cons of using an offset printer for your book and give you hints on finding a pool of reliable printers. (You find out how to select the winning printer in "Hiring the Right Offset Printer for Your Needs," later in this chapter.)

The pros and cons of offset printing

The advantages of offset printing include

- A consistently high image quality
- The fast and easy production of printing plates
- Lower per-copy printing costs than other printing options

The disadvantages of offset printing include

- Offset printing requires a significantly larger upfront investment because you have to pay for hundreds or thousands of books to be printed at once.

- You have to have a relatively large print run, which means you need to maintain an inventory until the books are sold. You also run the risk of not selling all your books if demand doesn't meet expectations.

- You're responsible for handling many more of the book publishing-related tasks that a POD company may otherwise handle.

Finding reputable offset printers

You can find a reliable book printer in many ways:

- **Special interest magazine ads:** These mags include
  - *Writer's Digest:* www.writersdigest.com
  - *The Writer:* www.writermag.com

- **Referral databases:** These databases are available to members of writing and publishing organizations. For example, if you're a member of The Independent Book Publishers Association (PMA), check out the "Suppliers and Services" section on their Web site (www.pma-online. org). Here, a small publisher can obtain a referral for a book printer that advertises with the organization. Several dozen full-service book printers are listed, along with contact information and a short description of each company's specialties.

✔ **Online searches:** Of course, you can also find a book printer by doing a search online (use the search phrase *book printing*)

Many of the best offset printers for books are located in the northern Midwest of the United States (especially Michigan and Ohio) because of their proximity to Canadian paper mills, meaning they have some of the lowest costs for paper. When first looking for a printer, self-publishers should get comparative quotes from such standards in the industry as Thomson-Shore, Data Reproductions, and Bookmasters.

✔ **Yellow Pages:** Look under *Printers, Book Printers,* or *Offset Printers.*

You may submit your book's galleys electronically to the printer, and your negotiations with the printer can be done by phone, fax, mail, or e-mail, so there's no need for the printer to be located in your immediate geographic area. After your books are printed, they can be shipped anywhere.

Choosing the Features of Your Traditionally Printed Book

The interior of most trade paperback books are published using 50-pound white or natural colored paper with black ink. If you choose to use a fancier paper stock or a different color paper, or if you use two or more ink colors within the book's interior, the book may look better, but your printing costs increase. Likewise, if you choose to do something fancy with your cover, this choice, too, impacts your printing costs.

By using standard paper stock and basic printing options, you can still create and publish a book that's highly professional looking and visually appealing. For most books, with the exception of high-end coffee table books or photo books, your goal should be to publish a book that, in terms of quality of paper, looks just like any other book you'd purchase at a bookstore — or better. With professional layout (see Chapter 8) and a good cover design (see Chapter 9), your printer should be able to produce books that meet or exceed your expectations without charging you for a wide range of extras.

To be happy with the end result of your book, try some of these suggestions:

✔ Visit a bookstore and find books you want yours to imitate.

✔ Work closely with the printer to communicate exactly what you envision.

✔ Be open to advice and creative suggestions.

The following sections help you decide what you want your book to look like. After you select your book's features, gather price quotes from potential printers and narrow your choices until you decide on one (see "Hiring the Right Offset Printer for Your Needs," later in this chapter).

Visit www.printindustry.com/glossary.htm for a glossary of common printing terminology. Understanding terminology used by printers helps you better determine and communicate your needs and understand price quotes.

Trim size

The trim size of your book refers to its dimensions. A book's trim size impacts its page count. With a smaller trim size, fewer words fit on the page. Therefore, the book has a higher page count and appears thicker. That same manuscript printed in a book with a larger trim size has a smaller page count and potentially cuts printing costs. The drawback, however, is that the book appears shorter, because it contains fewer pages. You want to decide your book's trim size before you begin page layout to save yourself a lot of extra work. See Chapter 8 for details about page layout and design.

For a trade paperback (the most common type of self-published book; see the next section), common trim sizes include

- 6-x-9 inches
- 8½-x-11 inches
- 5½-x-8½ inches
- 7-x-10 inches

Depending on the print run, most printers are willing to produce books with any trim size that's 8½-x-11 inches or smaller.

Hard covers versus soft covers

Printing softcover trade paperbacks (which are paperback books that use a thicker interior paper stock than newsprint and come in a variety of trim sizes) or mass market paperbacks (which are the size of paperback novels that use newsprint paper for the internal pages) is significantly less expensive than printing hardcover books. However, hardcover books look more formal and typically command higher cover prices. Although a mass market paperback book, such as a novel (with a trim size of 4-x-6¾ inches), almost always sells for under $8, a trade paperback book can have a larger trim size and have a cover price from $9.95 to $39.99 (or more).

Most self-published books or books published by small publishers are published as trade paperbacks. These books come in a variety of trim sizes, offer full-color covers, and can be almost any length. They're also suitable for both fiction and nonfiction type books and are the most economical to print, especially in small to medium size print runs (under 5,000 copies).

Cover stock and coatings

The quality of the cover and the cover jacket is particularly important. Covers come in different thicknesses (point size) and with certain coatings. For example, for a trade paperback book, it's common to use a 10-point or 12-point paper stock. You can then opt to add special coatings — glossy or matte finishes — to the cover. You can also add UV protection to prevent discoloration from sunlight. Pretty cool, huh? You may get excited if your book ever sits in a window display, but you'd hate for it to have sun damage!

The quality of the cover and the cover jacket for hardcover books is particularly important, because the cover price of the book is significantly higher and people expect to receive a high-quality product. For a hardcover, you have a wide range of options in terms of cover stock and the stock used for the book's jacket. Your options vary by printer. Typically, the thicker the paper stock you use, the more expensive the printing is. You're also adding costs if you ad coatings or laminates.

As you find out in Chapter 9, people do judge a book by its cover! In addition to having a catchy title and a well-designed cover, you want your cover to look professional and convey quality. Before making decisions about printing your book's cover, take a look at some other published books (especially your book's competing titles) and examine the quality of their covers. Choose some samples you like and then have your printer offer you quotes to create a similar cover from a printing specifications standpoint.

Binding types

Books can be bound in a variety of ways. The binding refers to how the pages are held together. The most common types of binding include

- **Perfect binding:** Most self-publishers opt for perfect binding, which uses glue to attach the pages to the book's cover. This binding type is most commonly seen among books sold through bookstores. *Self-Publishing For Dummies* is an example of a perfect-bound book. One benefit of perfect binding is that readers can clearly see the book's spine when the book is displayed sideways on a bookshelf.

- **Ring binding:** Holes are punched in the pages, which are then inserted into a traditional three-ring binder. This binding is ideal if pages need to be taken out or replaced either by the publisher or reader. A ring binder is mostly used for training manuals and other publications used in conjunction with a training program or seminar.

- **Comb binding:** Plastic comb binding uses a piece of plastic with "teeth" that fit into rectangular holes cut into each sheet of paper. Comb binding is mainly used for books printed at a local print shop in very small quantities. Keep in mind that bookstores and retail stores typically won't sell books with this type of binding, and the plastic binding itself could crack or break. This type of binding also doesn't look too professional.

- **Coil, wire, or wire-O binding:** This binding (also called spiral binding) refers to one piece of plastic (coil) or wire that forms a continuous coil that holds pages together by weaving in and out of many small holds cut into the book's pages. This type of binding is ideal for cookbooks and other types of books that need to lie flat, without being held.

- **Thermal binding:** A heat fused cloth tape or plastic strip is used along the side of the pages to seal them together. This binding is an option for small print runs, typically when the book isn't going to be sold at retail.

- **Saddle stitch binding:** Staples are used to hold folded over pages together. This binding technique is used more for binding booklets and magazines. Staples can also be used along the edge of the book and then concealed with cloth or paper tape. This type of binding can't be used for thick books, and you don't have a traditional spine that can display text. So, displaying the book sideways on a bookstore's shelf isn't practical.

- **Case binding:** This binding method is used for hardcover books and involves using thread to sew the pages together. If you're creating a hardcover book, this is a sturdy, classic-looking binding.

For very small print runs, where you print or photocopy your book at a local print shop (see Chapter 12), comb, coil, wire, thermal, or saddle stitch binding may be appropriate. To see these types of binding, visit these sites:

- Book Binding Pros: www.bookbindingpros.com
- FedEx/Kinko's: www.fedex.com/us/officeprint/main

Paper weight and color

The weight of the paper used for the interior of your book refers to its thickness. Using a thicker paper stock improves the look of the book from a quality standpoint and makes the spine of the book thicker, but remember that by using a thicker (heavier) paper, your printing costs may increase.

A certain kind of paper is usually used with different book types. For example:

- A hardcover book might use a slightly heavier paper than a trade paperback.
- A trade paperback often uses a 20-pound white or off-white paper (but there are options).
- Full-color books often use a brighter white paper with a glossy finish.
- Mass market paperback books are typically printed on a less expensive, newsprintlike paper.

The use of color in the interior

Adding color gives you creative freedom and adds a tremendous amount of visual appeal to your book if used correctly. For example, the interior of most books are printed on white paper with black ink, but you can use two-, three-, or even full-color spreads in your book to add visual appeal, highlight important information, or categorize information.

The more colors you incorporate into your book's interior design, the higher your printing costs may be.

Interior art, photos, and illustrations

Depending on the type of book you're publishing, incorporating artwork, photographs, illustrations, charts, diagrams, or figures of any kind add to the visual design of the book and makes it easier to convey certain types of information. Although a novel typically doesn't incorporate any artwork, a how-to book on plumbing, for example, may use photographs or other graphic elements to help the reader identify certain parts of a plumbing project.

When you start to include more types of artwork in your book, your printing costs may start to climb. These costs vary based on the technology used to layout and design your book and the process that's used to print the books.

To keep costs down, make sure that you supply artwork to the printer in a format of at least 300 dpi and has clear, true photographic quality. Most printers charge either by the hour or by the image digitally edited or enhanced artwork that appears in your book. Printers supply guidelines for artwork of various types. Stick to these guidelines.

Inserts

Depending on the type of book you're publishing, you may want to bind some type of insert into the book, such as a CD, subscription card, perforated coupon, checklist, stickers, or a fold-out poster. Most printers who are equipped to handle inserts, however, charge extra for this service, based on the type of insert. Prices vary by printer. You're also responsible for providing the insert in a format that's ready to be bound into the printed books. These formats also depend on the printer that you're working with.

Adding an audio CD, DVD, or CD-ROM into your book can increase your printing costs by up to $3 per copy but allows you to increase your cover price dramatically because of the value of the added content you're offering.

Hiring the Right Offset Printer for Your Needs

Various printers use different equipment and specialize in different types of print jobs. In the following sections, I give you a few issues to consider upfront, explain the importance of customer service and proper pricing, and clue you in on what happens after you hire the printer of your choice.

What are a few upfront considerations?

To start with, you want to choose a printer based on the following:

- **The company's experience in publishing books similar to yours:** Ask to see sample books with similar printing specifications to what you anticipate needing.

- **The professional quality of the output:** When you initially contact a printer, ask to see actual printed samples of the company's work. Upon request, a professional book printer can send you a handful of sample books it has printed so you can evaluate the quality of the work.

- **The equipment available:** For books printed by an offset printer, companies often outsource the job to a printing company or facility located overseas. Where the book is printed becomes important to you only if it in any way impacts the overall quality, professional appearance, cost, and printing schedule for your book.

- **Scheduling issues:** After you decide exactly how you want your book printed and you're gathering price quotes (see "Is the price right?" later in this chapter), determine the time needed for the initial printing and

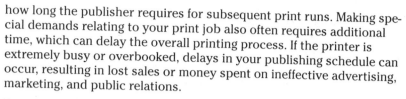

how long the publisher requires for subsequent print runs. Making special demands relating to your print job also often requires additional time, which can delay the overall printing process. If the printer is extremely busy or overbooked, delays in your publishing schedule can occur, resulting in lost sales or money spent on ineffective advertising, marketing, and public relations.

Every step in the book-printing process takes time. Rushing this process can lead to costly mistakes. I've seen some mistakes such as photographs being printed upside down and glue in the binding that's still wet.

- ✔ **Payment terms:** For first-time orders, many printers require at least a 50 percent down payment with the balance due on shipment. For any order, make sure that the terms are agreed on upfront and that you have the terms in writing.

- ✔ **Warehousing and order fulfillment services:** Some printers warehouse your books and handle order fulfillment on your behalf (for a fee, of course). The storing of your books can ultimately save you money because you don't need to have the books shipped from the printer to your own warehouse (at your expense), and then have those same books shipped from your warehouse to your customers. You can also save time and money by having your orders fulfilled directly by the printer, assuming the printer offers competitive rates for these services.

Unless you've found a printer through a referral from a reputable organization or someone you know, do a bit of research about the company before making a hiring decision. Contact your local Better Business Bureau or ask to speak with past clients. (Visit the Better Business Bureau's Web site at www.bbb.org and click "Locate a Bureau.") It's not uncommon for printers to be family-owned or to have been in business for 50 or more years, so look for a well-established and reputable company to work with.

How is the customer service?

After making contact with a printer, you may be assigned an account representative. This person is your primary contact person at the printing company. He or she answers your questions, negotiates pricing with you, and helps guide your book through each stage of the printing process.

Interview the rep assigned to you so you can tell whether you can have a solid working relationship. Ideally, you want to work with a representative who understands your needs and who's willing to invest the time in working closely with you. You should have faith in this person's knowledge and be able to work well together. You want someone who's readily available to answer all your questions, addresses your concerns, and makes sure that every phase of the printing process goes according to plan and stays within your budget (especially if this is your first time working with a book printer).

Is the price right?

The printing business is highly competitive. Have printers spec out your job and offer a price quote, and then shop around for other quotes to ensure that you're being offered a good deal. There's always room to negotiate!

Providing crucial information

Although you can begin making contact with printers anytime, you can't begin soliciting bids for your print job or gathering price estimates until you've determined exactly what your needs are. Each of these considerations impacts your costs and what your printed books look like.

Printers typically have a form that you fill out for quote requests, but in order to obtain an accurate quote, be prepared to provide the following information about your book (I cover these issues in detail earlier in this chapter):

- ✔ Desired trim size (the dimensions of your book)
- ✔ The book's length (the total number of pages)
- ✔ Whether you're publishing a hardcover, trade paperback, or mass-market paperback
- ✔ The cover stock
- ✔ Number of colors to be used on the book's front and back cover
- ✔ The type of binding desired
- ✔ The paper stock and color
- ✔ Ink color
- ✔ Whether color is used in the book's interior
- ✔ Whether the book contain an insert, such as a CD, DVD, or CD-ROM

In addition, be prepared to provide information about the following items:

- ✔ **Contact information:** Include your name, address, e-mail address, and so on.
- ✔ **Book-specific items:** List the title of your book, whether you've acquired your own ISBN, bar code, copyright, and other book-specific items (see Chapter 7 for details) or whether the printer needs to do these tasks on your behalf (typically for an additional fee).
- ✔ **Format:** Include the format of the content of your book and the book's front and back cover art and how it is supplied to the printer.

✓ **Initial print run (quantity of books to be printed):** Some printers accept orders for as few as 100 books. However, to dramatically reduce the printing cost per book, receive quotes for 500, 1,000 and 2,500 (or more) copies, assuming you anticipate being able to sell this quantity of books over the long term and don't mind having to inventory them until they're sold. For small print runs, seriously consider using POD technology (covered in Chapter 11).

✓ **Timeline:** How quickly you need the printing job done. Most printers charge extra for "rush" jobs. Figure out your overall publishing schedule and find a printer that can work within that schedule.

✓ **Packaging:** Whether the book needs to be shrink wrapped and boxed in a specific way. Special requests typically cost extra.

✓ **Shipping:** How and where you want the books shipped after they're printed. You're responsible for shipping charges, so you need to decide how you want the books shipped and how quickly you need them to arrive (see Chapter 16 for shipping details). The faster the shipping method, the more you pay, especially for heavy boxes of books.

✓ **Additional services:** Include copy editing; layout and design; cover design; preparation or editing of artwork to be used within the book; having multiple proofs created; rush printing services, and so on.

For the most accurate quote, you also may need to provide the printer with a copy of your book's manuscript or galleys (the laid-out and designed pages).

Reviewing quotes carefully

After you provide all the information in the previous section, the printer then can provide you with a written price quote. This quote should list all the print job's specifications exactly. If anything isn't listed, it should be discussed and a new quote should be issued before accepting it. The quote then lists all the prices associated with the print job, including a total price.

Many book printers have Web sites that calculate instant quotes. This service can be useful when estimating a budget, but use these quotes for estimate purposes only, and be prepared for a higher final quote.

After receiving a price quote that looks reasonable, sit down with the printer (or talk over the telephone) and go over every line of the quote to ensure that you understand what everything means. Ideally, you should also have the printer provide you a sample of another book that's already been printed that looks similar to yours, so you can see firsthand what to expect.

If you decide to move forward after receiving a written price quote, you sign the quote indicating you've accepted those terms. Sometimes you then submit a deposit (often nonrefundable) and/or apply for credit terms with that printer.

Beware of hidden and unexpected charges when calculating your printing budget and evaluating quotes. When you get a quote, it's based exactly on the printing specifications you initially provided. Any deviation from what's listed on the price quote may result in additional charges depending on who makes the changes. Make sure that you understand exactly what services are included in the quote you're given and that you understand exactly what the final printed books look like.

Shop around for the best prices and services based on your needs. If you receive two vastly different price quotes, determine why before choosing the company that provided the lowest quote. One printer may be quoting the job based on less expensive paper, for example.

What happens after you hire a printer?

After you agree to a price and officially hire the printer, determine exactly how your galleys (the edited and laid-out interior pages) and cover artwork need to be submitted and in what format. You also need to sign a contract or work order with the printer to establish a formal relationship. To avoid delays and extra fees, be sure to adhere to the guidelines provided by the printer, especially when it comes to preparing photographs and illustrations to be printed in the interior of the book and developing the book's front and back cover. Providing digital photographs in the wrong resolution or in the wrong format can negatively impact their appearance within the book (Chapter 8 has more about photo sizing and formatting).

The printer you choose becomes one of your publishing company's most important service suppliers. If your book sells well, you want to be able to quickly reorder books or use the same printer for future publishing projects. Your goal should be to build a long-term relationship with the printer of your choice. To do so, check out these steps:

- ✔ Develop a basic understanding early on about costs and scheduling.
- ✔ Openly communicate with the printer throughout the process.
- ✔ Make sure that all your needs, questions, and concerns are addressed.
- ✔ Make sure that your printer understands your needs and what you envision your final printed books should look like.

For more details about working successfully with any type of printer you've hired, check out Chapter 13.

Chapter 11

Print-On-Demand for Demanding Self-Publishers

*O*ne of the most cost-effective ways to self-publish a book and have many of the often confusing steps in the publishing process handled on your behalf is to pursue Print-On-Demand (POD) self-publishing. POD is fast and inexpensive and offers authors many options to create and publish their own book. Authors can also make their book available to potential readers through online distribution channels and potentially through bookstores and other retail outlets. POD utilizes the latest printing and publishing technologies to create a wide range of options for authors. For most people interested in pursuing self-publishing, POD is an extremely viable option.

This chapter explains POD and offers the information you need to take advantage of this relatively new technology to publish your book through turnkey POD solutions. These *turnkey solutions* take much of the guesswork and busy work out of publishing and distributing any type of book because they handle virtually all the tasks on the author's behalf. While the author is responsible for writing and editing his own manuscript, these companies handle everything from layout and design to distribution. Self-published authors pay for a publishing package based on their needs but don't have to worry about things like obtaining an ISBN, getting the book listed with online booksellers, or filling orders from customers.

Taking a Quick Tour of Print-On-Demand Technology

POD is very different from traditional offset book printing (which I cover in Chapter 10), although the end product is the same. Here are the major differences between offset printing and POD technology:

- ✓ **Traditional offset printing:** In this technique, an inked image is transferred from a plate to a rubber blanket and then to the printing paper. The book's cover is printed separately and then the entire book is bound to create a finished product.

- ✓ **POD technology:** When POD books are printed, high-end, 600 dpi (dots per-inch) laser printers are used. These industrial-quality laser printers print on 20-pound white bond paper, using black toner, to print the pages of the book, one copy at a time, as needed. A separate, full-color printing process is used to print each book's cover (reproduced at 300 dpi). The POD books then use proprietary binding technology, allowing for either a perfect-bound or coil-bound book to be created. (For binding information, see Chapter 10.)

Some POD publishers offer additional customization options for final printed books, allowing authors to request (for an extra per-copy fee) higher-quality, 24-pound white paper for their book's inside pages. Full-color pages can also be incorporated within the book, and you can add CDs or other flat objects that are pasted inside the book's back cover (also for an additional fee, which impacts the book's final cover price). Check out "Working with companies to manage money issues," later in this chapter for more about fees you may pay.

Looking at the Pros and Cons of Print-On-Demand

POD is definitely a popular choice among self-publishers for a variety of reasons. This section focuses on the many benefits of POD, as well as some of the potential drawbacks.

The benefits of Print-On-Demand

POD offers many benefits, especially to first-time self-publishers and people looking for complete publishing solutions that aren't too expensive. Check out what I'm talking about in the next few sections.

Avoiding a lot of hassle

POD makes getting published easy for any author and to have the majority of the hassle taken out of the process. The biggest benefit of this technology is that a complete turnkey solution is offered, so you don't mess with the every-day things of the publishing business. (See "Surveying the Print-On-Demand Process," later in this chapter for more details.)

Make sure that the POD company you choose gives your book project the one-on-one attention needed and that no pre-created templates are used when creating your book's front cover. Using a template makes the cover design process much faster but limits the designer's creatively and takes away the opportunity to create a unique book cover. Chapter 9 has cover design details.

Saving money

Back in 1995, the world of publishing changed dramatically with the introduction of POD technology. For decades, if an author wanted to have her book published, her options included working with a major publishing house or publishing her own book with offset printing, which was an extremely costly endeavor. Even today, most authors don't have $10,000 to $20,000 to invest in the offset publication of their own book plus additional funds to properly market, promote, and distribute. Now, in a matter of weeks and for an investment of between $300 and $1,500, anyone can have a book published and made available to the public.

Here are the major differences between the two printing processes:

- ✔ If you published your book through traditional offset printing technology, to make the process cost effective, hundreds or thousands of copies of the book would need to be printed during each print run. This means the publishing house or author needs to potentially pay thousands of dollars upfront to have a book designed, printed, and warehoused, even before a single copy is sold. For anyone who needs only a small number of books, POD is an extremely viable and cost-effective option.

- ✔ Conversely, POD requires only a small initial financial investment primarily because the technology used allows for just one copy of the book to be professionally printed and bound at a time after orders for the book are actually received. After the initial set-up process with a POD publisher, when an order is placed for a POD book, it immediately gets printed and shipped to the customer, retailer, or distributor, typically within one to three business days. That means that you don't have to invest in or store mountains of books until they're sold.

If you know you want to self-publish your book, whether you choose to use POD versus traditional offset book printing (see Chapter 10) or even eBook publishing (see Chapter 12), you need to crunch some numbers to determine what makes sense based on your budget, sales expectations, and ability to market and distribute your own book.

To determine if POD is worth it for your book publishing project, perform a simple cost-benefit analysis. The printing costs per copy by using POD are significantly higher than using traditional book printing methods, which take away from your per-copy profit potential. But, the initial financial investment is significantly lower. With POD, virtually all the major steps involved with bringing your book to print (after the manuscript is written and fully edited) are handled on your behalf. You pay for these services as part of the publishing package you purchase, but the time and money you save can be significant in the long run, and you take on much less of a financial risk when you publish your book using POD.

Want to crunch some numbers? Based on the number of copies you antici-pate selling, calculate how much profit you can earn per copy sold when comparing POD with other publishing options. This can be accomplished by figuring out your costs and comparing them. When you make contact with a POD publisher, they can help you calculate your costs after you know basic information like the length of your book and what printing specifications you're looking for. Chapter 6 helps you plan your publishing budget.

Enjoying speed and versatility

After your manuscript is completely written and edited, POD allows you to have your book published in a matter of weeks, not months or years. You can choose from a wide range of printing specifications, including the book's trim size and paper stock, then print books as they're sold — even if it's one copy at a time. POD requires a much lower financial investment and greatly reduces the self-published author's risk.

The drawbacks of Print-On-Demand

Depending on how you plan to market and distribute your book, POD can be an extremely viable publishing solution. It does, however, have certain draw-backs. The following sections explore some of them.

Rejecting returns and standard credit

The biggest drawback of POD is that most of the companies don't accept returns from booksellers, retailers, and distributors. All the major publishing houses do accept returns (typically within 90 days) if a book doesn't sell. By not accepting returns, booksellers or distributors must commit to buying and then selling all ordered copies of your book and often must order multiple copies (at least ten) in order to receive a standard 40 to 60 percent discount off of the cover price.

Another related drawback is that booksellers and distributors aren't given industry-standard credit terms. All orders must be pre-paid. Lack of buying on credit combined with the no returns policy make it extremely difficult for authors who use POD to sell their book through traditional booksellers and other retail stores because these places don't pay in advance and cycle their books for returns when they don't sell. Therefore, if people want to purchase your book, they need to make their purchase directly from the POD company, from the author, or from an online service such as Amazon.com or Barnes & Noble.com (see Chapter 14 for details about these services).

One way around these drawbacks is for you, the author, to pre-purchase a large quantity of books and sell them directly to distributors or booksellers and offer industry-standard discounts and returns. This procedure, however, may greatly reduce your book's profit potential because you pay around 40 to 60 percent of the book's cover price to purchase copies of your own book for resale. In this situation, it's often more cost-effective to use more traditional book printing methods as opposed to POD; see Chapter 10 for details about offset printing.

Handling issues with layout and design

When it comes to the layout and design of books, in some cases, POD also has small drawbacks:

- The resolution and the way photographs and artwork are incorporated into the book
- The type and quality of paper used for the internal pages
- The use of full-color within the inside pages

Although the author has many options when choosing the printing specifications of the book using POD, this is a different printing technology than what the major publishing houses use to print their books. This high-end laser technology is quickly improving, but there are certain issues that relate to the quality of photographic images and the type of paper that can be used for a book's internal pages. Each POD publisher uses slightly different technology, so it's important to request actual samples of books and discuss printing limitations with the company you choose to work with.

If cost isn't an issue, offset printing is always better, but you're talking an investment of thousands of dollars — not hundreds.

Surveying the Print-On-Demand Process

Just like with traditional offset book publishing (which I cover in Chapter 10), using POD to design, publish, distribute, and market your book is a multi-step process. The good news is that many of the POD companies handle a lot of the confusing steps in the process on your behalf. In the following sections, I steer you through the major steps in the POD process and explain what a POD company needs from an author to start the printing process.

As soon as you begin working with a POD company, you get a project manager who is your primary contact. This person walks you through the entire self-publishing process using POD and can answer your questions.

Looking at the major steps

After the completion of your manuscript, you should make sure that your text undergoes rigorous editing, as I discuss in Chapter 5. Many POD companies can help you hire an editor, for an additional fee, but most assume that your manuscript is ready to be laid out and printed after it's received.

After your manuscript is ready to begin the POD process, follow these major steps:

1. **Select a POD company, such as iUniverse, Trafford, or Wheatmark.**

   I discuss these companies in detail later in this chapter.

2. **Submit your manuscript to the POD company.**

   You also turn in your artwork, the Author's Agreement (provided by the POD company), your payment, and a variety of other materials (see the next section).

3. **Complete the layout and design process (including the scanning of artwork as needed), along with your book's cover creation process.**

   This step can take between two and six weeks, depending on the company you work with. But you have creative input during each stage of your book's development process.

   If you want to maintain total control over the design of your book, you can opt to handle the book's internal page layout and design, as well as the creation of your book's front and back cover, yourself. Meeting the POD company's exact technical specifications is necessary, however. Some POD companies offer a discount if you handle the layout and design of your own book and provide it in the form of a ready-to-print PDF electronic file. Chapter 8 focuses on book layout and design.

4. **You receive an author proof of your book from the POD company.**

   The proof is a mock-up showing exactly what each page of your book looks like. This stage is your final chance to make last-minute edits and ensure that the layout and design of the book is exactly as you envisioned it. You have about 14 days to submit any corrections or changes. (I cover proofing in more detail in Chapter 13.)

5. **Make revisions and prep the final book for publication.**

   This chance is your final one to make edits, fix errors, or improve the content of your book before it's printed and made available to the public. Proofread your book carefully!

6. **Begin promoting your book through advertising, marketing, and public relations.**

   Remember, this step is important because you're solely responsible for it. Plan your public relations, marketing, and advertising carefully so you can maximize your budget and reach the most potential readers. See Part V of this book for full details.

7. **Start selling and distributing your book.**

   Your POD company ensures that your book is listed on services such as Bowker's BooksInPrint.com (a comprehensive directory used by bookstores and libraries that lists all books currently in print), Amazon.com, Barnes & Noble.com, and Borders.com. The POD company also notifies major book distributors about the publication and availability of your book.

   The POD company also drop-ships copies of your book to your customers as orders are received. So, whether it's an individual, a bookstore, or a distributor that orders your book, the POD company prints books and fulfills orders as they're received. (These services are built into the fees and commissions you pay to the POD company.)

Many of the POD companies that offer turnkey solutions also offer a wide range of extra services to help you market and promote your book. In some cases, these services are included in the publishing package you purchase. You may, however, have to pay extra for them based on your needs. Check out "Working with companies to manage money issues," later in this chapter for more about fees you may pay. Chapter 13 also includes general information about working successfully with any printer you hire.

Knowing what a POD company needs to get rolling

To ensure that your book turns out exactly the way you envision it, provide the POD publisher with everything they need. This includes the internal pages of your book (after they've been fully edited, laid out, and designed) as well as your book's cover artwork. This section focuses on preparing the materials your POD publisher needs from you.

Materials for layout and cover design

When your manuscript is complete and edited and you've collected all the photos, illustrations, and artwork to be included in the book, you're ready to turn your work over to a POD company for the layout and design process.

If the POD company handles your page layout and design and your front and back cover design, plan on providing the following materials:

- ✔ A print out (hardcopy) of your entire edited manuscript

- ✔ An electronic version of your manuscript (in Microsoft Word) format

- ✔ Copies of any graphics, images, artwork, or photographs to be included within the book complete with figure reference numbers. Make sure that each piece of artwork is properly labeled and meets the technical specifications spelled out by the POD company you're working with. (See Chapter 4 for more about artwork in your manuscript.)

Many POD companies have a limit regarding the number of photographs or pieces of artwork that can be included within the book (if you want more, there may be additional fees). The number of photographs or pieces of artwork allowed varies based on the publishing package you purchase and the POD company you work with. By paying extra, however, an unlimited number of photographs or pieces of artwork can typically be incorporated into your book.

- ✔ PDF files of your page layout and design (if you've done it yourself) that are ready to print. See Chapter 8 for details on how to do this. In many cases, the POD publisher you hire handles your page layout and design for you. If this is the case, you can offer ideas or even sketches of what you'd like your book's pages to look like.

- ✔ A sketch or draft of the book's front cover and/or information about the cover you need designed by the POD company. If you've had your cover pre-designed by a professional graphic artist or have done the design work yourself (see Chapter 9 for details), you need to supply the final cover artwork in a format that meets the POD company's specifications.

One way to ensure that your book's interior layout and design comes out the way you envision it is to look at other books and provide the graphic designer with actual samples you like. You can even take design elements from several different books to create something unique for your book.

Information about the book and its author

When you initially begin working with a POD company, you need to provide specific information about your book and your vision for it. Some of the details you're asked for include

- ✔ Your book's complete title and subtitle (if applicable)

- ✔ The category or genre the book fits into, such as fiction, how-to, self-help, poetry, cookbook, and so on

- ✔ The main subject matter your book covers

- ✔ The book's intended audience

✔ The desired trim size of your book (usually a minimum 5-x-5 inches and maximum 8¼-x-10¾ inches for perfect-bound books)

✔ The type of book you want — trade paperback, hardcover, and/or eBook (see Chapter 12 for information on eBooks)

✔ The type of binding you prefer (see Chapter 10 for details on binding types)

✔ A short description of your book (one or two sentences)

✔ A more in-depth description of your book (a paragraph or two)

✔ Keywords or phrases that could be used by a potential customer when they're searching for your book (be prepared to provide up to a dozen keywords or phrases)

✔ Biographical information about the author

✔ A photograph of the author

✔ The completed author questionnaire provided by the POD company (if applicable)

✔ The signed Author's Agreement provided by the POD company

✔ Your payment to the POD company

Picking a Great Print-On-Demand Company for Your Book

The POD business has grown dramatically in recent years and many companies are starting to offer these services to self-published authors. This section focuses on a few of the more established and better known POD publishers that offer complete turnkey publishing solutions.

Finding and thoroughly researching companies

When it comes to choosing a POD printing solution for your book, you have many options. I cover three prominent POD companies later in this chapter; you can find additional companies online using any Internet search engines and the search phrase *Print-On-Demand book publishing.*

All POD companies aren't alike. Each offers slight differences in the services offered and prices charged, based on what's included in the respective POD publishing packages. You may discover that some POD companies offer a la carte layout and design, POD printing, distribution, and promotional services to authors instead of complete turnkey solutions. Depending on how much of the self-publishing process you want to handle yourself, this option may be a viable for you.

To find the right POD company capable of meeting your needs, first focus on what your needs are in terms of your book's design, printing, publishing, distribution, and marketing. After that, follow these guidelines:

- **Find a POD company you can afford.** Keep in mind, most of the POD companies offer several different publishing packages for authors at different price points. Each package includes specific services.

- **Research the company's history and reputation.** Make sure that the company has experience publishing books similar to yours and is well-established. Interview a representative from the company and request to see actual samples of work. Also, ask for a list of references or information about past clients.

- **Look for quality.** The print quality of POD books can vary, and in general doesn't quite meet the consistent standards of offset printing. Whenever possible, it's wise to find samples of POD books from a particular company not provided by that company, because the company tends to select the best print runs for samples. Even with a single print run, the print quality can vary, just the way the quality of laser copies can vary with the amount of toner in the machine, how old it is, how carefully quality is monitored, and so on.

- **Choose a company that offers the specific services you need and can benefit from the most.** Some POD companies focus more on book design and printing, while others are better equipped to assist you in marketing, promoting and distributing your book.

As you prepare to have your book published through a POD company, here are a few other important things to consider:

- The initial cost of the publishing package being offered

- The services included with the publishing package

- How and when royalties are calculated and paid to the author

- The discount at which you can purchase copies of your book from the POD company

- The amount of time the POD company needs to publish your book from the time it receives the manuscript

- How much control, if any, you have over the book's cover price

✔ How much marketing, advertising, and public relations support you plan to receive from the POD company and what form that support may take

✔ What discount is offered to bookstores, retailers, libraries, and book distributors and whether returns are accepted by the POD company

✔ Whether the POD company offers credit terms to established distributors, booksellers, libraries, and other retailers, or if all orders must be pre-paid

Before choosing a POD company, always read the company's *Author Agreement* and other contracts carefully. These documents are legal and outline the services to be offered and their related fees. Then calculate your overall budget. Determine approximately how many copies of your book you need to sell in order to break even on your investment, then determine if that sales figure is feasible, based on the distribution, sales, marketing, advertising and publicity opportunities you anticipate being available to you (see the next section for money matters).

As an author, you pay the POD company a pre-determined fee for a specific publishing package, and then you're able to purchase copies of your published book at a discount of up to 60 percent off the book's retail cover price. Each POD company offers several publishing packages at different price points.

Also remember that unlike when you work with a major publishing house, when you use POD to publish your book, you retain all rights to your book, including the copyright. See Chapter 6 for the full scoop on copyright.

Working with companies to manage money issues

The POD company you choose helps you make important decisions about your book's cover price, while ultimately impacting your profit margin. This section deals with some of the financial issues and decisions you need to contend with as a self-publisher using POD.

Watching out for hidden costs

Many first time authors don't pre-calculate all the costs associated with publishing their book. Using a turnkey POD solution helps control costs, but there are still many expenses you can incur in addition to the POD publishing package you purchase. These expenses include editing services, acquiring artwork, graphic design, and publicity.

Determine exactly what services are included in the POD publishing package you're purchasing and what additional services you need and have to pay for, and feel free to ask your contact person any and all questions.

POD companies specialize in publishing and distributing your book — not marketing and promoting it. Getting word out about your book is solely the author's responsibility. You can, of course, hire professional salespeople and public relations people to help you. If you don't properly promote your book, no matter how good the book actually is, it won't sell. It's that simple. See Part V for the lowdown on publicity, marketing, and advertising.

Pricing your book

Every book has a cost per copy to print, based on the number of pages and its binding. Most POD companies provide you with the exact printing cost per copy and require that your book's cover price be at least 2½ times the printing cost per book.

This pricing model ensures that you, as the author, as well as the POD company, can make ample profit on each copy of the book sold. This pricing model also allows for a standard 15 to 60 percent discount off the book's retail cover price to be offered to recognized book distributors, booksellers, and libraries that order your book.

As the author, you also want to be able to purchase copies of your book from the POD company at between 40 to 60 percent off the book's cover price and have the option to resell books directly to customers for the book's cover price. Most POD companies also initially supply you with a pre-determined number of free copies of your book, based on the publishing package you buy.

Here's an example: In 2006, the printing cost of a 260-page trade paperback book was $9.03 per copy. The minimum cover price for that book is $22.57 (2½ times the per-copy printing cost). As the author, you could increase your profits by boosting the cover price to $24.95 or $29.95 (or higher), based on how much you believe potential readers are willing to pay for your book. When you use POD, as the author, you have the option to purchase books at a discount (ranging from 40 to 60 percent off the cover price). You then have the option to resell those books at the cover price in order to earn your profit.

Some POD companies give authors input into their book's cover price. Others don't. Your book's cover price can have a tremendous impact on its profit potential. Pricing it correctly can mean the difference between earning a profit and losing money on your publishing venture over the life of your book. Check out Chapter 7 for details about setting your book's cover price.

Calculating your royalties

Every POD company has a different formula used to calculate an author's royalties. As books are sold, you receive a royalty based on a pre-determined percentage of the gross profit earned per book. Some POD companies offer up to a 60 percent royalty on gross profit from each copy sold. Another part of this equation is based on how the book is sold, either directly by the author or POD company, through a distributor, through an online bookseller, or through a traditional retailer. Make sure that you understand the formula your POD company uses to calculate your royalties.

To calculate how much of a royalty you earn per book, determine if the customer pays the full cover price or purchases the book at a discount. Here are some scenarios:

- ✔ **Direct sales:** If your book's cover price is $29.95 and one copy is sold directly to an individual from the POD company for the full cover price, here's how to calculate your royalty:

  - Take the cover price (in this case, $29.95) and subtract the printing costs (in this case $9.03). This leaves $20.92 in gross profit.

  - As the author, if you receive a royalty of 60 percent of the gross profit, you'd earn $12.53 on the sale of that book.

- ✔ **Retail booksellers:** If the book is sold through Amazon.com or a traditional bookstore or distributor, which purchased the $29.95 book at a wholesale price of 50 percent off of the book's cover price ($14.98), here's how to calculate your royalty.

  - Subtract the printing costs ($9.03) from the discounted book price, which leaves a gross profit of $5.95.

  - As the author, you'd then earn a 60 percent royalty on $5.95, which is $3.57 per copy sold.

  With this drastic difference in royalties, your obvious goal, to be able to make money, is to sell hundreds or thousands of copies of your book.

- ✔ **Author sales:** You purchase copies of your book directly from the POD company as the author, and you probably receive a 40 to 60 percent discount off the book's cover price, depending on the quality of books ordered. This means that you'd purchase the $29.95 book for $17.97 (40 percent off), then be able to resell it directly to customers at $29.95 and earn $11.98 per copy.

You can sell copies of your book to your existing customers and clients when you make author appearances, give lectures, or sell books directly from your Web site. By using this scenario, however, you're responsible for fulfilling orders and potentially maintaining an inventory of books. Fear not, though; I give you details on order fulfillment, inventory, and shipping in Chapter 16.

Royalties are typically paid by the POD companies to the author on a quarterly basis. This timeline varies, however, depending on the POD company you work with. Some companies may pay on a monthly or semi-annual basis. Be sure to ask your contact person about royalty payments before you sign a contract so you know what to expect.

Checking Out a Few Prominent POD Companies

Three POD companies offer turnkey solutions for authors interested in self-publishing their book:

- ✔ **iUniverse:** Phone (800) AUTHORS: Web site www.iuniverse.com
- ✔ **Trafford:** Phone (888) 232-4444; Web site www.trafford.com
- ✔ **Wheatmark:** Phone (888) 934-0888; Web site www.wheatmark.com

I describe these companies in the following sections, but keep in mind that these are just a sampling of the many printing and publishing companies that offer turnkey POD solutions. I mention these three companies because they're prominent in the industry. Check out "Finding and thoroughly researching companies" earlier in this chapter for tips on finding additional companies and checking their credentials.

Amazon.com has launched its own POD service for writers and authors called BookSurge. Using this service guarantees placement on Amazon.com and Amazon.com's worldwide affiliates. BookSurge also allows books to have full-color inserts and be printed in paperback or hard cover with a wide range of book trim sizes and paper stocks. Call BookSurge at (866) 308-6235, ext. 128, or visit the following Web site: www.booksurgepublisherservices.com.

iUniverse

iUniverse offers a variety of publishing services to help individuals publish, market, and sell books. For authors interested in POD, iUniverse offers several publishing packages, ranging in price from $299 for its *Fast Track* package to $799 for its *Premier Plus* package.

- ✔ The *Fast Track* package offers limited services, including basic page layout and design along with basic cover design.
- ✔ The *Premier Plus* package features all the services you need to design and lay out your book, create the front and back covers, and make trade paperback, hardcover, and/or eBook editions of your book available. The package also includes acquiring the book's ISBN, barcode, copyright, and Library of Congress Card Number on your behalf.

In as little as 30 days after supplying iUniverse with your fully edited manuscript, your book can be published and ready to be purchased on online booksellers and from more than 25,000 booksellers and e-retailers worldwide.

Other publishing services included with the more expensive publishing packages offered by iUniverse include

✔ Determining the retail cover price of your book

✔ Distribution (all books published by iUniverse are available for sale at www.iUniverse.com)

✔ Editorial evaluation

✔ Marketing toolkit

Manuscripts to be published by iUniverse must be at least 10,000 words in length (this word count results in a 48-page book). If you want to include up to 25 graphics or photographs within your book, an additional fee of $100 exists. For 26 to 50 images, add $200 to the cost of the publishing package.

According to iUniverse, the company publishes both hard- and softcover books in a variety of sizes. Visit the company online for more information.

Trafford

Trafford is a pioneer and leader in the POD industry. The company's publishing packages range in price from $699 for its basic "Legacy Classic" package to $1949 for its comprehensive *Best Seller Plus* package.

Each publishing package offers a variety of services designed to offer authors a complete publishing solution, based on their needs. Unlike iUniverse, Trafford gives authors some input into the retail cover price of their book. This input can impact your profit potential dramatically because you can select a lower cover price than what the printer recommends, but your profit margin per book decreases.

Trafford offers discounts for various reasons:

✔ For booksellers, distributors, and libraries; however, no returns are accepted

✔ For authors who do their own interior page layout and design, as well as create their own front and back book cover

To help you calculate your costs and anticipated revenue from your book, Trafford offers a Publishing Profit Calculator on its Web site. A free, 20-page publishing guide can also be downloaded.

Trafford also lists books on Amazon.com, Barnes & Noble.com, and Borders.com, and it also notifies BooksInPrint.com and other services about the publication of new books.

Wheatmark

Wheatmark is an example of a smaller POD publishing company that offers many of the same services as its larger competitors, as well as services companies such as iUniverse and Trafford don't offer. Here's a sampling of their services:

- ✔ Wheatmark works with authors to market and promote the books that initially sell over 2,000 copies.

- ✔ Wheatmark offers industry-standard wholesale discounts to all booksellers and distributors, and they accept returns.

- ✔ Wheatmark employs highly trained graphic designers who work with authors on original cover designs for each book.

- ✔ Wheatmark specializes in publishing trade paperback books in variety of trim sizes.

- ✔ Wheatmark boasts that it offers better discounts to authors, a higher level of personalized service, and competitively priced publishing packages.

Wheatmark offers its standard POD publishing package to authors for $799; however, it has a menu of a la carte extra services, ranging in price from $69 to $299 each. Although the company includes an ISBN and related barcode with its publishing package, it charges extra to register the copyright with The United States Copyright Office on your behalf. (Head to Chapter 7 to find out how to register copyright yourself.)

All books published using Wheatmark's POD services are automatically listed with Amazon.com, Barnes & Noble.com, Borders.com, and BooksAMillion.com and are made available on Wheatmark's own online bookstore. The company also works closely with Ingram Book Company, one of the country's leading book distributors. By listing a book with Ingram, the book is made available to any bookstore nationwide. For more information, visit Wheatmark online.

Chapter 12

Checking Out Some Non-Traditional Printing Options

Many people think of a book as a printed paperback or hardcover that's professionally bound and something you'd find in a typical library or bookstore. Most traditional books take on this form.

There are, however, other ways of distributing your book-length manuscript to potential readers. This chapter explores a couple of non-traditional publishing options: the creation and distribution of eBooks (electronic books) and the use of a local print shop for small quantities of books.

The Basics of eBook Publishing

Even though eBooks haven't reached acceptance in the mainstream quite yet, publishing an eBook is an easy, inexpensive, and technically savvy way to reach readers. In the following sections, I define eBooks and their audience, and I explain the pros and cons of turning your manuscript into an eBook.

Examining eBooks' setup and audience

eBooks are full-length books that are distributed in electronic form, typically via the Internet. They can be purchased online, downloaded, and read on a computer, personal digital assistant (PDA), Smartphone screen, or printed out on the reader's own printer. In terms of layout and design, the internal pages of the eBook look similar to a traditional book. In the following sections, I explain how to read eBooks and describe their typical audience.

How do you read an eBook?

To read an eBook, it's necessary to have eBook reading software on your computer or PDA device. This software is typically distributed free of charge and allows eBook pages to appear as traditional book pages on a screen.

One of the biggest problems with eBooks is that there are at least a dozen different eBook formats, each requiring a different type of reader. Some of the more popular eBook readers include

- ✔ Microsoft Reader (`www.microsoft.com/reader/default.asp`)
- ✔ Adobe Reader (`www.adobe.com/products/acrobat/readstep2.html`)
- ✔ eBook Reader for Palm (`www.adobe.com/products/acrobat/readerforpalm.html`)
- ✔ Pocket PC (`www.adobe.com/products/acrobat/readerforppc.html`)

For more about these programs, see "Formatting your eBook," later in this chapter.

The Sony Reader is another device for reading eBooks released in 2006. The unit is about the size of a trade paperback book and weighs nine ounces. It holds about 80 full-length eBooks in memory. The eBooks can be purchased from Sony's own online eBook store, called Connect. The Sony Reader also displays PDF files and plays MP3 audio files. For details about this innovative eBook reader, check out `products.sel.sony.com/pa/prs/index.html`.

Who actually reads eBooks, anyway?

When eBooks were first introduced, the hope was that they'd quickly replace traditional books, just as CDs made LPs and even cassettes virtually extinct. Well, that never happed. Most readers seem to prefer to hold a traditional book in their hands and manually turn the pages when they're reading.

Yet, a niche and slowly growing audience for eBooks does exist. The good news is that some avid readers simply enjoy the convenience of downloading text to read on screen. For example, if you're a frequent business traveler, you can take along your laptop or PDA and hold the full contents of several books and have access to them anytime you wish.

Making your book exclusively available as an eBook dramatically limits your potential audience. Therefore, it's a sound business strategy to publish your book in *both* traditionally printed and eBook form.

Understanding eBook benefits

Publishing an eBook has big benefits:

- ✔ **The cost of actually publishing an eBook is virtually free.** You don't incur printing costs or warehousing fees. After the book is created in eBook format, it's ready to be sold in any quantity.

- ✔ **eBooks can be unlimited in length and contain any type of text, photographs, or graphics.** The length of the book and extra graphic elements don't impact production cost or the publisher's requirements when setting retail pricing.

- ✔ **eBooks can be edited and modified quickly and cheaply.** After the document is created, it can be edited or revised in a matter of minutes.

- ✔ **Distribution of an eBook can be done via a Web site, e-mail, or on CD-ROM.** From the publisher's standpoint, an eBook is simply a digital file that can be distributed just like any other digital file.

  Also, many companies have discovered that making just the user's manuals or technical reference materials for their products available in eBook form is an extremely cost effective solution for distributing this material. (See "Distributing your eBook," later in this chapter for details.)

From the reader's standpoint, the benefits of eBooks are the following:

- ✔ An eBook can be read anytime and anywhere, and multiple eBook titles can be stored on a computer, PDA, or Smartphone.

- ✔ The text in an eBook can be searched just like when you read a Web site and use hyperlinks and searches within an eBook to jump around the text and quickly find specific information you're looking for.

- ✔ The price of an eBook is typically about half of what a traditional printed book costs, and who doesn't like a bargain?

Recognizing potential eBook drawbacks

Some potential drawbacks of publishing an eBook include

- ✔ **Having trouble reading eBooks:** For example: After someone purchases an eBook, he has the option of printing out the entire document on a printer, but this takes time and uses up ink (or toner) as well as paper.

- ✔ **Reaching the broadest eBook reading audience:** This audience is small to begin with, so your eBook must be created and distributed in multiple eBook formats, such as Portable Document Format (PDF) (for Acrobat Reader and Acrobat eBook Reader), Microsoft Reader format, and Palm and Pocket PC eBook Reader format.

✓ **Gathering a small audience:** In addition to being interested in the subject matter of your book, an eBook reader needs to be savvy enough to use an eBook reader on a computer or PDA and be willing to use this technology to actually read a book-length document on their screen.

✓ **Having trouble with displaying details:** eBook readers for smaller devices, such as PDAs and Smartphones, have difficulty displaying detailed graphics and photos.

The Details of Putting Out eBooks

When it comes to eBook publishing, after your content is created, you need to format that content so it can be read and accessed by people using the most popular eBook readers. You also must develop pricing for the eBook edition and then find the best ways to distribute your eBook. The good news is that publishing eBooks is much cheaper than publishing traditionally printed books. The problem, however, is that the profit potential is significantly lower. This section focuses on how to create an eBook edition of your book.

Most self-published authors benefit from publishing their book in printed form and offering an eBook edition. This extra edition allows you to reach the broadest possible audience. Publishing only an eBook edition saves you a fortune but greatly limits your audience.

Formatting your eBook

For every popular eBook format, there are a handful of tools designed to help you format and transform your book-length manuscript into an eBook. This process can be simple or require a lot of effort, depending on how fancy you want your eBook to look and how many different formats you want to publish your eBook in. In the following sections, I cover three popular formats.

The PDF Store Web site (www.pdfstore.com) offers a wide range of eBook publishing tools and resources designed to assist first-time eBook publishers and authors. Here, you find eBook publishing software packages, such as NitroPDF and Palm eBook Studio, which can be used to format eBooks for Palm easily. You can also download virtually all the popular eBook reader programs from this site for free.

To add professionalism, many eBook publishers design their eBook pages just as they would for a traditional book before publishing and distributing it. To accomplish this task, load your manuscript (Microsoft Word format) into a page layout and design program, like Quark, Microsoft Publisher, or Adobe InDesign CS2 (see Chapter 8), to properly format each page so it takes on the appearance of a book. The formatted document can then be converted into a PDF file or another eBook format and distributed electronically as an eBook.

The Adobe Reader format

You can take any Microsoft Word document and use Adobe Acrobat to create a PDF file that can be read using either Adobe Reader or Adobe eBook Reader. This process takes just a few minutes. The PDF file can then be distributed as an eBook.

Adobe Acrobat is a software package published by Adobe that can be used to create PDF files from almost any type of computer document, such as Microsoft Word or any application in the Microsoft Office Suite. To open and read a PDF file on any computer or PDA, Adobe Reader, Adobe eBook Reader, or a compatible program must be used. These programs are free and already installed on millions of PCs, PDAs, and Smartphones around the world. Versions of Adobe Reader are available for the PC (Windows), Mac, Symbian, Palm, and Pocket PC operating systems.

The biggest benefit to publishing your eBook in Adobe Reader format is that it's the most widely used eBook Reader software in the world and available on a variety of platforms. Therefore by publishing your eBook in this format, you're able to cater to the needs of a large eBook reading audience. The Adobe Web site (www.adobe.com) is an excellent resource for discovering eBook platform and how to best use it as part of your publishing efforts.

The Microsoft Reader eBook format

Microsoft Reader is used for reading eBooks on a PC or laptop computer. Two other versions of this eBook reading software are also available for the Pocket PC and Windows Mobile operating systems, making it possible to store and read eBooks on PDAs and Smartphones that run under these Microsoft operating systems.

Formatting an eBook to be compatible with Microsoft Reader is easy, as long as you adhere to certain compatibility guidelines, which the Web sites listed below describe. eBooks can be created using Microsoft Word, Microsoft Publisher, or a variety of other page layout and design tools. To find out more about the Microsoft Reader format and how to format eBooks to the proper specifications, download these free eBooks:

- ✔ *Layout Guide for Microsoft Reader:* www.microsoft.com/reader/ developers/downloads/layout.asp
- ✔ *Microsoft Reader Source Materials & Conversion Guide:* www. microsoft.com/reader/developers/downloads/source.asp

The Palm eBook Reader format

One of the most successful distribution methods for eBooks has been through Palm OS compatible personal digital assistants (PDAs). By loading eBook reader software (such as eReader or eReader Pro for Palm OS) into your Palm OS compatible PDA or Smartphone, eBooks can be stored in the hand-held device and read on the screen, anytime and anywhere.

Formatting your eBook to be compatible with Palm eBook Reader can be done by using specialized formatting software or any program that allows you to create PDF files.

Several software packages are available to help eBook authors and publishers format and publish their eBooks in the Palm OS and Pocket PC format. One of the most popular packages is eBook Studio, which can be downloaded or demoed at `www.ereader.com/product/detail/15001`. For more information about how to publish an eBook so it's compatible with Palm OS devices, visit the PalmSource Web site at `www.palmsource.com/interests/ebooks`.

Pricing your eBook

Generally, most eBooks are priced at about half of what the same traditionally printed book title would sell for. So, if the trade paperback edition of your book sells for $19.95, the eBook edition might sell for $9.95. Head to Chapter 7 for details on how to set the cover price of your printed book.

Depending on how you plan to market and sell your eBook (see the next section), you can formulate the best possible suggested retail price, based on what you believe people are willing to pay. Be sure that the price you set for your eBook covers your costs associated with writing the manuscript and includes any marketing, advertising, and distribution you plan. If you plan to create and host a Web site to sell your eBook, there's a cost associated with this. This cost should be built into your eBook's retail price. Likewise, if you know you need to pay an eBook store a high commission for selling your book, this too needs to be calculated into your cover price. Generally, you want to charge one price for your eBook. Don't offer the same book and content at vastly different price points from different Web sites.

The cheaper your eBook is, the more copies of it you may sell. Established online eBookstores (which I cover later in this chapter) often help you set a reasonable retail price for your eBook.

Distributing your eBook

You can distribute your eBook in three primary ways:

- ✔ Create your own Web site to promote, sell, and distribute
- ✔ Sell your eBook online, through established eBookstores
- ✔ Distribute your eBook for free with a product purchase

I cover these methods in the following sections.

Just as you can use many different sales and distribution methods to sell traditionally printed copies of your book, you can also tap different distribution methods to sell your eBook edition. For example, you can offer the book through the established eBookstores and sell it directly to readers via your own Web site. When you make personal appearances, you can also sell the eBook edition on CD-ROM. Based on what your sales goals are and who your target audience is, focus on distribution methods that help you best reach your intended readers.

Selling through online eBooksellers

The established online eBookstores sell your eBook on your behalf and fulfill the orders, and they pay you a preset licensing fee or royalty, which is typically 40 to 60 percent of the selling price.

The biggest benefit to distributing your eBook through established eBooksellers is that the people shopping at these sites are typically avid eBook readers who already have the technological know-how to download and read eBook content. The drawback is that these eBooksellers often charge you a commission to promote your book on their site.

To have your eBook listed on various eBookstores' Web sites, contact each of them separately and fill out a publisher contract and agreement. A few popular eBookstore Web sites include

- ✔ www.ebooks.com
- ✔ www.ereader.com
- ✔ http://ebooks.palm.com
- ✔ www.ubibooks.com
- ✔ www.amazon.com

Due to lack of demand, Barnes & Noble no longer supports or sells eBooks from its retail stores or Web site.

Web site marketing

One of the biggest benefits of creating your own Web site and selling your eBook online is having a totally automated business opportunity and revenue generator. After the Web site is set up and your eBook is published and ready for download, all you need to do is promote the Web site to potential readers. Visitors to your Web site can then find out more about your eBook, perhaps read an excerpt, purchase the eBook online using a major credit card or PayPal, and automatically download the book and start reading. Check out Chapter 21 for details on how to create a stellar Web site for your book.

Having a killer Web site

For promoting and selling eBooks online, a type of Web site exists that is referred to as a *Killer Mini Site.* It features just one main Web page but includes a focused sales message designed to sell your eBook. A Killer Mini Site format works well for selling a wide range of how-to and nonfiction eBooks. A typical Killer Mini Site consists of a header graphic, headline, testimonial, product information section, benefits section, a call to action, a guarantee, and a summary all on one Web page. Ask your Web site design company or ISP for information about how to design, write, and launch a Killer Mini Site for your eBook.

Handing out a freebie

If your company publishes book-length owner's manuals, user's guides, or technical materials for its products, it can save a fortune by making these books available in eBook form on CD-ROM (as opposed to printed form) or as a free download from its Web site when the product is purchased. Thousands of companies are now using eBooks to distribute information instead of printing manuals, guides, and other materials.

For in-house use, employee training manuals, annual reports, press kits, and other lengthy documents can also be transformed into eBooks for easy and inexpensive distribution.

Heading to a Local Print Shop

Suppose you're about to give a lecture or teach a seminar and you want to create a workbook for participants to take home. Perhaps you have an idea for a book that lends itself better to a workbook format, bound in a three-ring binder (allowing pages to be removed with ease). For small print runs, your local print shop probably offers the perfect printing and binding solution. In the following sections, I give you the pros and cons of using a print shop and tips for ensuring that your book looks as professional as possible.

Knowing when to use (and when to avoid) a print shop

Consider photocopying your book, manual, or guide if

- ✔ The print run is relatively low (under 100 copies)
- ✔ A trim size of 8½-x-11 inches is suitable
- ✔ Your book doesn't have traditional retail distribution
- ✔ You want the ability to add and remove pages from the final document
- ✔ You don't want to invest the time and effort in designing and laying out an entire trade paperback or hardcover book

The advantages of using a print shop to publish a book include the following:

- ✔ **Printing cost:** Your local print shop probably offers high-speed copiers capable of quickly copying, collating, and even binding documents from 25 to 500 pages (or more) in length. The good news is that when photo-copying your book, there are no minimum print runs, so if you need one copy or 100 copies, you pay the local print shop just a few cents per page for photocopying services, plus a bit extra for binding.

- ✔ **Cover price:** Manuals, workbooks, research reports, and how-to guides targeted to business professionals can command a significantly higher cover price than a traditional trade paperback book.

- ✔ **Convenience:** You can visit a local print shop, have your documents printed and bound (often while you wait or within a few hours), and then pick up the finished product without having to pay shipping costs or waiting for the published books to be shipped to you. Working with a local printer also allows you to oversee the printing firsthand. You may want to shop around for a local printer that offers competitive pricing as well as the best high-end printing equipment capable of generating the most professional looking output.

Maintaining a professional look

If you're going to photocopy your book and have it bound at your local print shop, the end result may look more like a business report than a published book. And without an ISBN number and associated barcode (see Chapter 7 for details on these items), the photocopied document isn't suitable for retail sale.

Follow these hints to ensure that your book looks as professional as possible:

- ✔ **Make double-sided copies.** Many photocopiers can easily create col-lated, double-sided copies. This process saves paper and adds a more professional look to the finished product.

- ✔ **Make sure that the photocopier you use is high-quality and generates professional looking output.** The print shouldn't be washed out due to low toner. Ask to see samples of past work.

✔ **Make color copies.** Although using a high-speed copier to make black and white copies of your book or manual is cost effective and ideal for many projects, a color copier can be used to reproduce full-color images, photos, or other artwork. Many print shops can use a color copier and thicker paper stock to create an eye-catching cover, which can then be laminated to add a professional touch to your photocopied project.

✔ **Use quality paper stock.** To enhance the look of your photocopied document, consider using a higher quality paper than standard 20-pound white paper. Photocopying a large number of pages on brightly colored paper (using black toner) can make the document hard to read. For the main pages, stick to white, off-white, or cream-colored paper.

✔ **Choose a good binding.** The binding you choose also impacts the professional appearance of the finished product. (See Chapter 10 for details on binding methods.) You also can have holes punched along the left margin of your pages and insert them into a three-ring binder. (If you're using a three-ring binder and photocopying a significant number of books over the long term, consider having the binder custom imprinted with full-color text and graphics.)

✔ **Focus on creating a professional overall design.** Every aspect of design and layout, use of graphics, fonts, typestyles, and white space on each page makes a difference. Chapters 8 and 9 focus on how to create professional looking page and cover designs using programs such as Adobe InDesign CS2, Microsoft Publisher, or QuarkXPress.

Many print shops can print directly from an electronic file, so create pages with a nice layout and design, save the document as a PDF file, and then print copies as they're needed at your local print shop. This method is a less formal method of using Print-On-Demand, which I cover in Chapter 11.

Chapter 13

Working Successfully with Any Printer

There's nothing worse than working hard on your book, creating great content, and then having the project ruined by a shabby print job. The poor quality could ultimately make your book look amateurish and cause you to lose credibility among your readers. So printing is one of the major important steps in your publishing process. The methods you use and the printing company you hire determine how much you spend on production, how long it takes to have your books printed, and the overall look and quality of your finished books.

Finding a printer who's knowledgeable and qualified is important, but just as important is staying in contact with your printer during each step of the printing process. Developing a good rapport with your printer helps ensure that every step of the printing process goes smoothly and that the finished product is something you can be truly proud of. In this chapter, I take you on a quick tour of the general printing process and provide you with important questions to ask any printer as you work together. I also give you the scoop on smoothly handling proofreading and wrapping up any loose ends before your books enter the world.

Walking through the General Printing Process

The two major printing options you have are traditional offset printing (see Chapter 10 for details) and Print-On-Demand (POD) publishing (see Chapter 11 for details). Although the two methods use different technology, they mostly follow the same general printing process. Important steps in this process include

- ✓ **Defining your exact printing needs:** Determine the book's trim size, page count, ink colors, and type of paper to be used.

- ✓ **Finding a printer capable of meeting your needs:** Obtain referrals and contact printers. See Chapters 10 and 11 for details on finding referrals for offset printers and POD companies.

    The Graphics Arts Information Network (GAIN) is a professional association composed of graphic designers and printers. From this group's Web site (`www.gain.net`), you can obtain referrals for printing companies, read informative articles and industry news headlines, and find out about related industry associations.

- ✓ **Researching potential prices and negotiating your best price:** After you know exactly what your print job entails, solicit quotes from a handful of printers and negotiate the best price.

    - **Obtain a price quote from an offset printer.** Use one of two ways: Visit a printer's Web site and fill out an online questionnaire and have a quote e-mailed back to you, or call or visit a printer and discuss your needs in person.

    - **Check out POD companies.** POD businesses usually have package deals with preset prices. Some offer an a la carte menu of printing options and allow you to pick and choose the printing specifications for your book for a totally customized print job.

- ✓ **Turning over the final materials of your book to the printer:** This step requires simply submitting your materials in electronic form (as a PDF or PostScript PRN file, depending on the printer's requirements).

    - **Traditional offset printing submission:** You most likely handle the design and layout of the interior pages and the creation of the book's cover either by yourself or with the help of a professional designer. (Chapter 8 has the scoop on layout; Chapter 9 has details on cover design.) Review and make any necessary corrections to those laid-out files first (see the proofing checklist later in this chapter for edits to watch for), and then submit those materials to the printer.

- **POD submission:** After you review and make any necessary corrections to your manuscript, turn it over in a Microsoft Word document for layout and design and work with the POD company to develop a cover design.

✔ **Having a proof created by the printer:** This creation gives you a sample of what your final product looks like after it's printed.

✔ **Making any last-minute edits or changes to the proof and then approving them:** Review your proof carefully. This stage is your absolute last chance to make changes and correct any errors. See "Surviving the Proofing Stage," later in this chapter.

✔ **Printing and binding your books:** This process varies based on your preferences and the printing method you're using (see Chapter 10 for offset printing and Chapter 11 for POD companies).

✔ **Shipping or warehousing your books:** Unless you're using POD, after your books are printed, they're boxed up and shipped to your warehouse (or any address you provide); I cover shipping and warehousing in more detail in Chapter 16. Some printers also handle warehousing and order fulfillment on your behalf, but be aware that an extra charge exists for these services.

Getting on the Same Page with Your Printer

Ensuring that your book turns out exactly how you want it requires both you and your printer to be on the same page (pun intended). You need to develop a basic understanding of printing terminology and have a vision for your finished product. It's also necessary to ensure that your printer understands exactly what you're trying to achieve and how the printed books should look. A misunderstanding or failure to communicate may cause mistakes that could become extremely costly to fix.

In the following sections, I show you how to ask the right questions, understand technical terminology, and share your vision of your book with your printer during the printing process.

Asking appropriate questions

Initially, before settling on which printer or POD publisher to hire, you need to gauge the printer's level of expertise, experience, and willingness to work with you on your publishing project. See Chapter 10 for help choosing an offset printer or Chapter 11 for help selecting which POD publisher to work with based on your individual needs.

To assess these qualifications, ask questions to help you move forward with your process. These inquiries should relate directly to the process, scheduling, and expectations (both what's expected of you and what you should expect from your printer). Try out the following list of questions to get you started:

- ✔ Have you printed books that meet similar specifications to mine? If so, can I see some samples of your work?

- ✔ What options can you offer in terms of cover and paper stock?

- ✔ From the time I provide my manuscript, what's your turnaround time for printing books?

- ✔ Do you need front and back cover artwork in advance?

- ✔ How will the books be shipped to me, my distributor, or warehouse after they're printed?

- ✔ For offset printers, what price breaks can I receive based on printing various quantities?

- ✔ In what electronic format do you need me to provide my book's cover design and internal pages?

Becoming technically savvy

If your printer relies on using technical lingo to describe everything, but doesn't take the time to explain things in ordinary terms, either seek out a different printer or brush up on your printing terminology. Many offset printing companies and POD publishers are happy to have your business and are capable of printing your book. Choose a company that employs people you're comfortable working with and one that doesn't make your head spin.

For an online glossary of printing and graphics terminology, visit one of these Web sites:

- ✔ www.albionmich.com/cards/printingdef.htm

- ✔ www2.print-logics.com/printing_terminology.htm

- ✔ www.montana.edu/cpa/printshop/upglossary.html

- ✔ www.customprint.com/Terminology.htm

Relaying your message

Communicating your vision for what you want your book to look like is critical. The printer and any other folks working on your book during the printing process need to understand exactly what your book should look like in order to meet your expectations. It's up to you to educate them about what your book's about, who the target audience is, and what you're envisioning from a creative standpoint.

One way to do this is to find books at the bookstore or library that you want yours to replicate in terms of the printing specifications (trim size, cover stock, paper stock, and so on) and show those samples to your printer. It's much easier for printers to match actual samples than it is for them to interpret your verbal description.

Surviving the Proofing Stage

Just before the presses start to roll, the printer or POD publisher provides you with a proof. This sample is what your book looks like when it's printed. Depending on the printing process and the company you use, the proof form may vary. You may receive a proof in electronic PDF format or an actual printed and bound copy of your book.

If your book has multiple colors, ask to see a high-resolution full-color proof that accurately shows how the colors look. The colors you see on your computer screen vary greatly from how they look in final print.

Whatever form the proof takes, it's now your responsibility to review every page of the proof and correct any errors. (Depending on the printing company, you may be charged extra to make corrections at this point; nevertheless, this is still the last opportunity to make them.) After you accept the proofs and sign off, the book goes to press and the printer assumes no responsibility for any mistakes or errors that should've been caught by you.

In the following sections, I steer you through a proofing checklist and give you tips on hiring a professional proofreader.

Following a proofing checklist

By this point, you and your editor (see Chapter 5) should've reviewed the manuscript several times. If any changes still need to be made at the proof stage, they should be minor, unless you're correcting a mistake made by the printer.

TIP

This final development requires you to review the proof multiple times, looking for specific types of errors. Take your time when completing this process. The following list is chock-full of things to look for when reviewing your proof for the last time before your book actually gets printed. For each item on this checklist, review your proof looking for just that type of mistake or problem:

❏ Correct spelling mistakes.

❏ Perform a final check of all names, phone numbers, Web site addresses, statistics, facts, and figures to make sure that everything is accurate.

❏ Correct grammatical errors.

❏ Fix any layout and design mistakes, such as mislabeled and misplaced photos or figures and their captions, headings and subheadings, page numbers, or running headers or footers.

❏ Ensure that text or content hasn't been accidentally left out.

❏ Make sure that no characters are missing at the end of headings, paragraphs, or sentences.

❏ Double-check the order of the chapters (and then numbering of the chapters) and sections within your book and that all elements of the content are in the right place, including the book's front matter and back matter (see Chapter 4 for more about these elements).

❏ Make certain that all figures and graphics are correctly placed, referenced, and numbered.

❏ Certify that all photos and artwork are correctly positioned (not upside down or flopped).

❏ Review all captions to make sure that they correspond to the correct figures or photographs.

❏ Check that the page numbers are all in sequence and correctly positioned on each page.

❏ Double-check all margins to make sure that they're straight and consistent throughout the book.

❏ Make sure that all chapter or page number references within the book are accurate (for example, if the text says, "As seen in Chapter 4 . . ." or "See page 123 . . .," that the appropriate page, chapter, or section is referenced).

❏ Check all fonts and typestyles for correct displayed and that all chapter title pages, headings, subheadings, and so on are uniform in their appearance and formatting.

❏ Review the print quality, ensuring that it's uniform, clear, and professional looking, especially when it comes to the photographs, artwork, and graphics.

Catching a last-minute error is one step. The next involves instructing the printer on exactly how to correct each error. This process is best done in writing (not verbally or via e-mail) to avoid miscommunication. Ideally, you want to mark up the actual pages of the proof with a blue or black pen, and fax or hand deliver those edited pages to the printer. After the corrections are made, request a revised proof (even if you're charged extra for it). You want to make sure that all corrections have been made accurately.

Hiring a professional proofreader

When you hire your professional editor, you can also negotiate with her to be responsible for your final proofreading before the book goes to press. Major publishing houses, however, use a professional *proofreader* (someone different from the editor) to handle this task. For an additional fee, you can hire a professional proofreader to review your manuscript with a fine-tooth comb. I advise this extra step if you have the budget to hire this specialist.

A professional proofreader has experience looking for common and not-so-common layout and design errors as well as grammatical and spelling errors. These people are extremely detail-oriented, and they know exactly how to ensure your book's professional look.

To hire a professional proofreader, follow the same guidelines as hiring an editor or graphic designer:

- ✔ Check out the popular freelancer Web sites.
- ✔ Ask people you know for referrals.
- ✔ Check out the qualifications of the person you're interested in hiring.
- ✔ Hire someone with extensive experience proofreading books.

The cost of a proofreader varies greatly based on the length of your book, the experience of the proofreader, and the time it takes to proofread the book. A proofreader, however, is considerably less expensive than an editor.

Whether you choose to hire a professional proofreader is a personal and financial decision. But remember, your book always benefits from having another pair of eyes review it carefully before it goes to press. Using your copy editor for this job can work (and save you money), but proofreading does require a slightly different skill set than editing.

Wrapping Up Your Work with a Printer

The process of having your book published is almost complete. After you turn over your book to the printer, you can expect to receive printed copies of your book usually within five to ten business days. When you review the final books, check them carefully to make sure that the printer has done his job correctly. Was the correct cover and paper stock used? Was the binding done correctly? Is the quality of the overall work up to par and of professional quality?

If there's a problem with the print job, you need to contact the printer directly to discuss a remedy. If the problem was caused by an error on your part, chances are you'll to pay to have the problem fixed. If the error was on the printer's part, the printer should take full financial responsibility for correcting the error, even if the books have to be reprinted.

If the books you receive from the printer are ready for sale, you're in excellent shape. Make sure that the printer keeps copies of your files so you can order additional copies of your book quickly. Ideally, reordering your book at this point (if you used an offset printer) should require little more than a phone call.

Now that you have printed books in hand, you're officially a published author! Congratulations! It's now your job as a self-published author to start selling and promoting your book heavily in order to generate sales.

Part IV

Making Your Book a Bestseller: Distribution Methods

The 5th Wave   By Rich Tennant

In this part . . .

How your book ultimately gets distributed determines how readers are able to find and purchase it. One realistic option is to sell your book online. Many self-published authors also achieve success by selling their own book through traditional channels. Coordinating distribution for your book is what this part is all about. In addition, I give you the scoop on handling warehousing, fulfillment, and shipping, and I provide tips for wider distribution with a major publisher.

Chapter 14

Selling Your Book through Popular Online Booksellers

. . . .

. . . .

For the self-published author, your book's listing on online booksellers like Amazon.com (www.amazon.com) and Barnes & Noble.com (www.barnesandnoble.com) may be your primary outlet for nationwide distribution. When your book lacks national retail distribution, making it available on Amazon.com and Barnes & Noble.com is extremely important for generating sales. Also, when you're doing an interview with the media or telling people about where to obtain a copy of your book, it's easy to say, "It's now available on Amazon.com, Barnes & Noble.com, or from my Web site, www.[booktitle.com].com."

This chapter is all about how to generate sales and positive reviews by having your book listed with popular online booksellers. I focus on how to create the best possible listings for your book in order to capture the attention of potential readers and describe other ways to promote your book to online booksellers.

Another online option is selling your book through your own promotional Web site; see Chapter 21 for more details.

Creating an Effective Listing

The listing for your book on Amazon.com, Barnes & Noble.com, or any other online bookseller site is an opportunity for you to sell your book to potential readers. In essence, you create a digital brochure. The more informative and sales oriented your listing is, the better chance you have of getting someone to click the *Buy Now* icon to purchase your book.

The major online booksellers have literally hundreds of thousands, perhaps millions of book listings. While all contain basic bibliographic data, you have the ability to expand on the book's listing information and greatly improve your chances of getting your book noticed and selling it on these online services. In the following sections, I show you essential details to include in a listing and tips for writing a listing sure to capture readers' attention.

Excellent elements to include in a listing

When you create your book's listing for Amazon.com or Barnes & Noble.com, you're required to include basic information such as the book's full title, the author's name, publisher information, the price, the ISBN, the page count, and the trim size. You also want to provide a detailed description of the book that's sales oriented and some information about the author.

Your listing on an online bookseller should provide all the information a potential reader needs to convince him to purchase your book online, right on the spot. My book *The Bachelor's Guide to Life* (iUniverse) is a self-published book. However, based on the listing on Amazon.com's Web site in Figure 14-1, the average reader wouldn't know it. The book's listing is just like a listing you'd find for a book published by a major publishing house.

Creating an effective listing and providing additional information about your book, beyond what's required, help generate interest in your book. Some of the information you should consider adding to your book's listing includes

- **A detailed description of your book:** This info should be well written and contain all the information someone wants to know about the book. The materials you create as part of your book's press kit (see Chapter 18) and your book's back cover copy (see Chapter 9) can be utilized.

- **An author bio:** Providing information about the author helps establish the book's credibility and promote the author as an expert in the field. If it's allowed, also include an author photo within the listing. See Chapter 18 for more about author bios and photos.

- **The book's front and back cover image:** You created the book cover to be a marketing and sales tool for your book. Your book cover should help entice potential readers to buy your book.

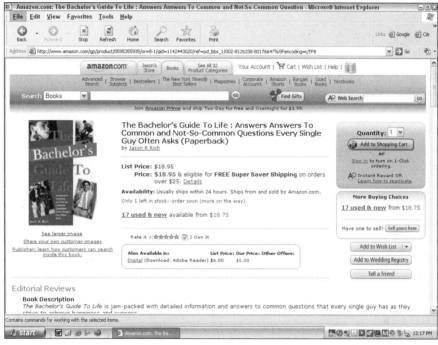

Figure 14-1:
A listing for
a self-
published
book can
look just like
one for a
book from a
major
publisher.

✔ **Additional images from the book (if possible):** Providing additional images or graphics from your book can be beneficial if you want to offer a bigger preview of what the reader can expect.

✔ **Your book's Table of Contents:** Providing a Table of Contents allows you to convey exactly what information is included and the order it's presented in.

✔ **A sample chapter from your book (or at least six to ten pages):** Providing a sample chapter is one way to capture potential readers' attention and draw them into what your book offers. This material is particularly useful for fiction; however, it can be used effectively for almost any type of book.

✔ **Excerpts of published reviews about your book:** You, as the author, think that your book is fantastic. But potential readers are more apt to trust professional and well-known book reviewers, journalists, and reporters. After your book begins receiving positive publicity, offer excerpts from these good reviews and editorial coverage.

✔ **"Message from the Author" and/or "Message from the Publisher":** Some popular online booksellers allow the author and/or publisher to post information targeted directly to potential readers within the listing.

Many potential readers find your book on Amazon.com's or Barnes & Noble.com's Web site by doing a search based on subject matter, topic, or category. Therefore, it's important that you categorize your book correctly with online booksellers and create a description and related content that makes it easy for someone to find your book, based on keyword, category, subject, author's name, and/or title searches.

Terrific tactics for writing a listing

As you write your listing, keep your book's target audience in mind and be sure to include information that those readers will be interested in. Focus on what's new or innovative about your book. What sets your book apart from the competition? Why should someone read it? The following sections offer detailed advice on how to write a creative, high-impact, and sales-oriented listing for your book.

Target all types of readers and Web surfers

Create a listing that caters to the masses because online services are used by several types of readers:

- **People who know what they want:** These folks go online type in the exact title or ISBN to find it and then order it online. (These people don't bother to read the listing because they already know what they want.) It's important that the book's title, ISBN, author, and book cover image be accurate and up-to-date, so you don't confuse the reader.

- **People who browse by subject matter:** When someone enters a subject or topic as a search phrase as they're using Amazon.com or Barnes & Noble.com's Web site, a handful of book titles and descriptions are displayed. Browsers know they want a book on a specific topic, but they haven't yet selected a specific title. In this moment, your chance to sell your book to this potential reader has increased, so by creating a well-written and informative listing, your book may be set apart from the competition.

- **People who have heard about your book:** If someone has heard about your book, his interest may be piqued and now he wants to know more. Naturally, today, most people would look up the information online. Your listing should be able to transform their casual interest into a sale.

- **People who search for topics of interest:** These people know they want to order a book, but they haven't necessarily selected a topic or specific book title. They're browsers. When they find something they want, they order it. Your book listing should engage these people and get them interested in your book.

Avoid babbling

You want to create an informative, comprehensive, and well-written listing for your book, but you must remember that the attention span of Web surfers is extremely short. Keep your listing as concise as possible, but make sure that it targets your book's potential audience.

Within the description of your book, not only should you focus on what the book includes and who it's written for, but also describe what makes it unique and how the reader benefits from reading it. Why should someone read your book and not another book covering the same topic?

Use a creative, upbeat writing style when writing the listing for your book. Offer the reader a preview of what to expect and get them excited about the prospect of buying and reading your book. This type of content appears on your book's back cover (Chapter 9 has cover details).

As you begin to create a listing to appear on Amazon.com's or Barnes & Noble.com's site, spend time browsing these services. Look at the listings for current bestsellers, as well as for books more directly related to your subject matter. Determine what approach works best and generate ideas for your own listing (but don't plagiarize other people's words or listing content).

Submitting Your Listing to Popular Online Booksellers

In many cases, after your book receives its ISBN, is registered with the *Bowker's BooksInPrint.com* directory, and is made available through one or more of the major book distributors (such as Ingram or Baker & Taylor), obtaining a basic listing on the sites of Amazon.com and Barnes & Noble.com is easy and in some cases automatic. (See Chapter 7 for more about obtaining an ISBN and registering with Bowker's. See Chapter 15 for details about how to sell your book to major distributors that automatically get their inventory listed with the popular online booksellers.)

Depending on the self-publishing method you use, you may be considered the author, not the publisher. For example, if you use Trafford, iUniverse, or one of the other popular Print-On-Demand (POD) publishers (see Chapter 11), that company would be considered the book's publisher. Therefore, the company should obtain a listing for your book with Amazon.com and Barnes & Noble.com. After the listing is created, however, as the author, you can fully customize it. See "Creating an Effective Listing," earlier in this chapter, for ideas on how to create a listing that makes the most impact.

If you're both the author and the publisher (because you used a traditional offset printer; see Chapter 10), establishing a listing for your book probably will be your responsibility, unless this is a service your printer will handle on your behalf. In the following sections, I explain how to submit a listing to Amazon.com, Barnes & Noble.com, and other online booksellers.

Listing your book on Amazon.com

There are three main ways to get your book listed with Amazon.com:

- ✔ **Join the Amazon.com Advantage program:** This service allows publishers to utilize Amazon.com's service to sell and distribute their books, music, videos, and DVDs. To participate in this service, there's a small annual fee (under $30) and a 55-percent sales commission on every sale. For details about this program, visit `www.amazon.com/exec/obidos/ subst/partners/direct/advantage/home.html/103-7617088- 4850247`.

- ✔ **Participating in Amazon.com's Pro-Merchant Program:** This program is a method of selling a large volume of used, collectible, and remainder books through the Amazon.com Marketplace service. For more information, visit `www.amazon.com/exec/obidos/tg/browse/-/1161308/ 103-9734249-4187021`.

- ✔ **List your book with a major publisher:** By getting your self-published book carried by a major distributor, such as Ingram or Baker & Taylor (see Chapter 15 for details), a listing will automatically be created on Amazon.com. After the listing is created, as the author/publisher, you can then edit and expand it.

For most self-publishers, this route is the most viable way of getting a book listed with Amazom.com, especially because many turnkey publishing solutions offered to self-publishers include having the book made available through one or more major distributors.

Listing your book with Barnes & Noble.com

Many turnkey self-publishing solutions include having your book listed with Barnes & Noble.com (which you, as the author) can then customize. If you become your own publisher, however, you need to register your publishing company and your individual book titles with Barnes & Noble.com directly.

At the bottom of the Barnes & Noble.com main page, click *Publisher and Author Guidelines* to access information about getting your book listed with Barnes and Noble's popular online bookseller service. The process involves first becoming a Vendor of Record, and then submitting content about your book electronically. In the following sections, I guide you through the phases of submitting a listing to Barnes & Noble.com.

Having your book distributed through Barnes & Noble.com isn't the same as having it sold through Barnes and Noble retail stores. If you're interested in obtaining distribution through the company's retail chain, visit the following Web site: www.barnesandnobleinc.com. See Chapter 15 for additional information on retail distribution.

Filling out the application

If you're a self-publisher as well as an author, becoming a Vendor of Record involves completing an extensive online questionnaire. You need to provide details about your company, your tax ID number, and other financial information, among other items, to show that you represent a legitimate and established publishing company.

After completing this form, if your book is approved, you receive an order for two copies. This process allows your book to be listed with the service and added to Barnes & Noble.com's inventory system. Additional orders will then be placed, based on demand for your book.

Self-published books are considered for distribution through Barnes & Noble.com's site only if the books have an ISBN assigned, a cover price over $1, and either traditional hardcover or paperback binding (see Chapter 10 for more about binding). All books sold to Barnes & Noble.com are on a returnable basis.

The forms and contracts you need to complete to have your book distributed through Barnes & Noble.com are legal documents, so review them carefully before signing and submitting them.

Submitting bibliographic information and a cover image

After being approved as a Vendor of Record, submit detailed content about each book. This info includes bibliographic information (pertaining to the book's title and author), as well as merchandising data (including a detailed description of the book, the cover image, and other information used to create your book's listing on Barnes & Noble.com). Information should be submitted to Barnes & Noble.com 180 days prior to publication or as soon as possible thereafter.

When submitting information about a new book, you must include the following information:

- ✔ The book's ISBN
- ✔ Title
- ✔ Author
- ✔ Publisher (If you haven't used a turnkey publishing solution, you need to list your own publishing company as the book's publisher)
- ✔ Format (such as hard cover, trade paperback, eBook, and so on)
- ✔ Price
- ✔ Publication date
- ✔ BISAC Audience
- ✔ BISAC Subject (see Chapter 7 for more info about BISAC)
- ✔ Discount (offered to Barnes and Noble)

Also send a digital image of your book's cover, in TIFF or JPEG format, at 100 to 150 dpi resolution, with the longest side of the digital image being between 75 and 2,000 pixels. A clear image of the book cover that meets the technical guidelines of Barnes & Noble.com must be provided with each new book listing.

In addition to bibliographic content and the cover image, you may want to include optional information. See "Excellent elements to include in a listing," earlier in this chapter, for information on gathering this optional info.

For help along the way, e-mail the following contacts:

- ✔ Submit your content information via e-mail to `titles@bn.com`.
- ✔ If you have questions about submitting a new book listing, send them via e-mail to `PublisherAuthorInquiry@book.com`.
- ✔ To update your book's listing after it's been posted online, e-mail changes to `corrections@barnesandnoble.com`, and be sure to reference the book's title and ISBN.

Approaching other online booksellers

Literally hundreds of other online booksellers are smaller than Amazon.com and Barnes & Noble.com but can help you sell your book to its intended audience. Each online bookseller has its own criteria for getting your self-published book listed and made available for sale on the service. Visit each online bookseller's Web site and follow the links for author or publisher submission guidelines. Two sample online booksellers are

- Books-A-Million.com (www.booksamillion.com)
- Zooba (www.zooba.com)

Generating Excellent Online Reviews

Although having your book reviewed in the *New York Times* or any other newspaper or magazine definitely helps generate interest and sales for your book, many readers rely on other readers to help them make book selections.

Many popular online booksellers allow people to write reviews of any book and give the book a rating (one to five stars). In addition to displaying all reviews written for each title, a cumulative average score is displayed with each listing. So, even if a potential reader doesn't spend the time reading all of the posted reviews, in a matter of seconds, anyone can glance at a book's average rating and determine how other people liked the book. Would you buy a book that's received an average rating of two stars, when a competing book has an average rating of five stars?

Having a handful of good reviews attached to your book's listing with Amazon.com and Barnes & Noble.com helps establish your book's credibility and works as a very powerful sales tool. After all, many people rely on what other readers have to say, in addition to reading the promotional description and hype you've included about your book as part of the listing (see "Creating an Effective Listing," earlier in this chapter, for details).

In the following sections, I give you the scoop on having folks you know post reviews and reviewing other books yourself so you can get noticed.

Asking others to post reviews

As soon as your listing appears with Amazon.com and Barnes & Noble.com, have a few close friends, relatives, or coworkers who've read your book post a positive review with both online booksellers. The more positive reviews you generate, the better. Just make sure that the reviews posted by people you know are believable and not too over-the-top. (Oh, and while you're at it, feel free to post a five-star, incredibly positive review for *Self-Publishing For Dummies* on both Amazon.com's and Barnes & Noble.com's Web sites!)

Relying on strangers to post positive reviews about your book is an honorable thing to do, but most readers are more apt to invest their time in writing bad reviews about books they feel somehow ripped them off. Unfortunately, motivating people to write reviews about books they've really enjoyed is harder than getting people to trash your book online.

Becoming a reviewer yourself

While people are busy reviewing your book and hopefully making your book's listing with Amazon.com and Barnes & Noble.com more impressive, as an author, you can also post reviews of other books that your target audience may also be interested in. In other words, you can review your competition and utilize their book listings to promote your book. Readers who visit your competition may be compelled to visit your book's listing and choose your book over others. How to do it? Keep reading!

Within your reviews for other books, position yourself as an expert in your field and as an author, and mention the title of your book. For example, say, "As the author of [insert book title], I've read and reviewed many books on this topic. This one offers . . ." Just make sure that the reviews you write are accurate, honest, and not too promotional when discussing your own book. Always maintain your professionalism and be courteous to your fellow authors.

Taking Advantage of Other Resources from Online Booksellers

In addition to creating a well-written and comprehensive listing for your book, consider utilizing as many of the other tools and resources available to authors and publishers on the popular online booksellers' Web sites as possible. I cover a sampling of them in the following sections.

Promotional opportunities with Amazon.com

To promote your book, try the following resources:

 ✔ **AmazonConnect:** This service gives authors an opportunity to communicate directly with their readers through e-mail. Messages (in blog-like format) from the author are also displayed as part of the book's listing. As you develop a following as an author, use this service to tell people more about your book, yourself, and future projects. Visit `www.amazon.com/gp/arms/directory/ref=sd_allcatpop_ac/002-5992920-5756805` for details about this service.

✔ **Author Profile Pages:** These pages are available to authors who have books being sold at Amazon.com. Using the service's online tools, authors can create a one-page Web site that offers information about themselves, messages to readers, links to their books, a link to their personal Web site, and other information of interest to readers. This service is free; authors simply need to complete online registration. For more information, visit `www.amazon.com/connect`.

✔ **Amazon Associate:** By becoming an Amazon Associate, you can create your own online bookstore to sell your books and generate commissions from sales. This opportunity is open to everyone, but for authors, the service offers yet another way to promote your book and generate revenue. You also earn a commission on book sales for titles that you didn't write or publish. Visit this following Web site for details: `associates.amazon.com/gp/associates/join/103-7617088-4850247`.

Promotional opportunities with Barnes & Noble.com

To get your book started, check out Barnes & Noble.com's resources:

✔ **Meet The Writers:** Barnes & Noble.com has a fast growing editorial feature, called *Meet The Writers,* which profiles authors. To be considered to receive this coverage, send an e-mail request, complete with information about yourself and your book, to `writers@book.com`.

✔ **Author Recommendations:** This service allows customers and readers to read book recommendations and reviews from well-known and established authors. For details, visit `www.barnesandnoble.com/writers/writers2_cds2.asp?PID=10181&z=y&cds2Pid=9481&linkid=666857`.

✔ **Discovery Awards:** If your book has won any literary awards, Barnes & Noble.com also profiles award-winning book titles and authors. Barnes and Noble sponsors its own annual Discovery Awards program, which recognizes new authors. The service also profiles National Book Award winners for fiction and nonfiction. To find out how to nominate your book for the annual National Book Awards, check out `www.nationalbook.org`. You have to pay a $100 fee for entering each title into the competition.

Chapter 15

Distributing Your Book through Traditional Channels

*T*his chapter focuses on how to obtain traditional distribution for your self-published book. It describes some of the hurdles you face and ways to potentially overcome them. I would love to say that self-publishing offers all the benefits and profit potential as having your book published by a major publishing house and that self-publishing has no drawbacks whatsoever. But, unfortunately, that's not the case. Although self-publishing is a viable and potentially lucrative publishing option, its biggest drawback is the challenges you face in trying to obtain traditional retail distribution for your book.

There is some good news though, so don't lose heart. With a bit of work and salesmanship, you should be able to get your book into some independently owned bookstores and specialty retail stores. You can try your hand at distribution through direct mail and niche groups like trade associations. Plus, by working through a major wholesaler or distributor, any bookstore could potentially order your book for a customer, even if the store doesn't stock it on its shelves.

The Challenges of Securing Major Retail Distribution for a Self-Published Book

Self-publishers can face a variety of challenges when attempting to obtain distribution through retail bookstores, especially the major chains. Here are a few of those hurdles:

- **Buying on credit:** Major publishing houses, distributors, and wholesalers offer bookstores credit terms (up to 90 days) when orders are placed. When you use most self-publishing solutions, orders must be paid for in advance. To overcome this obstacle, you need to inventory your own books at your expense, but that means laying out the money needed, shipping the books to the bookseller with industry-standard credit terms, and waiting to be paid. Unfortunately, as the author, if you're buying your books at 40 to 50 percent off the cover price, this discount is the same you offer to booksellers. Therefore, at best, you'd break even on the sale or earn a five to ten percent profit but tie up your money for up to three months in the process.

- **Accepting returns:** Major publishing houses accept returns on unsold books. Unless you're establishing your own publishing company (see Chapter 6 for more about this task) and handling your own printing, warehousing, and distribution, returns aren't typically accepted by companies offering self-publishing solutions. Again, as a self-published author, you could inventory your own books, and then take on the risk that you'd receive returns 30, 60, or 90 days later.

- **Lacking a sales team:** Major publishers have sales teams with established relationships with key buyers at the major distributors, wholesalers, and bookstore chains. As a self-publisher, you can overcome this obstacle by hiring an independent trade salesperson with industry connections (see "Grabbing the Attention of Mass-Market Retailers and Bookstore Chains," later in this chapter for details on doing this). However, for this to work, you also need to overcome the previous two obstacles.

There are a few independent trade sales reps that work with self-published authors with only one or two titles, but finding one capable of selling your book, especially if the topic is niche-oriented, can be a challenge.

- **Having a single title to sell:** Major publishers offer multiple titles at once. Most buyers are extremely busy and won't focus their time on evaluating and purchasing just one book title from a small publisher. The way around this obstacle is to hire an independent trade salesperson who sells a handful of titles simultaneously from several small publishers. But, you first need to overcome all the previous obstacles described.

Don't count on retail distribution to achieve sales success for your book. You need to use some or all the other sales and distribution methods discussed in the rest of this chapter to sell large quantities of your book. I also cover other ways to sell plenty of books and earn a respectable profit from those sales elsewhere in this book:

✔ Selling books through the major online booksellers, including Amazon.com and Barnes & Noble.com (see Chapter 14)

✔ Selling your book through your own Web site (see Chapter 21)

✔ Selling your book at author appearances, book signings, lectures, seminars, and workshops (see Chapters 19 and 22)

After you achieve some level of success, if you still have your heart set on being able to visit a bookstore anywhere in the country to see your book displayed on the shelf, consider selling your book to a major publishing house; head to Chapter 17 for more details on this option. And you can always try contacting national chains directly; check out "Grabbing the Attention of Mass-Market Retailers and Bookstore Chains," later in this chapter for more information.

Working with Wholesalers and Distributors

As far as self-publishers are concerned wholesalers and distributors are pretty much the same. (The two terms are used interchangeably.) The easiest way to get your book into retail stores is to make it available through one or more of the major wholesalers and distributors that already have established relationships with key retailers. Each distributor, however, has different criteria for choosing publishers to work with and actual book titles to inventory and sell.

If you're working with a well-established Print-On-Demand (POD) publisher (see Chapter 11 for POD details), that company may already have an established relationship with one or more of the major distributors. If not, you need to contact the distributors yourself. In the following sections, I introduce the major distributors that you can work with.

For help obtaining retail distribution and getting the attention of a major distributor, consider joining PMA, The Independent Book Publishers Association. This organization offers a wide range of educational programs and resources for self-published authors and small publishing houses. Through the organization's targeted publications, you can advertise your book to thousands of booksellers nationwide. Membership is about $110 per year. Find out more information by calling (310) 372-2732 or by visiting www.pma-online.org.

Baker & Taylor

For over 176 years, Baker & Taylor has been a pioneer in the book publishing industry. It's now one of the largest book distributors in the nation and a supplier to virtually all the United States' leading booksellers and libraries.

One of the company's representatives is able to help you set up an account and introduce you to the services offered by this company. The key benefit to working with Baker & Taylor is that virtually all bookstores, libraries, and other retail outlets that sell books have an established relationship with them. After your book is listed with Baker & Taylor, booksellers can easily order your book. Visit Baker & Taylor online at `www.btol.com` or give them a call at (800) 775-1800.

Ingram Book Company

Ingram Book Company is the industry's other largest book distributor in the United States. Typically, Ingram only works directly with publishers offering more than ten book titles, so self-published authors need to work with established companies to meet their needs. So your books are carried by one of the largest wholesalers in the world while your operations, costs, and other publishing risks are minimized, Ingram has established a relationship with each of the following companies:

- ✔ **Publishers Marketing Association (PMA):** PMA is a trade organization that tries to advance the professional interests of independent publishers Visit `www.pma-online.org` to stay informed about their dynamic industry.

- ✔ **Lightning Source:** This company is one of Ingram's subsidiaries and is a POD Publisher. Check them out online at `www.lightningsource.com` or call (615) 213-5815.

- ✔ **Biblio Distribution:** Biblio formed in 2001 to represent books published by small trade publishers by offering warehousing, distribution, sales, and other operation services. Contact Biblio at (800) 462-6420 or www.bibliodistribution.com/distribution.

- ✔ **Greenleaf Book Group LLC:** This group offers nationwide distribution and comprehensive production and supply marketing services. Call (800) 932-5420 or visit `www.greenleafbookgroup.com`.

For more information about getting your book distributed through Ingram Book Company, visit `www.ingrambook.com/new/publishers.asp`.

Other major distributors

Even if you can't get the attention of Ingram or Baker & Taylor, many smaller book distributors are capable of handling your book and getting it into book-stores. Some of the other well-established book distributors include

- **Alliance Book Company:** Phone (678) 361-3953
- **Book Clearing House:** Phone (800) 431-1579; Web site www.bookch.com
- **Bookazine:** Phone (800) 221-8112; Web site www.bookazine.com
- **BookMasters, Inc.:** Phone (800) 537-6727; Web site www.bookmasters.com
- **BookWorld Services, Inc.:** Phone (941) 758-8094; Web site www.bookworld.com
- **Consortium Book Sales:** Phone (800) 283-3572; Web site www.cbsd.com
- **Independent Publishers Group:** Phone (312) 337-0747; Web site www.ipgbook.com. Check out IPG later in this chapter for more details.
- **Koen-Levy Book Distributors:** Phone (800) 257-8481; Web site www.koen.com
- **National Book Network:** Phone (301) 459-3366; Web site www.nbnbooks.com
- **New Leaf Distributing:** Phone (800) 326-2665 or (770) 948-7845; Web site www.newleaf-dist.com
- **Partners Book Distributing:** Phone (800) 563-2385
- **Publishers Group West:** Phone (800) 788-3123; Web site www.pgw.com
- **SCB Distributors:** Phone (800) 729-6423; Web site www.scbdistributors.com
- **Wilson & Associates:** Phone (281) 388-0196; Web site www.wilsonpublishing.com

Many of the above distributors consider representing a book published by using POD, but you may have to agree to have a pre-determined inventory of books on hand. These terms can be negotiated with the distributor after interest is expressed in your book. If you use a traditional offset printer to publish your book, these companies definitely consider working with you, assuming you meet their requirements.

For more information, contact any of the above distributors and be prepared to submit a complete package that includes

- A published copy of your book (or galleys)
- A detailed description of the book, as well as your marketing materials (see Part V for more about marketing and advertising)

✔ Copies of published reviews and media coverage

✔ A description of your marketing, advertising, and public relations plans

✔ Information about the author

✔ Retail and potential wholesale pricing (see Chapter 7 for more about pricing your book)

Approaching Independent Booksellers

Independent booksellers typically have their own in-house buyers (often the owner or manager of the store) and welcome the opportunity to work with small and independent publishers in order to offer a selection of books that their competitors don't (those competitors are the major bookstore chains).

Working with independent booksellers offers the self-publisher an opportunity to break into traditional retail stores. After you demonstrate strong sales through a handful of independent retailers, you have an easier time selling the rights to your book to a major publishing house, if this is your goal. It also provides another distribution method for selling copies of your book, especially if you can support the independent booksellers in your area by making author appearances or participating in a book signing.

Contacting these booksellers could prove to be a time consuming process that generates relatively few book sales. Independent bookstores each have to be approached separately from a sales standpoint, and each typically orders only a small number of books at a time. Many self-publishers discover they can better utilize their time and financial resources by selling books directly to consumers or focusing on using public relations and marketing to get consumers to purchase their book from an online bookseller (see Chapter 14 for details on online booksellers).

In the following sections, I explain how to create a sell sheet and give you pointers on contacting independent booksellers around the country.

Creating a sell sheet

The best way to sell to independent booksellers is to offer them credit terms and accept returns, and then target them with a direct mail piece that advertises your book. This piece, called a *sell sheet,* is a sales tool for your book. Major publishing companies create one-page sell sheets for each of their titles, so you should do this as well if you plan to sell directly to booksellers. Your sell sheet should be easy-to-read, visually appealing, professional looking, and convince bookstore buyers and other retailers to purchase, inventory, and sell your book.

Because you may only have one title to offer, you could create a single-page sell sheet, preferably using four-color printing on glossy paper, which can be distributed to buyers and used as a sales tool. To create an outstanding sell sheet, check out the following tips:

- Prominently display your book's title, cover image, and bibliographic information, which includes

    - ISBN

    - Cover price

    - Page count

    - Trim size

    - Author

    - Publisher

    - BISAC Subject/Audience information

- Include a short but detailed description of your book, along with its target audience in addition to the bibliographic information. You can use the same description that appears on your book's back cover. See Chapter 9 for details on back cover descriptions.

- Mention if the book is available through a major distributor, so booksellers know they can easily place an order for the book through the distributor it already has a relationship with. (See "Working with Wholesalers and Distributors," earlier in this chapter for more information.)

- Include any useful facts or statistics (in bulleted format is fine) that may help the sale of your book to booksellers. The list can include such info as the size of the potential audience or the industry your book targets.

- Include a short author bio and author photo (see Chapter 18 for more about author bios and photos).

- Design your sell sheet on your computer with software like Microsoft Publisher, QuarkXPress or Adobe InDesign CS2, or hire a professional graphic designer to create it for you (Chapter 8 has tips on finding a graphic designer).

- Print the sheet in full-color at a local print shop or search for a company online. The price of printing 1,000 full-color sell sheets on glossy paper may be around $600. A much less expensive option is to print the sell sheet in black and white, but this option looks less professional. The major publishing houses typically use full-color sell sheets, which industry people receive. Because you're competing with books published by major publishing houses, maintain a high-quality image.

Contacting independent booksellers

There are a variety of ways to contact independent booksellers across the country. Using one of the following directories may save you considerable time as you build your mailing list and pinpoint the booksellers you want to target with your sales efforts. In the following sections, I give you a few helpful resources for finding and contacting independent booksellers.

The American Booksellers Association's Web site

You can purchase a mailing list of independent booksellers and contact the buyer(s) separately to sell your books. The American Booksellers Association's (ABA) Web site offers an online directory of over 2,200 booksellers. The list can also be rented and made available on labels. Check out the site at www.bookweb.org/bookstores.

Book Sense

Several times per month, the American Booksellers Association publishes *Book Sense* — a newsletter that's distributed to more than 1,000 key buyers at independent booksellers nationwide. As a self-published author you want to list your book in this newsletter prior to its publication for an excellent way to announce the book to key industry buyers. (There is a $100 charge per title for this service.)

To find out how to obtain a listing in *Book Sense* and potentially receive additional editorial coverage, visit www.bookweb.org/booksense/publisher/3311.html.

For a book listing to be considered for publication, the information must be provided in a very specific format, which is outlined on the organization's Web site. Be sure to include the book's full title, author, publisher, ISBN, cover price, type of book (hardcover, trade paperback, and so on), publication date, and subject category. This information should be followed by a two-sentence (50-word maximum) description of the book, along with your contact e-mail address.

Additional advertising opportunities are available in *Book Sense* and other ABA publications, which are a cost effective ways of reaching buyers and decision makers at bookstores.

Because a *Book Sense* listing appears prior to the book's publication, the ABA recommends that self-published authors offer buyers and booksellers a free copy of the book's galleys (at the buyer's request) to review.

The Independent Publishers Group

The Independent Publishers Group (IPG) is an organization with an established book sales and marketing team that works with a small number of self-published authors and small publishers each year to help them establish national distribution through retail booksellers. This organization does more than simply act as a distributor; it also helps the self-published author market and promote a title using proven methods.

IPG charges a commission (based on sales) for its services. You can reach the company at (312) 337-0747 or hop online at www.ipgbook.com.

PMA, the Independent Book Publishers Association

PMA, the Independent Book Publishers Association, offers a "Trade Distribution Acceptance Program" that can help self-publishers market and distribute their book. You can reach the group at (310) 372-2732 or visit www.pma-online.org.

Scoping Out Specialty Retail Stores

Specialty retail outlets can include any retail store that isn't a traditional bookstore but that sells a small number of book titles. For example, independently owned gift shops and boutiques often sell books, while retail chains like Urban Outfitters sell novelty books that cater to its young and hip demographic. The Discovery Store is another example of a retail chain that sells a small number of books that cater to its customers.

Other specialty retailers that sell books (usually on specific topics of interest to its customers) include Best Buy, Staples, OfficeMax, Office Depot, Toys "R" Us, Newbury Comics, CompUSA, PETCO, PetSmart, and General Nutrition Centers (GNC).

This type of distribution strategy is ideal for books that focus on a niche-oriented topic. The advantage to pursuing specialty retail shops as a distribution outlet is that you could potentially increase awareness and sales opportunities for your book. The drawback is that as a self-published author working alone, getting through to the appropriate buyer and getting their attention could be a challenge.

The process of selling your books through specialty retail stores is very much the same as selling to independent booksellers (see the previous section). You need to contact the appropriate buyer at the retail store or chain. You may find that hiring an experienced salesperson is helpful so you can establish connections and have some assistance in the sales process. See "Grabbing the Attention of Mass-Market Retailers and Bookstore Chains," later in this chapter for the scoop on finding such a person.

You may need to allow specialty retail stores to buy on credit but not to return unsold books. These stores expect to buy the book in quantity at 40 to 60 percent off the cover price.

Distributing Your Book via Direct Mail

Another way to distribute your book is to focus on reaching your book's target audience by sending a direct mail piece. Direct mail pieces need to be well-written and create an incentive that the reader can't refuse. The mailer should also establish urgency, so the reader responds to your offer immediately. And don't forget: Your direct mail piece needs an order form for recipients to order copies of your book directly from you (providing a toll-free phone number or Web site can increase your chances of getting a response even more). Make sure that your order form requests all the information you need to process someone's order, including the buyer's name, address, phone number, payment information, shipping address, and so on. See Chapter 16 for more information on order fulfillment.

Your direct mail piece can be a powerful sales tool for your book. You only have a few seconds to capture the attention of the potential reader, so make sure that your mailer, whether it's a sales letter, brochure, or sell sheet (see "Creating a sell sheet" earlier in this chapter), piques the readers' curiosity.

After you've prepared your mailer, you need somewhere to send it, right? Using direct mail is most useful when you're targeting a very niche market. You can figure out who to send your piece to by purchasing a custom-tailored mailing list comprised of people you believe may be interested in your book. How to do it? Rent a targeted mailing list from a special interest group, trade association, or special interest magazine publisher that also targets your intended readers. You should also use a mailing list of your established customers or clients, if available.

Because of the costs associated with renting a mailing list and then printing and mailing brochures and sales literature (varies from a fraction of a cent per name up to several dollars per name), make sure to target your audience and ensure that the cover price of your book (and your profit from each copy sold) can justify this expense. When using direct mail, a response rate of only 1½ to 2 percent is considered normal.

Before investing a lot in direct mail marketing and distribution, find out more about this opportunity from other sources:

✔ The Direct Marketing Association is one excellent resource that's available online at www.the-dma.org.

✔ The National Mail Order Association is another organization that offers educational resources online to help small businesses learn direct mail techniques and strategies. Visit www.nmoa.com or call (612) 788-1673.

✔ If you want to give creating your own pieces a shot, pick up *Writing Copy For Dummies* (Wiley) by Jonathan Kranz.

Looking for less expensive options that directly target potential readers? Try the following:

✔ Utilize opt-in e-mail lists and targeted e-mail (which is very different from sending spam). See Chapter 21 for tips on using the Internet as a marketing tool for your book.

✔ Do some research and team up with a company that uses direct mail to sell its products or services and bundle your book mailing in with theirs. Offer a special discount to people who buy the product/service and your book.

Hooking Up with Trade Associations, Special Interest Groups, and Conferences

Many professional trade associations, special interest groups, and trade show/ conference planners sell books and educational materials to its members. As part of your market research (see Chapter 7 for more info), pinpoint groups and associations whose membership may be interested in selling your book, and then contact those groups directly. Consider offering a special discount to members or allowing the organization to publish excerpts from your book (for free) on their Web site in order to generate interest and sales.

In reality, any company, organization or group that sells books or that's set up to sell products at retail to customers, clients, or members, could potentially sell your book. The trick to making this happen is helping the decision makers at these organizations realize how selling your book can potentially benefit everyone involved and generate a profit, too. Your book's press kit and marketing materials, combined with telephone calls to key decision markets should do the trick. In some cases, offering these organizations a special discount on high-quantity orders can be enticing.

Now showing . . .

Industry-oriented and consumer trade shows are held throughout the world that focus on many different industries and interests. These gatherings bring together professionals working in an industry from all over the world. They allow for the exchange of information, provide a valuable learning opportunity, and offer excellent networking opportunities. When attending a trade show, bring plenty of press kits and marketing materials for your book to hand out for networking.

Many trade shows occur each year. One of the biggest industry trades shows is Book Expo America. Booksellers, buyers, major publishing houses, authors, distributors, wholesalers, the media, and a wide range of other people working in the book publishing industry attend this show, held annually in a different city each year. If you're looking for distribution, attending this trade show and perhaps renting a small booth to showcase your book could be beneficial. For details, visit the trade show's Web site at www.bookexpoamerica.com.

Trade shows provide excellent marketing and sales opportunities for your book and allow you to reach your target audience in person, so for a listing of other events like the Book Expo America, visit www.biztradeshows.com. To find out about trade shows that cater to a specific industry, look for event listings in industry trade magazines and newsletters.

If your book caters to people working in a specific industry or who gather for an industry or consumer-oriented trade show, consider renting booth space at these trade shows or conferences and selling your book directly to attendees and participants. Offering attendees a special discount and an autographed copy of the book are excellent sales incentives. But be sure that you can fit such expenses into your overall budget (see Chapter 6 for details).

Grabbing the Attention of Mass-Market Retailers and Bookstore Chains

For self-published authors and small publishers, breaking into the mass-market retailers or into major bookstore chains is extremely challenging. Realistically, you shouldn't expect to obtain this type of distribution for your self-published book. Getting the attention of a buyer who represents a major bookstore chain or mass-market retailer requires a lot more than you being a good writer. Major publishing houses have entire sales departments whose job involves cultivating relationships with these buyers.

To properly sell your book to the appropriate decision makers, you need to be highly professional, knowledgeable about the publishing industry, business savvy, persistent, and willing to dedicate the time, energy, and resources needed. You definitely need to step up and play in the big leagues, so to speak. Start your selling process early-on, because getting the attention of a buyer can take weeks or months. An alternative is to wait for your book to become successful, and then approach the appropriate buyers with proof that there's a huge potential market for your book. So here are a few things to get you to the plate:

✔ **Hire an experienced sales representative who has established connections with buyers associated with the mass-market retailers and bookstore chains.** Many sales representatives work with a handful of authors and small publishers simultaneously. Even though you have to pay for the services of a sales representative, your chances of having your book seen and evaluated by important buyers improve greatly if you hire the right person. The sales rep you hire should have experience working with the key buyers you want to target and have a good understanding of your book and who it targets. A successful sales rep has pre-established relationships with buyers that you benefit from.

✔ **Team up with the manufacturer or distributor of an established product that already has mass-market distribution and bundle your book with that product.** This maneuver requires approaching and negotiating with a company that offers a product of interest to the same target audience as your book. To do this, contact the sales or marketing department of the company whose product you'd like to bundle your book with. You need to pitch the idea and probably want to follow up with a written proposal outlining your plan and ideas.

Of course, you can contact the book buyers who represent the various mass-market retailers yourself. Contact the company's corporate offices and ask who the appropriate buyer is. Then, send that buyer a copy of your book and related sales materials. Keep in mind that you need to offer the mass market retailers and bookstore chains credit terms, plus a significant discount off the book's cover price (up to 60 percent), if they become interested in placing an order and selling your book.

Try contacting the following mass-market retailers

✔ **Wal-Mart:** To approach Wal-Mart, call Anderson Merchandisers at (800) 999-0904. This company exclusively distributes books, magazines, video, and audio products to Wal-Mart. To have your book evaluated for possible sale through Wal-Mart stores, send the following info:

- A copy of your book

- Sales materials (your book's press kit and marketing materials)

Address: Anderson Merchandisers, Attn: Marketing Dept. – New Title Solicitation, 421 South East 34th Avenue, Amarillo, TX 79103.

✔ **Barnes & Noble Retail Bookstores:** Self-published authors or small publishers can try to have their books distributed through Barnes & Noble's chain of retail bookstores. Barnes & Noble Retail Bookstores doesn't give preference to books sold through wholesalers like Borders does. Here is the info to send:

- A published copy of your book

- Marketing and promotional plans

- Trade reviews

- Information about what makes the book unique

Address: The Small Press Department, Barnes & Noble, Inc., 122 Fifth Avenue, New York, NY 10011.

Barnes & Noble.com is different than the company's chain of retail stores. See Chapter 14 for information on selling your book through popular online booksellers.

✔ **Borders Group:** Borders Group, Inc. is the parent company of Borders bookstores and Waldenbooks, two national chains of retail booksellers. To have your book considered for possible sale through these retail chains, send

- A copy of your published book

- Marketing and promotional plans

- Trade reviews

- Details about your distribution channel

- A description of your book

Address: New Vendor Acquisitions, Borders Group, Inc., 100 Phoenix Drive, Ann Arbor, MI 48108.

The review process takes approximately 90 days. Borders Group reports that having your book available from one of the popular book distributors greatly increases your chances of being considered for distribution through its retailers. See "Working with Wholesalers and Distributors," earlier in this chapter for more information.

Chapter 16

Getting a Grip on Warehousing, Order Fulfillment, and Shipping

In This Chapter

▶ Storing and taking inventory of your books

▶ Taking and fulfilling orders

▶ Sending your books to customers

---

*I*n many cases authors can reap financial rewards for selling their own books directly. These sales allow authors to increase earning potentials on each copy sold. But this potential does come with a little bit of work. You have to set up your own operation for warehousing, order taking, fulfillment, and shipping. Many self-published authors do these processes from their homes. This chapter helps you create your procedures.

After you begin selling books, whether directly to customers or to booksellers or retailers, you need to establish some type of formal business (mainly for tax purposes). Chapter 6 helps you set up your publishing business.

Here are a few ideas to ease you into the entire warehousing, fulfillment, and shipping process:

 ✔ **Figure out the least expensive way to ship books.** Research prices through the United States Postal Service, FedEx, UPS, and DHL.

 ✔ **Purchase the appropriate shipping supplies, so you have everything on hand.** This stock includes envelopes, packing tape, mailing labels, postage, and so on. You want to be able to fill and ship orders quickly and in an organized manner.

 ✔ **Hire a company to handle everything for you.** The company takes care of accepting telephone and online orders to warehousing your books, processing orders, and handling the necessary accounting and customer management. Hiring a company can get expensive and quickly eat away your profits, so check with your printer to see if it handles these services. You also can do an online search for *order processing* or *order fulfillment companies* or obtain a referral from an industry association's Web site, such as PMA, the Independent Book Publishers Association (www.pma-online.org).

Warehousing Your Books and Managing Inventory

Selling your own books requires maintaining an inventory (warehousing books) to fill orders. In the following sections, I explain the importance of safely storing your books and carefully monitoring your inventory.

Storing your books safely

If you use offset printing (see Chapter 10 for details) to publish a large quantity of books, you wind up with a bunch of large cartons filled with books that need to be warehoused. If you use Print-On-Demand (POD) (covered in Chapter 11), you can keep a much smaller quantity of books on-hand and reorder more as needed.

Many self-published authors use their basement, garage, or attic to store their book inventory. This storage is convenient if you plan to sell books directly to readers, booksellers, or retailers and wish to work from home.

Check out these important tips for keeping books in excellent condition:

✔ Keep the books in a climate-controlled, clean, and dry environment.

✔ Store cartons on pallets (a few inches above the ground), especially if you're storing boxes in your basement and you have flooding issues.

✔ Pack the books in large, sealable plastic containers to ensure that they stay clean and dry until they're sold and ready to be shipped.

✔ Consider running a dehumidifier in your storage room if the room is damp because exposure to water or moisture quickly damages the books to the point where they're unsuitable for sale.

✔ Purchase additional insurance to protect your inventory against damage or theft, especially if you're storing a large quantity of inventory within your home; this inventory is for a business, so your homeowner's or renter's insurance policy may not cover it (contact your insurance company for more information).

If you don't have a basement or attic available, another option for warehousing large quantities of books is to rent space from a self-storage facility in your area. The cost for this space is about $30 to $50 per month. Make sure that the storage facility is climate controlled and that you store the books in airtight and waterproof containers for their protection. You may also need to acquire special insurance if you use a storage facility.

Taking stock of your inventory

A wise business operator regularly maintains a good grasp of the inventory levels. You need to establish a simple way to handle inventory control so you always know how many books you have on hand. Monitoring inventory also means being able to anticipate demand and pre-ordering additional inventory at the appropriate time so it's available when you need it. If you're selling just one product — your book — you can calculate inventory levels by hand. Keeping detailed invoices also helps with this process.

After you begin selling a significant number of books, consider investing in some basic inventory management software for your computer. Some turnkey eCommerce Web site solutions have built-in inventory management tools. Quicken Premiere Home and Business 2006 is an excellent software package for managing many aspects of your small, home-based business operations and finances. For more info on this program, visit www.quicken.com.

Handling Order Taking and Fulfillment

Depending on how you plan to sell your books, your order taking and fulfillment operations may be different:

- ✔ You may sell your books in person at a variety of events.

- ✔ Some authors advertise their books in print publications, on the radio, or through a direct mail campaign, so establish a toll-free phone number to accept orders.

- ✔ You may want to create an eCommerce Web site to accept orders online.

- ✔ Set yourself up to accept orders by mail and obtain a P.O. Box (for your privacy) and then display the mail order address in your ads (see Part V for more on advertising).

As orders are received or sales are made, document them promptly and fulfill the orders ASAP. Make sure to process payments, manage a database of customers, and print invoices, too. I cover all these processes and more in the following sections.

Whatever methods you use to accept orders and interact with customers, the service and professionalism you offer to those people need to be top notch. When you begin selling books directly to customers, whether those customers are booksellers or individual readers, those people expect to be doing business with an established company. You can easily run this company from your home on a part-time basis as long as customers are able to easily place orders and those orders are promptly processed and shipped. This process requires you to establish carefully thought out procedures for all aspects of the ordering process.

Offering different order options

There are many ways to sell your books, such as in person, via mail order, through an 800 number, and through your own Web site. The following sections offer some additional detail about these various options.

Taking orders in person

If you sell books in person at author appearances, seminars, trade shows, and other events, be prepared. Bring a generous supply of books (so you don't run out) and a small table or trade show display to sell the books from (if the vendor doesn't supply a table). Be ready to accept cash, check, debit card, or credit card payments. Along with the payments, generate simple receipts for customers with a duplicate copy of the receipt for your own records.

Accepting checks can be a problem, because checks bounce, causing you to lose money on the sale. You don't want to waste the time or money involved in tracking down the lost sales of bad checks. If you're willing to take the financial risk, accept checks. Otherwise, accept other forms of payment.

Selling books in person allows people to meet you and purchase the book right on the spot, without having to place and wait for an order. People often prefer the instant gratification of obtaining what they purchase right away.

Working with mail orders

Some customers may prefer to send their orders through the mail. If that is the case, then you need to be prepared. Here are a few tips:

- ✔ Include an order form that people can fax or mail as a viable way to sell books.
- ✔ Offer a printable order form on your Web site for people unwilling to make online purchases.
- ✔ List an address in print ads to encourage orders by mail.

When accepting forms of payment through the mail, you can take all forms, but remember that checks can cause you big headaches. It's best not to accept checks, especially on small ticket items like books. It's not worth the risk.

Establishing a toll-free phone number

Establishing an incoming toll-free number to accept orders is easy. The toll-free number can be programmed to ring on your existing home, cell, or office phone. To order your own toll-free number, call your local phone company or a long distance telephone service provider.

The following list is a small sampling of companies that offer inexpensive, incoming, toll-free service:

- ✔ **Freedom Voice Systems:** Rates start at 4.5 cents per minute, plus a low monthly fee. A variety of extra features and services, such as voicemail and call forwarding, are included. Call (800) 605-9858 or visit www.xtreme800.biz.

- ✔ **RingCentral:** Rates start at 3.9 cents per minute with a low monthly fee. Service includes voicemail, call forwarding, and other useful features. Reach the company at (800) 574-5290 or visit their Web site at www.ringcentral.com.

- ✔ **Smart800:** Rates start at 4.9 cents per minute, plus a small monthly fee. A variety of extra features and services, such as voicemail and call forwarding, are included. Phone (877) 357-0757; Web site www.smart800now.com.

- ✔ **TollFreeNumber.org:** Rates start at 3 cents per minute with a low monthly fee. Service includes voicemail, call forwarding, and other useful features. Call (800) 951-9411 for more info or go online at www.tollfreenumber.org.

Having a toll-free number means that you pay by the minute for each incoming call, so if you're on the phone for five minutes with each customer, the cost of that call needs to be built into your cost of doing business and the cost of goods sold (and subtracted from your potential profit). See Chapter 6 for more about working with a budget.

After you have a toll-free phone number set up for people to call and place their orders, have someone well trained on hand to answer the phone during business hours. If someone calls to place an order, you could lose the sale if that caller hears your voicemail instead of a live person.

If you're not available to answer your incoming calls, hire a non-automated answering service capable of order taking. Be prepared to write a script for the people answering the phone, so they know what to say, how to describe your book, and how to gather the information you need to process orders. You typically pay for a service by the call. Some also charge a monthly fee. You can find answering services listed online or in the Yellow Pages.

Launching an eCommerce Web site

An eCommerce Web site is slightly different from a regular Web site because it's equipped with a shopping cart module that allows someone to place a secure order online using a major credit card or PayPal. Adding a shopping cart to a Web site or creating a simple eCommerce Web site for your book is relatively easy and inexpensive.

Many turnkey companies offer easy-to-use eCommerce Web site creating and hosting tools, for as little as $10 per month. These companies include

- ✔ Yahoo! Small Business: `sbs.smallbusiness.yahoo.com/merchant`
- ✔ ProStores: `www.prostores.com`
- ✔ GoDaddy.com: `www.godaddy.com/gdshop/ecommerce/cart.asp`

These turnkey eCommerce solutions also help you set up a merchant account so you can accept credit card payments online. The beauty of these solutions is that all of the tools are available online and absolutely no programming knowledge is required to create and operate the site.

For help creating an effective eCommerce Web site to sell books online, read my book *The Unofficial Guide to Starting a Business Online,* 2nd Edition (Wiley), or check out *E-Commerce For Dummies* (Wiley) by Don Jones, Mark D. Scott, and Richard Villars. You can find additional information about building a Web site for your book in Chapter 21.

Accepting payments

Selling books, whether in person or online, requires you to be able to accept different forms of payment in order to generate the most possible sales and offer convenience to your customers. To accept credit card payments, you can establish a merchant account. You also can accept payments via PayPal, cash, and checks. I cover all these options in the following sections.

You may accept most payments by credit card. When you sell books in person, you can, of course, also accept cash and checks. However, many people prefer the convenience of making purchases using their credit or debit card. When selling online, accepting cash isn't an option and few people take the time to mail in a check or money order if they're shopping online.

Opening a merchant account for credit card payments

To accept credit cards, you first need to establish a merchant account through a bank, a financial institution, or a merchant account service provider. After credit card payments are authorized, either manually or automatically (through your eCommerce Web site), the funds are transferred directly into your bank account within one to three business days.

Typically, establishing a merchant account requires a one-time set-up fee and an ongoing monthly fee. You also need to pay a small service charge on each sale made. Depending on the volume of business you're doing, you can shop around for the lowest fees.

Here are a few strategies for setting up a merchant account and finding the best deals available from banks or merchant account providers:

- **Before shopping around, estimate your anticipated number of monthly transactions and sales volume.** If you have a small number of high volume sales (to booksellers or distributors, for example), your ideal fee structure may be different than if you're processing many smaller transactions and selling individual copies of your book.

- **Compare prices and beware of hidden fees.** The majority of merchant accounts charge a percentage of the volume processed. This term is called the *discount rate.*

- **Ask about rate review policies.** After you establish a working relationship with a merchant bank, request a reduction in your discount rate after several months. Even a small reduction in your discount rate saves you money in the long run.

- **Read all the contracts and agreements carefully!** Make sure that you understand the terms of the contract, including how long the contract is in effect and what all the fees are. You can even hire a lawyer to review the contracts before you sign them.

- **Make sure that the merchant account you sign up for allows you to accept orders online but also make in-person sales, if those are your plans.** The merchant account should be able to work seamlessly with your eCommerce Web site.

To find merchant account service providers and compare rates, use any Internet search engine, such as Yahoo! or Google. Enter the search phrase *merchant account.* If you're using a turnkey solution for your eCommerce Web site (covered earlier in this chapter), the service provider often offers merchant account services (for an additional fee). Here's a small list of merchant account service providers:

- **Card Service International:** Phone (888) 869-5520; Web site `www.csicard.com`

- **Credit Merchant Account Services:** Phone (203) 483-5751; Web site `www.merchantaccount.net`

- **Merchant Account Company:** (800) 956-1990; Web site `www.merchantaccount.com`

- **Merchant Accounts Express:** (888) 845-9457; Web site `www.merchantexpress.com`

Using PayPal

PayPal was created to be a safe, convenient, and easy way for people to make purchases online. It's another option you can offer as a safe way to accept payments from your customers. PayPal offers merchants a variety of different, low-cost services, which are especially attractive to small business operators. Best of all, as a merchant, you can set up your account and begin receiving PayPal payments in a matter of minutes. Funds from sales are transmitted to your bank account instantly.

The main drawback to PayPal is that for someone to use it to make a payment, he must be a PayPal member, unless you establish your merchant account through PayPal. After someone has an established PayPal account, he can make purchases using a major credit card, debit card, or checking account number. Consumers can also maintain funds in their account for purchases.

For more information, visit the PayPal Web site at www.paypal.com and click the *Merchant Tools* tab at the top of the screen.

Taking care with cash

If you're going to accept cash, especially at busy events, make sure that you have a cash register or cash box that remains safe, especially if you get distracted. As the author, if you're interacting with potential readers, signing books, and answering questions, have someone else nearby actually handling the money and selling your books for you.

It's also important to write out receipts for customers who pay with cash. Make sure that you have a duplicate copy for your records. If customers have questions or complaints later, you have a copy of the receipt to settle disputes.

Checking out checks

Accepting personal checks is risky. It's easy for someone to bounce a check or put a stop payment on the check. If this happens, you not only lose the purchase price of the book, but also you're charged an extra fee by your bank or financial institution. As you get started selling books, you may want to offer this as a payment option, but ultimately, you're better off accepting cash, PayPal payments, and debit or credit cards. If you're going to accept a check, get the buyer's information (address, phone number, driver's license number, and so on.) The problem is, for the value of the check (the cover price of your book), it's probably not worth pursuing if it bounces.

Doing the paperwork

Every business requires its operators to handle a variety of different types of paperwork to track customers, record orders, process those orders, and manage finances. Proper recordkeeping is essential.

To handle much of your recordkeeping and paperwork, you can use a comprehensive, vertical market software application designed for mail-order businesses, off-the-shelf contact management and accounting software, or online tools provided by the eCommerce Internet Service Provider (ISP) you opt to work with (I cover eCommerce Web sites earlier in this chapter). These online tools help you manage customer records and the paperwork associated with all aspects of order fulfillment. Of course, you can always do your recordkeeping the old-fashioned way — using paper, pencil, and a calculator, if you're not technologically savvy.

ACT! is a powerful contact management software application available from Sage Software that allows you to keep track of customers, print shipping labels, and generate personalized invoices and correspondence with ease. Check out the product online at `www.act.com`.

The following types of information you handle most when doing paperwork:

- ✔ **Orders:** Maintain a detailed list of all incoming book orders. You can use a database program, spreadsheet, or hard copy files.

- ✔ **Customer database:** Maintaining a database of your customers is extremely helpful, especially if you plan to publish additional books in the future or want to sell these same customers additional products or services. Having order information at your fingertips is helpful and important. For each customer, make sure that you have a full name, address, phone number, ordering details, method of payment and its details, and the way you shipped the product.

- ✔ **Sales receipts:** A *sales receipt* is issued to the customer when a sale is made, typically in a retail or in-person environment. It's a good idea to keep a copy of your sales receipts for recordkeeping purposes and to be able to track orders.

- ✔ **Invoices:** An invoice can be used as a sales receipt or it can be created if you're shipping books to customers and receiving payment later. Whether you use invoices or sales receipts depends on how and where you sell your books.

- ✔ **Returns:** Keeping track of returns helps you maintain accurate inventory records and manage your finances. It's faster and easier to keep track of returns with inventory-management or mail-order-management software.

Because you're running a business, doing the appropriate paperwork and filing tax returns as needed keeps you out of trouble with the IRS and helps you better manage your finances, track profits and expenditures, and generate the most revenue possible from your publishing venture. Hiring a bookkeeper to manage your day-to-day paperwork may be helpful. An accountant can also help you set up procedures for handling this paperwork, but having these people do all of the recordkeeping for you can get costly, so maybe take a class or two on financial management.

Shipping Your Books to Customers

Setting your publishing company up to accept orders and sell books also includes having the ability to ship orders to customers, whether it's 100 books to a distributor, ten books to a bookseller, or one book to a customer. In the following sections, I give you the basics on shipping rates and supplies.

Surveying shipping rates

When it comes to shipping books to customers, you have a variety of options. The service you use should depend on your budget and how quickly you need your books to arrive at their destinations. Overnight couriers like FedEx are going to be much more expensive than First-Class or Priority Mail from the U.S. Postal Service. However, if you absolutely, positively need to get your book someplace overnight, FedEx or another overnight courier is the way to go. For most self-published authors, the book rate from the post office or a standard ground service from a courier is an inexpensive, viable option.

The United States Postal Service

The United States Postal Service (USPS) offers a variety of services for merchants to ship their goods. You can order stamps and shipping supplies online (www.usps.com) and find out about the following shipping methods:

✔ **Priority Mail:** The USPS offers free envelopes for flat-rate Priority Mail, and the postage for the envelopes starts at $4.05 per package. Priority Mail typically takes two to three business days (including Saturday) for delivery.

✔ **First-Class Mail:** First-Class Mail is a bit cheaper than Priority Mail, but you have to pay for the envelope. First Class mail can take one to five business days to be delivered.

- **Book Rate or Media Mail:** This method is the cheapest shipping method from the USPS. When you use Book Rate shipping, a one-pound package costs around $1.59 to ship.

  Book Rate does dramatically slow down how long it takes for your shipments to arrive at their destination. Book Rate can take up to ten days or longer for delivery.

If you're filling a large number of orders (and I hope you do!), consider renting a postage machine and buying a postage scale. A postage machine can help you keep accurate records of your postage expenditures and also reduce trips to the Post Office to purchase stamps. Here are some options:

- Pitney Bowes offers a variety of different postage machine options. Visit www.pb.com for more info.

- Stamps.com allows you to purchase and print postage from your computer and printer. Visit www.stamps.com.

Major shipping companies

For larger shipments or overnight shipments, consider establishing an account with a major shipping company:

- **DHL:** Phone (800) CALL-DHL; Web site www.dhl-usa.com
- **FedEx:** Phone (800) GO-FEDEX; Web site www.fedex.com
- **UPS:** Phone (800) PICK-UPS; Web site www.ups.com

These accounts can be set up by using a major credit card by visiting any of these couriers' Web sites. After an account is set up, you can print shipping labels and schedule pick ups from your computer.

Setting up your shipping department

To save time and money, stock up on shipping supplies in order to promptly fill orders. Necessary supplies include

- Bubble wrap or packing peanuts
- Invoices
- Packing tape
- Padded envelopes
- Scissors

- ✔ Shipping labels
- ✔ Small boxes
- ✔ Stamps or a postage machine

To stock up on shipping supplies, visit your local office supply superstore, or check out other shipping supply suppliers online. Your options include

- ✔ Boxes.com: www.boxes.com
- ✔ Bubble Fast: www.bubblefast.com
- ✔ Go Packaging: www.gopackaging.com
- ✔ Office Depot: www.officedepot.com
- ✔ OfficeMax: www.officemax.com
- ✔ Packaging Supplies: www.packagingsupplies.com
- ✔ PaperMart: www.papermart.com
- ✔ Staples: www.staples.com
- ✔ Uline: www.uline.com
- ✔ VeriPack: www.veripack.com

Make sure that your packages don't arrive damaged. Either use an appropriate size envelope, a padded envelope, or wrap the book in bubble wrap. Your customers will be happier and your business won't suffer from shipping damaged goods.

Chapter 17

Selling Your Book to the Big Boys for Better Distribution

Self-publishing certainly has its benefits, especially for unproven, previously unpublished authors or established writers who are able to market directly to people interested in the topic they're writing about. One of the biggest drawbacks to self-publishing, however, is the difficulty you face trying to obtain national distribution.

Selling your self-published book to a major publishing house offers multiple advantages. You can also sell your book in foreign countries or negotiate the subsidiary and serial rights for wider distribution, as you see in this chapter.

Sending Your Book to a Major Publisher

Suppose you're an author who's already pursued self-publishing, achieved some success, and is now looking to improve distribution and sales of your book by working with a major publishing house. In the following sections, I show you the benefits of working with a major publisher and smart methods for approaching one. I also explain basic types of publishing deals and tell you how to handle potential rejections.

The book publishing industry is competitive. Even if a major publisher decides to publish and distribute your book, you may not receive the full support of the company's sales, marketing, public relations, and advertising departments. So, while your book could reach booksellers' shelves, unless you take an active role in promoting it as the author, it may not receive the support it needs. It may make sense to invest more money in marketing or establish better distribution and continue your self-publishing efforts.

Understanding how a major publisher can help you

A major publisher can offer a wide range of resources you probably don't have as a self-published author. These resources include

- ✔ A team of editors and creative people who can help redesign and enhance your book's interior and cover
- ✔ Established relationships with printers
- ✔ An experienced sales and marketing team with existing relationships with buyers representing major bookstore chains nationwide, as well as libraries, independent booksellers, distributors, and wholesalers
- ✔ A team of public relations specialists who can create and implement a comprehensive campaign for your book
- ✔ A marketing and advertising team capable of properly reaching your book's target audience on a national level
- ✔ Warehousing and distribution facilities
- ✔ An accounting department that tracks sales, handles all finances relating to the book, and distributes author royalties accordingly

You give up significant control over your book working with a major publisher, and you earn a significantly lower royalty on every copy of the book sold. But with the resources of a major publisher behind you, you can enjoy the following benefits:

- ✔ You may sell many more copies of your book than you would as a self-published author.
- ✔ The publisher takes on all of the financial responsibilities relating to designing, printing, distributing, selling, and marketing your book.

After spending between $5,000 and $20,000 (or more) to have your book self-published initially, you could be paid an advance upfront by the publisher who buys your book.

Approaching a major publisher

You want to grab the attention of the major publishing houses, right? You've already self-published your book; you've received a handful of favorable reviews and some positive media coverage; and you can show respectable sales for the title based on the distribution and resources you've had at your disposal. You may now be able to accomplish your goal. In the following sections, I give you tips on hiring a literary agent, researching potential publishers, and crafting a proposal to get your book in front of the big boys.

Having a literary agent represent you

The first step to approaching a publisher is to find an established literary agent who really believes in your project and helps you sell the idea to publishers. Many major publishing houses work only with authors represented by literary agents. A literary agent is someone who's experienced working in the book publishing industry, who's established contacts with publishers, and who represents you and your book ideas to those publishers. A literary agent earns between 15 and 20 percent of your earnings, based on the advance, royalties, and/or licensing fees paid by the publisher.

A literary agent helps you

- ✔ **Prepare and fine-tune your proposal for a publisher:** This proposal is your sales packet that introduces yourself to the publisher and gets them excited to learn about your book. Focus on benefits to the publishing house. Why should they publish your book? (I cover proposals later in this chapter.)

- ✔ **Represent your book by contacting publishers on your behalf:** A respected agent will often be able to get your proposal read by publishers that would otherwise ignore submissions from self-published or inexperienced writers.

- ✔ **Negotiate a deal (and related contracts) with a publisher that's interested in your book:** Whenever an author and a publisher work together, a detailed, legal contract must be written and signed by both parties. This contract outlines the terms of the deal and describes the exact responsibilities of the author and the publisher. (I cover publishing deals later in this chapter.)

Looking for a literary agent? Check out the *2006 Guide to Literary Agents* (Writer's Digest Books). The book is an annual directory listing more than 600 established literary agents; it includes detailed information about the types of clients each agency represents and how to make contact with them.

Look for an agent who specializes in the type of book you've written and who has contacts with the major publishing houses that may be interested in your project. An agent must agree to represent you, but you also must decide if the agent's experience, qualifications, contacts, and publishing knowledge will help you get your book published by a major publishing house.

Even though it's not critical to have an agent, unless you're familiar with how the publishing industry works and have your own connections with executives (editors and publishers) at major publishing houses, you may want to work with a literary agent when trying to sell your book.

Researching potential publishers

You can contact the publishing houses yourself without using a literary agent, but first, do some research to pinpoint a handful of publishers that specialize in the type of book you're hoping to get published. When approaching larger publishers, you need to contact the subsidiary or imprint within the company that's most appropriate. (Many publishers have subsidiaries or imprints that are smaller divisions specializing in specific types of books. For example, a major publisher may have a fiction imprint, a nonfiction imprint, a business books imprint, a children's book imprint, and even a cookbook imprint.)

Even if you're using an agent, you can do research to determine which publishers may be interested in your book. This lets you have an intelligent conversation with your agent about his approach to selling your book.

Two popular directories list details about book publishers.

- *Writer's Market* **(Writer's Digest Books):** This directory is published annually. It offers a comprehensive list of 4,000 potential markets for writers, including book publishers. Each listing describes the types of books a publisher specializes in, along with relevant contact information and submission guidelines.

- *Jeff Herman's Guide to Book Publishers, Editors, & Literary Agents* **(Three Dogs Press):** This annual directory is available in bookstores.

After you've created a list of potential publishers to target, determine who the acquisitions editor is at each publishing company, subsidiary, and/or imprint. This person is your ultimate contact. Initiate contact by making a telephone call to the acquisitions editor. During this call, introduce yourself, describe your book in 30 seconds or less, and determine if there's a potential interest. If so, follow up by sending a full proposal. If you have an agent representing you, he's responsible for making contact with the publisher on your behalf.

Creating a winning proposal

Even though you already have copies of your self-published book in your hands, you still need to develop a detailed proposal. If you're working with a literary agent, he helps you fine-tune your proposal and customize it for each publisher you're submitting to. This proposal should include the following:

- A detailed description of your book (one or two pages), including what it's about and information about what the book contains

- An explanation about what sets your book apart from the competition

- A detailed outline of the book (several pages long), including a chapter-by-chapter summary

- A summary, including quantitative and qualitative facts, figures, or statistics, of the book's target audience, including its size

- Your biography, including information about what makes you an expert on the topic you've written and your related experience

- A copy of your self-published book, along with copies of reviews and press coverage you've received

Each proposal should be accompanied by a well-written, attention-getting cover letter that's specifically addressed to the acquisitions editor at the publisher. As much as possible, customize the cover letter and proposal to each individual publisher. This letter should be typed and printed in a formal business letter format. You want to make the best first impression possible with this letter, so what it says and the way it looks are equally important.

Most publishers receive dozens, perhaps hundreds, of proposals every week. Your proposal must be professional and fall within the editorial scope of what the publisher typically publishes. It needs to stand out and demonstrate that there's a need and viable market for your book on a national scale.

Examining different publishing deals

Just as there are thousands of publishers, as well as imprints and subsidiaries within those publishers, there are many types of publishing deals that can be structured. If you're working with a literary agent, he can help you evaluate and negotiate the best deal possible. The four most common scenarios are

- ✔ The publisher pays a one-time, flat fee for the manuscript and becomes the sole copyright owner of the material. You provide the manuscript on a work-for-hire basis.

- ✔ The publisher pays a licensing fee to print copies of your self-published book.

- ✔ The publisher pays an advance, plus royalties on all copies of the book sold. This means you'd receive money upfront and ongoing royalty payments based on sales of your book. The advance is usually fully recoupable from future sales. (When you receive an advance, that money is deducted from your initial book sales. Think of your advance as a loan against your future income. If, however, your book doesn't sell enough copies to pay back the advance, you don't have to refund the money out of your pocket.)

- ✔ The publisher pays royalties only, based on sales.

The advance or royalty you can expect from a publisher varies greatly. Many publishers base the advance it offers to the author on anticipated first-year sales. Depending on the size of the publisher and a variety of other factors, a book advance could be anywhere from $5,000 to $25,000 or more. The percentage of royalties paid also varies greatly but is typically something that can be negotiated with the publisher.

Before signing your contract with the publisher, have your literary agent carefully review it. If you're not working with an agent, hire a lawyer to review the contract to ensure that your interests are protected. Contracts written by major publishers vary greatly. Some protect the author's interest more than others, but all of them always protect the publisher's legal, business, and financial interests. Make sure that you understand all the terms within the contract and know your responsibilities.

If you make a deal with a publisher, you give up significant control over the project as a whole. Ultimately, the publisher needs to approve all content within the book. The publisher also has final say over the book's interior and cover design, how the book is marketed, and how much of its resources get put behind your book. In some cases, you don't even get consulted when certain decisions are made. Your primary obligation is simply to submit a manuscript that adheres to the outline pre-approved by the publisher.

"Sorry, not interested": Handling rejection

Getting your book published by a major company is a competitive process. Publishers are becoming much more careful about the projects they publish and how resources are allocated. Unless you're a celebrity, a well-known business leader, a juror in a high-profile trial, or a recognized expert in your field and there's a potentially large market for your book, capturing the attention of a publisher, especially a large publisher, is going to be difficult.

With that said, though, being able to submit a self-published copy of your book with your proposal when contacting a publisher certainly gives you some added credibility. But remember that no matter how good your self-published book really is and how professional your proposal comes across, not all publishers jump at what you're offering. So, expect some rejection when you submit your proposal to publishers.

With rejection comes perseverance (that's perseverance on your part). Submit your proposal to multiple publishers you believe might be interested in your project, and never take rejection personally. In most cases, you either never hear back from the publisher (implying that they're not interested) or you receive a short rejection letter. Don't give up!

If you happen to speak with an acquisitions editor who ultimately rejects your book, ask her why she made the decision and what could be done to improve the proposal or book. Use whatever feedback you can get constructively, keeping in mind that the rejection is based upon someone's opinion. However, you probably don't want to make a follow-up call to the editor after you receive a rejection. This could make you look unprofessional or desperate. One alternative is to write a short, friendly e-mail to the editor. You're better off having your agent call on your behalf if you're looking for constructive feedback.

After you submit your proposal to a publisher, be patient! The decision can take weeks or months and that includes your proposal reaching the top of an acquisitions editor's stack of proposals. Then, if the editor likes the project, a publishing company's editorial board and sales department still must often approve the idea.

Meet a literary agent

Jeff Herman is the president of the Jeff Herman Agency (Web site: `www.jeffherman.com`). He's represented authors as a literary agent since 1987 and is responsible for helping to bring more than 500 books into print. He's also the author of *Jeff Herman's Guide to Book Publishers, Editors, & Literary Agents* (Three Dog Press) and *Write the Perfect Book Proposal* (Wiley).

Herman has worked with many first-time authors. For someone interested in getting a book published, he recommends using a literary agent but stresses the importance of finding the right agent. "Most literary agencies are mom-and-pop businesses that employ less than 10 people. Each agent is individually quirky and has his own taste and preferences. An agent who's successful is by definition someone who's very selective about the authors and projects he chooses to represent. So most agents, including myself, wind up rejecting over 90 percent of the proposals we see. An agent builds up his credibility with publishers by carefully screening projects and only pitching viable books. If an agent loses his credibility, he loses access to publishers, which renders him ineffective as an agent," explains Herman.

When a self-published author approaches a respectable literary agent, Herman explains that in most situations, the agent and most publishers treat that book as a previously unpublished work, because most self-published books don't have bookstore distribution. "A self-published book is just like an unpublished book from my perspective as an agent. Major publishers are focused on selling books to the booksellers. So, if a self-published book has never been distributed through bookstores, even if it's sold a million copies, as far as the publisher is concerned, it's an unpublished book," says Herman.

A self-published author can benefit from using a literary agent in the same way as any other author. Herman says, "I look at what the self-published book can do moving forward. If the book has already sold 5,000 copies, I ask right away if it could potentially sell an additional 5,000 copies if a publisher comes on board or if the market for the book is already tapped out. The literary agent takes the self-published book and helps the author create a proposal package for potential publishers, and then the agent uses his connections to get the book seen by decision makers at the publishing companies. An agent can never guarantee that a book will be acquired by a publisher. An agent can guarantee that the book is seen by decision makers at major publishing companies."

For someone looking to work with a literary agent, Herman explains that the author should never have to pay a reading fee to the agent. "No reputable literary agent charges an author a fee to read a proposal or manuscript. An agent earns money by selling books to publishers and collecting commissions," he added. "Having a self-published book doesn't put you at a disadvantage when trying to sell a project to a publisher. You'd be surprised how many current bestsellers started out as self-published books. If as a self-published author you plan to continue to sell copies of your own book, be sure to negotiate for the ability to purchase copies of your book at a significant discount if you begin working with a publisher. This agreement allows you to continue earning a good margin on the books you sell yourself, but you can rely on the publisher to do what you couldn't do yourself, which is to get your book into the bookstores."

Even if a publisher rejects your book, you can still resubmit it six months (or more) later. Often, the publisher's focus changes, based on trends and how the publishing industry is doing. There's also a high rate of turnover among acquisitions editors and other decision makers at many publishing companies.

Tapping the International Market

Some books have sales potential not just in the United States but also in one or more countries throughout the world. Having your book sold overseas may require that it be translated into other languages. However, if the content of your book is of interest to readers in other countries, tapping the international market could become an extremely viable revenue stream. In the following sections, I give you an overview of licensing your book to foreign publishers and selling your self-published book directly overseas.

Licensing your book to foreign publishers

Many major publishing houses (as well as self-publishers) have found success in tapping the international market by contacting overseas publishers and offering them an exclusive licensing arrangement. In exchange for licensing fees (or an advance, plus royalties), the overseas publisher obtains the rights to publish, market, and distribute your book in the territories it does business in. The overseas publisher also incurs the cost of translating your book into other languages, if applicable. This method probably is the most cost-effective and easiest way to obtain international distribution for your book.

A literary agent helps you determine if your book has international appeal and then makes contact with overseas publishers and negotiates publishing and distribution deals on your behalf. See "Having a literary agent represent you" earlier in this chapter for more about finding an agent.

Directly selling your book overseas

Just as you've developed a distribution channel for your self-published book in the United States and kicked off marketing, advertising, and public relations campaigns for it (see Part V for details), you can do the same things in other countries. This process, however, requires a strong knowledge about how business in done in each country you want to directly sell your book in, and you need to develop local business contacts within those countries.

Another potential difficulty with selling your book directly to readers overseas is printing, shipping, and inventory. One option is to work with a Print-On-Demand (POD) publisher in each country or region where you believe there's a viable market for your book (see Chapter 11 for more about POD). You also can sell your book to international wholesalers and distributors (see Chapter 15 for general info on wholesalers and distributors).

Amazon.com, for example, has several subsidiaries in various countries:

- ✔ Canada (www.amazon.ca)
- ✔ The United Kingdom (www.amazon.co.uk)
- ✔ Germany (www.amazon.de)
- ✔ Japan (www.amazon.co.jp)
- ✔ France (www.amazon.fr)
- ✔ China (www.joyo.com)

After your book releases, you can list it with online booksellers in foreign markets. See Chapter 14 for more information about online booksellers.

Selling the Subsidiary or Serial Rights to Your Book

Subsidiary rights refers to licensing or selling permission for other companies to rework your book into various other types of products, such as videos, movies, or television shows. The term also refers to selling rights to an overseas publisher or book club interested in publishing its own version or edition of your book. (See the nearby sidebar "Join the club: Generating huge sales" for more about book clubs.)

Depending on the topic of your book, subsidiary sales and licensing can become extremely lucrative. Hollywood often pays hundreds of thousands or even millions of dollars for the movie or television series rights to a bestselling work of fiction or a true story. There's also money to be made selling instructional DVDs and videos based on successful how-to books. Licensing your book to an established audio book publisher also is a viable option for self-publishers. (Head to Chapter 22 for details on creating spin-off products from your book without selling your rights.)

Another viable revenue stream for self-publishers is through selling the *serial rights* to your book to magazines, newspapers, or other publications. This sale allows a publication to publish large portions of your book, including excerpts, serializations, and condensations (an abridged version of your book), in exchange for paying you a fee.

Join the club: Generating huge sales

Book clubs are mail order houses that allow members to sign up and purchase books at discounted rates. For example, a new member may be able to buy six books for the price of one but then be required to purchase two or three additional books at the book club's normal, but discounted, price sometime during the next one or two years. Members can purchase any number of books beyond their membership commitment at the club's discounted rates.

Book clubs aren't as popular as they once were, but if you can get a book club interested in recommending and selling your book, the interest almost always leads to impressive sales. You can find listings of book clubs and related contact information in directories, like *The Literary Market Place* (R.R. Bowker) and *Writer's Market*. The Book Club Offers' Web site

(www.book-club-offers.com) features an online comparison between the most popular book clubs in America.

In addition to general interest book clubs, there are also a range of special interest book clubs that cater to people with specific interests: mystery; romance; science fiction; home improvement; cooking; children's books; books with gay, lesbian, or transgender themes; pets; or travel.

In many cases, the book club either purchases a large quantity of books from you or negotiates for subsidiary rights to publish its own edition of your book. In addition to generating sales, working with a book club is a powerful marketing tool, because the book club promotes your book to all of its members and perspective members. If you're working with an agent, allow him to handle negotiations on your behalf.

When you sell the serial rights to your book *before* it's actually published and distributed in book form, this is referred to as selling the *first serial rights*. If you sell or license the rights to this material *after* your book has been published, it's referred to as selling the *second serial rights*. Many publications are willing to pay more for the first serial rights because these rights give them the ability to offer their readers an exclusive.

An experienced lawyer or a literary agent can best handle marketing, negotiating, and selling the subsidiary and/or serial rights to your work.

Part V
Creating a Buzz: Publicity and Marketing

The 5th Wave   By Rich Tennant

©RICHTENNANT

"Your new book, 'Help – My Head's Caught
in a Pipe,' has been called by some to be
semi–autobiographical. Can you comment
on these rumors?"

In this part . . .

Creating a buzz about your book can be done by creating and implementing highly effective and comprehensive public relations, marketing, and advertising campaigns, which can be accomplished on almost any budget. Getting your book reviewed in the media, having feature articles written about it, obtaining guest appearances on radio and television shows, and creating high-impact advertising all help you sell books. To reach your book's target audience, using the Internet is also a highly effective tool. You can even create products based on your book's content and topic to generate greater revenues. This part focuses on how to promote your book to the public to start selling copies!

Chapter 18

Crafting Publicity Materials for Your Book

*A*dvertising and publicity do have one important difference: the impact on your wallet. Advertising (covered in Chapter 20) can cost a pretty penny, but generating publicity can be much less expensive. Even if you hire a public relations (PR) firm, the cost is often less than advertising and can be much more effective in generating book sales. Your alternative is to act as your own publicist and begin making contacts within the media world yourself.

Generate hype for your book at least 60 days before it hits the stores or becomes available for sale. Create excitement by developing and launching a well-thought-out PR campaign. Although your goal may be to obtain a guest spot on *Oprah* and to sell a million books overnight, more realistically, to generate positive media attention for your soon-to-be published book, contact a wide range of media outlets such as local, regional, and national newspapers; magazines; Web sites; and television and radio shows.

This chapter helps you prepare the publicity tools you need to begin working with the media in a professional way. You discover how to supply reporters, journalists, editors, and producers with the information they need, in the format they want, within a time frame that works well to meet their deadlines. Check out Chapter 19 for details on how to handle yourself with the media.

Going Over the Basics of Press Materials

Your success in generating publicity for your book is directly impacted by the quality of the press materials you create. A well-written and informative press release may pique the interest of a journalist and result in positive articles and/or reviews. A poorly written press release may be ignored by the media and result in no publicity. The press materials you create are used as a tool when executing your pre-planned publicity campaign.

The PR campaign you develop needs to do the following:

✔ Generate positive reviews of your book in newspapers, in magazines, and on Web sites

✔ Convince specific media outlets to do a feature article or segment about you as the author of your new book (the campaign includes profiling you as an expert on the topic you wrote about in your book)

✔ Help you get invited to be as a guest on radio and television talk shows

✔ Assist you in booking author appearances and book signings (which I cover in Chapter 19)

In the following sections, I explain why creating press materials for your book, listing the elements found in a traditional press kit, and covering the importance of including a solid PR message in your materials are important.

Knowing why your book needs a press kit

A press kit is a tool that you create to educate the media about you and your book. The items within your press kit all work together to communicate information fast and efficiently. In a nutshell, your press kit helps you to do the following:

✔ **Generate positive attention:** You want to create a professional looking press kit, which is the easiest and least expensive way to tell large numbers of people about your book. This kit can gain the attention of the media. After you get attention, convince the media to feature your book in their editorial coverage.

Most reporters are extremely busy, so the squeaky wheel gets the grease. Reporters and the like receive dozens of press kits and story pitches each day from people looking for publicity.

✔ **Clearly define your message:** Avoiding ambiguity may send your story to the top of the pile. Pitch your book in a unique way that tells an engaging story that the media wants to share with the public.

✔ **Describe unique features of your book:** Your press kit describes what's interesting, newsworthy, or exciting about your book and positions you as an expert who can speak with authority on the topic of your book. For fiction writers, your message focuses on the plot of your book, relevance or timeliness it has to real world issues, and the target audience.

Surveying a press kit's elements

Every element in your press kit complements each other in terms of content. This process can easily be done by using the same paper color, paper stock, font, typestyle, ink color, and overall design or color scheme for all elements. The media wants and needs exact information for their stories, so if your information isn't presented properly within the press kit, it may be ignored! Traditionally, a press kit contains the following items:

✔ A two-pocket presentation folder

✔ A one- or two-page press release about your book

✔ An author bio

✔ A photo of the author

✔ A business card of the author (that's you)

✔ Photo copies of previous articles written about your book

✔ A review copy of the book or a postcard/faxback form a reporter can use to quickly request a review copy of your book

✔ Promotional items (see Chapter 20), such as a bookmark, that you've created to hype your book

Customizing your message

As you develop the PR campaign for your book, focus on customizing the message you're trying to communicate to the specific media outlets you target. Remember who your audience is and focus on the best way to reach them. After you've defined whom you're trying to reach, focus on the best ways to reach those people. The following sections cover some ways you can target specific media outlets.

Media categorized by geography and audience

Being the publicist for your own book requires you to write a customized marketing message and pitch it to specific media outlets. These outlets need to have an interest in covering your book. Professional publicists categorize media outlets in a variety of different ways.

- ✔ **Regional and national media:** Describes the geographic coverage a media outlet reaches
- ✔ **Consumer-oriented media:** Comprises newspapers, magazines, radio, TV, and Web sites that cater to mass-market consumers
- ✔ **Niche media:** Includes special interest media outlets that cater to small, but highly focused, audiences
- ✔ **Industry-oriented media:** Targets people working in a specific industry

As you create your message, consider specific story ideas that the various media outlets may use. The PR message you create should be something journalists want to share with their audience or readers. Your PR message should quickly explain to a journalist how and why your book appeals to the audience that the journalist reaches.

Your press kit needs to be customized for various types of media outlets:

- ✔ **Print media:** Focus on providing the tools needed, such as artwork of your book's cover, details about your book, and information (and a photo) about the author.
- ✔ **Radio or TV:** Instead of including artwork in your press kit, you may want to include sample interview questions within your press kit and a video of past appearances you've made on TV shows.

Always personalize and customize your pitch letter specifically to the journalist, reporter, editor, or producer you're sending it to.

Special tips for electronic media

Print media refers to any media outlet, such as a newsletter, newspaper, or magazine, that's distributed in printed form. Electronic media, on the other hand, refers to any media outlet, such as a television station, radio station, or Web site, that distributes content electronically.

When you're targeting electronic media outlets, you're typically pitching yourself to be a guest on a specific show. The producer needs to know that you're knowledgeable, well-spoken, clean-cut, professional, and media savvy enough to be an entertaining guest. The easiest way to prove your demeanor is to provide an electronic press kit (EPK). (EPKs are discussed later in this chapter.) In addition to the items included in the traditional press kit, an EPK contains either audio or video clips of you appearing on other radio or television programs. This footage allows the show's producers, booking agents, and hosts to determine whether you'd be a good guest on the show.

After several radio or television interviews and a handful of newspaper or magazine features, create a printed list of where you and your book have appeared and include this list within your press kit. An impressive list of past media coverage showcases your credibility with other media outlets.

Making a Great Impression with the Press Kit Folder

All the elements of a professional press kit are typically housed in a two-pocket presentation folder. Blank folders are available at office supply stores; however, to establish a true professional image, have your press kit folders professionally designed and printed. The custom design typically costs between $1 and $3 per folder, with a minimum order of 500 or 1,000 units. I cover design and cost issues to consider in the following sections.

By making the investment and having custom-printed press kit folders created, you establish a professional image for your self-published book, your publishing company, and for you as an author.

Design details

Almost any professional printer can work with you to design and print your press kit folders. The best option for your press kit folder is a standard-size folder, that nicely holds 8½-x-11-inch sheets of paper. On the front cover of the folder, you can have your book's cover displayed. On the inside pocket flaps, you can have your contact information and/or Web site address imprinted, or have slits cut into the pocket flap so you can insert your business card. Discuss these options with your printer. (See Chapter 10 for more details about working with a traditional printer.)

If you're the author of multiple books, create a more generic press kit folder for you as an author instead of each individual book title (this method is more cost effective). Imprint your name, photo, or images of multiple book covers on the front cover of your press kit folder. Don't just use your newest book cover. You can also use your publishing company's logo as artwork on the press kit's cover if you're promoting multiple book titles.

Cost considerations

Be sure to ask your printer for samples of other folders, so you get design ideas. Some decisions that impact folder printing costs include the following:

- ✔ Paper stock and color used
- ✔ Coating or laminate added to the folder
- ✔ Single, multiple, or full-color printing
- ✔ Timeline

Regarding timeline, how quickly you need the completed folders may also impact cost (most printers charge extra for rush service, too). And depending on the printer, delivery of the finished product can take anywhere from five to ten (or more) business days, so plan production accordingly.

You're likely to save money if you supply your printer with camera-ready artwork of the images to be printed on your folders. Provide these images in print or electronic form, but be sure to meet your printer's guidelines.

Check out these companies for printing options:

- ✔ **Folder Express:** A full-service printing company that offers fast turnaround and top-quality custom-printed folders at highly competitive prices (Phone [800] 322-1064; Web site www.folderexpress.com)
- ✔ **Getz Color Graphics:** A full-service publishing company that specializes in working with self-published authors to print press kit folders, full-color postcards and promotional bookmarks (Phone [800] 562-7052; Web site www.getzcolor.com)

Writing an Attention-Getting Press Release

The most important document within your press kit is the press release. This one or two page release, written in a very specific format, provides the needed facts, but in a concise way. A press release must answer the following questions: Who? What? Where? When? Why? How?

The press release also needs to convince the reporter or journalist that you're news is actually newsworthy. If the publication date of your book ties into a specific event or holiday, make that information clear within the release.

What you say in your press release and how you say it depend on the type of book you're publishing and the PR message you're trying to convey. Somewhere within your press release, include the following information:

- A catchy headline announcing the publication of your book
- A release date for the press release
- Your contact information (or the contact information of someone working with you)
- A dateline
- Title and author
- Cover price, publisher, and page count
- The target audience and why the book appeals to readers
- Specific content and what makes it unique
- One or two short quotes from the author
- One or two sentences about how and where the book can be purchased

In the following sections, I walk you through the parts of a press release and share some winning tips for crafting your own.

The anatomy of a press release

Before you start writing your press release, focus on the message you're trying to convey and determine exactly who you want to receive the message. Now, figure out how to convey the information about your book in a catchy, up-beat, and concise way, keeping the press release to one or two pages. (One page is the ideal length; most reporters are too busy to read long documents.)

Figure 18-1 is a sample press release for a self-published book. Use it as a guideline for the proper way to write and format your book's press release.

The headline

The headline is the first line of your press release. In one or two lines (use as few words as possible), come up with a catchy way — through puns, statistics, or statements about your book — to attract the reader's attention. Format the headline specifically:

- Centered at the very top of the release
- Boldface type
- 14- to 16-point font
- No more than two lines and fewer than ten words, if possible

Answers To Common Questions Often Asked By Single Guys Featured In...
The Bachelor's Guide To Life

Contact: Peter Simmons
(800) 555-5555
Email: jr7777@aol.com

FOR IMMEDIATE RELEASE

Boston, MA / February 9, 2005 — Bestselling author Jason R. Rich (www.JasonRich.com) is proud to announce the publication of his latest book, *The Bachelor's Guide To Life* ($18.95/iUniverse). This 228-page fun and informative book is jam-packed with answers to common questions that single guys often have.

"Included within this book are interviews with well-known experts who share information and advice with bachelors about how to achieve happiness and success in their lives," explained Rich, who has written more than 32 books covering a wide range of topics. "*The Bachelor's Guide To Life* is the perfect gift for guys headed off to college, recent graduates first establishing themselves in the real world, as well as recently divorced men."

Each chapter of *The Bachelor's Guide To Life* focuses on one aspect of a single guy's life, such as finding an awesome job, living on a budget, dressing like a fashion icon, spending your free time, traveling bachelor style, personal grooming, and dating. Have questions about doing laundry, what to do on a date to impress the girl, or what type of shaving cream to use? Single guys will easily and quickly find the answers they need within this book, which is now available from Amazon.com and BN.com or can be ordered from any bookstore.

About The Author

Figure 18-1:
A successful press release contains specific information about your book.

Jason R. Rich is the bestselling author of more than 32 books, including two self-published titles. He's also a frequent contributor to numerous newspapers and magazines and an award-winning radio and television producer. For more information, or to schedule an interview with Jason R. Rich, please call (800) 555-5555, visit his Web site at www.JasonRich.com, or send an e-mail to jr7777@aol.com. Review copies are available to the media on request.

# # #

The release date

Below the headline type the words *for immediate release.* Make sure that this phrase is formatted as follows:

- ✔ In all caps (FOR IMMEDIATE RELEASE)
- ✔ Left-justified on the page
- ✔ Boldface type
- ✔ 12-point font

Contact information

The contact information lists a person, phone number, and e-mail address and is listed under the headline (on the right side of the page), so journalists or reporters can reach you quickly. Use the same font and type size as the main body of the press release. Even if contact information is already on your company's letterhead, repeat it in the press release at the bottom of the page.

Ideally, the contact person shouldn't be the same person as the author. You quickly earn more credibility with journalists if you appear to have a publicist. If you haven't hired a publicist, consider listing your secretary, business partner, spouse, or someone else as the main contact person.

Format the contact information as follows:

- ✔ Placed under the headline
- ✔ Right-justified on the page
- ✔ 10-point font
- ✔ Non-boldfaced type

The dateline

Under *for immediate release,* skip one line and add a dateline. This line includes the issuing city and state, followed by the date of the release. For example: "Boston, MA — September 21, 2006". After the date, include a dash (—), followed by the first sentence of the press release's lead paragraph. For the dateline only, not the rest of the release's text, use a specific format:

- ✔ Boldface type
- ✔ 12-point font

The lead paragraph

In the first sentence or two, you must grab the reader's addition, while providing key information about the release of your book. This key info includes your book's title, author's name, topic, publisher, audience, cover price, page count, and other related details (like where the book is available). Generally, don't write more than one or two sentences. Here's an example:

> Bestselling author Jason R. Rich (`www.JasonRich.com`) is proud to announce the publication of his latest book, *The Bachelor's Guide to Life* ($18.95/iUniverse). This 228-page fun and informative book is jam-packed with answers to common questions that single guys often have.

Format the lead paragraph as such:

- ✔ Left and right justified on the page (blocked)
- ✔ Non-boldface type
- ✔ 12-point font

The body

The next one or two paragraphs of the press release provide details about the new book: what sets it apart, who it targets, and why people may be interested in it. If your first paragraph doesn't fully answer the *w* questions (see "Writing an Attention-Getting Press Release" for *w* questions), then this is the information you need to convey. Also be sure to include a few short quotes and information on how to order the book.

The information in the body contains all the information you want the general public to know about your book. Many journalists lift information from your release and place it verbatim within their articles and reviews, so format your text as follows:

- ✔ Left and right justified on the page (blocked)
- ✔ Non-boldface type
- ✔ 12-point font

Information about the author

This separate paragraph, titled *About The Author,* describes the author's credentials and establishes him as an expert in his field. The information can also include reasons why the author makes an interesting guest on a television or radio talk show. This paragraph can also list the author's Web site address.

The final sentence of this paragraph states, "For more information, or to schedule an interview with [insert author's name], please call [phone number], visit [Web site], or send an e-mail to [e-mail address]. Review copies are available to the media by request." The contact person's full name, title, company name, mailing address, phone number, fax number, e-mail address, and Web site can be displayed at the bottom, if room permits.

The *About The Author* section of the press release is formatted as a separate paragraph within the body of the press release. The text is formatted as such:

- ✔ Left and right justified on the page (blocked)
- ✔ Non-boldface type
- ✔ 12-point font

The ending

At the very end of the release, skip two or three lines and include the following: # # #. This indicates the end of the release and no additional text follows. Format this line of text as

- ✔ Non-boldface type
- ✔ 12-point font
- ✔ Centered on the page

If your release continues to a second page, display *More . . .* at the bottom-right corner of the first page and indicate at the top of the second page that the page is page two of the release. At the top center of the second page, display a phrase like *Page 2 of 2.*

Tips for putting together a press release

The goal of the press release is to convey your unique PR message to a journalist in a standardized format. Although you definitely want to communicate the relevant facts, it's okay to tap your creativity to make your releases stand out. Here are additional tips to help you format and create your press releases so that they receive the attention they deserve from the media:

- ✔ **Print a press release on 8½-x-11-inch white paper.** Use a standard one-inch top and bottom margin and 1¼-inch left and right margin. Stick with a common, easy-to-read font, such as Times New Roman, Helvetica, or Arial. Ideally, you want to double-space the main body of the release, but if necessary, use 1½ line spacing to ensure that the text fits on one or two pages.

✔ **Visit PR Newswire on the Web (www.PRNewswire.com).** This Web site is a press release distribution service. Read a handful of actual press releases issued by companies, study each release's formatting and content, and determine what elements of those releases can be used to help convey your own PR message (see "Customizing your message," earlier in this chapter, for details).

✔ **Hire a freelance writer or PR professional to assist you with the writing and formatting of your press release.** One excellent resource for finding skilled freelance writers is www.eLance.com. Services cost between $100 and $500.

Using Successful Strategies for Writing Your Author Bio

The press release is designed to announce the publication of your book and describe to journalists and reporters what the book is all about. The author bio, however, needs to focus on you, the author. Describe yourself and your professional experience, and position yourself as an expert in your field. Format the author bio by using the following specs:

✔ One, 8½-x-11-inch page

✔ Single or double-spacing

✔ 12-point font

The author bio is also an opportunity to showcase your personality, through the tone in which your bio is written. After reading your author bio, the media rep will hopefully want to meet, interview, and feature you in his coverage.

Although following a certain format for your press release is vital, your author bio can be a bit less structured, although visually, the bio needs to complement your press release and the overall design of your press kit. See an example of an author bio in Figure 18-2.

The heading

Place your full name at the top of your author bio formatted as follows:

✔ Centered on the page

✔ Boldface type

✔ 16- to 18-point font

Jason R. Rich
Bestselling Author and Journalist

Street Address
City, State, Zip
(###) ###-####
www.JasonRich.com

Jason R. Rich (www.JasonRich.com) is the bestselling author of more than 32 books. With 21 years of writing and journalism experience, he continues to contribute articles to major daily newspapers and national magazines, as well as work as a freelance marketing and public relations consultant for companies in a range of industries.

Since 1985, Jason Rich has done literally thousands of interviews with well-known celebrities from television, motion pictures, and the recording industry. He's also interviewed hundreds of professional athletes, entrepreneurs, and top-level business leaders for a wide range of media outlets. For two television seasons, while writing *American Idol Season 3: All-Access* and *American Idol Season 4: The Official Behind-The-Scenes Fan Book* (Prima/Random House), he had exclusive behind-the-scenes access of the hit television series *American Idol*. As the only journalist backstage every day, he followed each contestant's journey from the auditions to the season finale.

Some of Rich's other recently or soon-to-be-published books include *The Unofficial Guide to Starting A Business Online, 2nd Edition* (Wiley), *Pampering Your Pooch: Discover What Your Dog Wants Needs and Loves* (Howell), and *The Everything Family Travel Guide to Walt Disney World, Universal Studios, and Greater Orlando, 4th Edition* (Adams Media).

Jason Rich is a graduate of Bentley College and currently lives just outside of Boston, Massachusetts, with his Yorkshire Terrier, Rusty.

# # #

Figure 18-2: An author bio showcases your expert credentials.

Directly under your full name, type your title or main credential. For example, say, "Author, [Insert Book Title]" or "President and CEO of [Insert Company Name]". Format this information with boldface type and 14-point font.

Beneath your name and title, skip a line or two, and then add your contact information, including your mailing address, phone number(s), fax number, e-mail address, and Web site address. Format this section with non-boldface type and 10- or 12-point font.

Some authors and publicists incorporate a small, black-and-white photo of the author on the author bio page. This option isn't mandatory but a photo is a good idea because it helps readers see who they're reading about and helps them to better relate to that person. Research has proven that for radio and TV appearances, in particular, press kits that contain an author photo generate more requests for interviews. See "Putting Your Best Face Forward with a Publicity Photo," later in this chapter for more details.

If you incorporate a photo into the body of this document, make sure the photo looks professional and isn't blurry or pixilated. Photocopying the release dramatically detracts from the picture quality and looks amateurish. The alternative is to include a professionally taken publicity photo within your press kit (which is ideal).

The body

After the heading of your author bio is complete, create three or four, well-written paragraphs that describe you, your credentials, your background and your story. Be sure to include your PR message within this bio and use wording that helps to convey your personality. Relate who you are and what you do to the topic your book covers and focus on the relevance between the two. What makes you the ideal person to write the book? Why should the media outlet you're pitching interview you? Some of the topics you may want to address within your author bio include

- Your professional background
- Your educational background
- Information about your book
- Why you wrote your book
- How and why you became an expert in your field
- Interesting, newsworthy, or unusual info about yourself

✔ One or two sentences containing personal information about your family, hobbies, interests and/or where you live (for example: "John Doe is a graduate of Harvard University and currently lives in Boston, Massachusetts with his wife and two children. When not writing, he enjoys traveling, sailing, and breeding Yorkshire Terrier puppies")

Not all of the above information applies to every author. Keep the topic of your book and your target audience in mind. The order in which this information is revealed is also entirely up to you; however, the very first paragraph needs to grab the reader's attention and quickly summarize who you are and why you're an expert (and also mention your book).

For the body text of your author bio, make sure that the text looks visually pleasing on the page (not cluttered). Use a consistent format:

✔ Non-boldface type

✔ 12-point font

✔ Justified text (both left and right margin justification)

✔ 1½ or double line spacing

If you want a booking as a guest on a talk radio or television program, the author bio is your best tool. The bio can persuade producers, talent bookers, and hosts that you'd be an ideal guest for their show. If you're chosen as a guest, help formulate intelligent interview questions. At the end of the author bio, many authors and publicists include a list of between five and ten sample questions for the talk show host to ask you during an interview. By offering these questions, along with background information about you and your book, you'll be providing the information interviewers need, without making them do research or too much pre-interview preparation.

Putting Your Best Face Forward with a Publicity Photo

Another element of your press kit is a publicity photo of the author. Many publications run photos of a book's author in conjunction with reviews or articles, but require the author or publisher to supply the photo. In the following sections, I discuss the look and price of your photo.

Photo particulars

If you're creating a traditional printed press kit, include either a 5-x-7- or 8-x-10-inch publicity photo of yourself. Place your full name, title (such as "Author, [insert book title]"), and contact information (at least your phone number and e-mail address) at the bottom of the photo.

Listing your contact information multiple times throughout your packet ensures that people can reach you. Your publicity photo is no different.

Here are some suggestions for creating an attention-getting picture:

- ✔ **Have a professional photographer take your publicity photo.** If you work with any professional photographer, they'll know exactly what to shoot, if you specifically request that a publicity head shot be taken.

- ✔ **Have a tight headshot.** This shot is a close-up photo, taken of your upper chest and head. This shot shows more detail and what the author looks like more than a full-body shot, and the headshot is considered standard.

- ✔ **Shoot black-and-white photos.** Newspapers prefer black-and-white photos for their publications.

- ✔ **Make a full-color picture.** Have this variety available by request. Magazines tend to use color images for their stories.

- ✔ **Consider the tone.** The publicity conveys a message about your personality and the tone of the book itself. If you're promoting a funny or upbeat book, for instance, make sure that the publicity photo suggests your fun and cheerful personality.

Pricing pointers

Shooting a professional looking photo can be pricy, but if you know where to look, you may snatch up a good deal. Check out these places for a quality photo within a reasonable price range:

- ✔ Glamour Shots
- ✔ The Picture People
- ✔ Sears
- ✔ Target
- ✔ Wal-Mart

Portrait studios typically charge under $50 for a publicity photo, while department stores also have inexpensive portrait options ($30–50). Before you have your photograph taken, make sure you'll own the copyright to the photo so you can easily have it reproduced as needed, by any photo processing lab. Most labs don't duplicate photos if you don't own the copyright.

You can check the Yellow Pages for portrait photographers in your area, but these independent photographers often charge several hundred dollars for a photo shoot.

At the time you have your publicity photo taken, ask to receive one 8-x-10-inch print and a copy of the file saved in high-resolution, electronic format, either on a disk or CD. Save the file electronically in either a TIF or JPG format. This format allows you to distribute your publicity photo electronically — via e-mail — on a CD, or via your Web site. If the photographer doesn't provide the photo in an electronic format, take the 8-x-10-inch print to any photo lab where it can be scanned into a computer and saved on a disk or CD for a small fee.

Photo labs can also reproduce your photo for a small fee. Depending on the quantity of publicity photos you need, have your photographer or a professional photo lab reproduce the photo for you. Plan on spending between $1 and $5 per 8-x-10-inch, black-and-white print if you have the photo reproduced at a photo lab.

An alternative to 8-x-10-inch prints is to use 5-x-7-inch prints. This option is slightly cheaper and just as easily reproduced. Only supply color photos if they're in a digital format and can be easily edited (into black and white) by the publication's photo editor, if appropriate.

A quality photo lab is different from those one-hour photo places in supermarkets, drugstores, and mass-market retailers. Check your local Yellow Pages for photo processing labs in your area. You can also seek a referral from a professional photographer.

An alternative to the photo lab, especially if you need several hundred copies of your publicity photo, is submit your master print to a national company like ABC Pictures (Phone [888] 526-5336; Web site www.abcpictures.com). This company specializes in reproducing more cost-effective publicity photos for authors and actors by using a lithograph printing process. For $90 (plus shipping), the company offers 500 8-x-10-inch, black-and-white photos, complete with typesetting at the bottom. Just supply one master photo in print or electronic form. ABC Pictures also creates full-color publicity photos by using the lithograph printing process for less cost than a traditional photo lab.

After you have your photo taken, allow a week to duplicate your publicity photos. Ideally, you want to have your press kit folders, publicity photos, and the printed materials within your press kit all completed around the same time, so you can begin distributing the completed press kits to the media and generate publicity for your book in a timely manner. I cover the distribution of press materials later in this chapter.

Writing a Knockout Pitch Letter

A pitch letter accompanies a press kit; it introduces you and briefly states why you're sending the press kit and what it contains. In other words, pitch your story in a way that perfectly addresses an audience interest as it relates to you and your book.

Personalize the pitch letter to a specific person. As you write the letter, make sure that it addresses the needs of the person you're sending it to and that the information you're sending is normally covered. For example, if your book is about sports, don't send your press kit and letter to the lifestyle editor or even the managing editor of a newspaper. Address your packet directly to the sports editor. See "Starting a target press list," later in this chapter, for more.

Write your pitch letter in a traditional business letter style and keep the length under one page. Here's what the format should include:

- **First paragraph:** Introduce your book.

- **Second paragraph:** Talk about why you're an expert in your field.

- **Third paragraph:** Showcase exactly why the recipient's audience is interested in your book and what you have to say. If you're pitching yourself as a guest on a radio talk show, describe some of the reasons why you'd make an entertaining and informative guest.

- **Final paragraph:** Invite the reporter, journalist, editor, or producer to review the enclosed press kit, request a review copy of your book, and contact you if they're interested in booking an interview or receiving more information. If you're e-mailing your initial pitch letter, you may also want to add a sentence inviting the pitch letter's recipient to visit your Web site to obtain more information. See Figure 18-3 for a template that you can use to create a pitch letter.

If you have a publicist, have him or her sign the pitch letter on your behalf.

[Company or Personal Letterhead]

[Date]

[Recipient's name]
[Title]
[Media outlet]
[Address]
[City, state, zip]

Dear *[Mr./Mrs./Ms.]*,

I am pleased to enclose information about an exciting, newly published book that's targeted to *[brief description of the book's target audience]* titled *[book title]*. *[Publishing company]* is publishing this title on *[publication date]*. Priced at $*[price]*, *[book title]* will be available starting *[publication date]* through Amazon.com, BN.com, and bookstores nationwide. As you'll see, this *[number of pages]*-page book's fun and timely approach to *[topic]* will definitely be of interest to your demanding audience *[readers, listeners, or viewers, as appropriate]*.

[Book title] was written by *[author's name]*, a leading expert in *[his/her]* field, with *[number]* years of experience. *[He's/She's]* currently a *[job title]* with *[employer]*. In this book, *[he/she]* shares *[his/her]* unique perspective and advice, plus offers detailed and easy-to-understand strategies relating to *[topic]*.

[Author's name] is also currently available for interviews. *[Reasons why author is an excellent person to interview for media outlet's audience]*

Review copies are now available on request. If you have any questions about the enclosed information, wish to receive a review copy, or would like to set up an interview, please call me at *[phone number]* or e-mail your request to *[e-mail address]*. I also invite you to visit the book's Web site at *[Web site URL]*.

Thank you in advance for your interest.

Respectfully,

[Author's name]

Figure 18-3:
Keep your pitch letter short and specific with this template.

Creating an Electronic Press Kit

An *electronic press kit* (EPK) showcases you in audio or video form and allows a media outlet to see exactly who you are, what you look like, and how well you speak before you're booked on a show. An EPK can be an audio CD, VHS tape, or DVD that contains a sample interview with you, information about your book, and/or clips from past radio and TV interviews you've done. If you're looking to get booked as a guest on TV and radio shows, seriously consider producing an EPK to compliment your traditional printed press kit.

Realistically, you probably don't need an EPK right away as you kick off your book's PR campaign. Wait until you have several really good local or regional radio or TV interviews under your belt, and then include a few on your EPK before pitching to national radio or TV shows. (A really good interview portrays you and your book in the best possible way, highlights your PR message, and is something you're proud to show people as a sampling of your work and the publicity you've received.)

Ideally, your EPK should contain a short video or audio-only interview with you and several clips from radio or TV interviews. Keep the length of your EPK under five minutes. The goal of this compilation is to showcase you as a well-spoken, media-savvy individual who is a great guest on radio or TV shows. Also post clips from radio and TV interviews on your Web site.

For help filming, recording, editing, or producing an EPK, contact any local video or audio production company in your area. You can find listings for these companies online or in the Yellow Pages. You have to pay the production costs associated with producing the EPK, which can cost anywhere from several hundred to several thousand dollars, depending on its complexity, length and what's involved in the actual filming.

To save money, some authors incorporate audio or video clips of past interviews on their Web sites, as opposed to having a separate audio CD or DVD produced and duplicated. Make sure to reference the Web site (and a specific link) in the press kit so producers and such can look up your clips online. See Chapter 21 for more innovative ways to use your Web site.

Distributing Your Press Materials to the Media

After you've gathered all of the elements for your press kit, the next step involves distributing your press kit and making contact with the media.

In the following sections, you discover how to begin finding and targeting members of the press. You also find out how important keeping a budget is, especially when distributing all your costly materials, and how to keep media lead times in mind as you send off materials.

Starting a targeted press list

The first step in kicking off any PR campaign is to carefully target the media and develop your own press list. Follow these steps:

1. **Sit down with a pad and pen.**

   Write down all the print media outlets you want to pitch your book to.

2. **Visit a large newsstand to see firsthand all the newspapers and magazines out there.**

   Don't forget to target special interest, niche and industry-oriented newspapers and magazines, if they're appropriate. (See "Media categorized by geography and audience," earlier in this chapter.)

3. **Create a separate list of TV and radio outlets you'd like to appear on as a guest or expert.**

   These outlets can include news programs where you're interviewed as an expert on a newsworthy topic that somehow relates to your book.

 Are you only looking for local or regional media attention, or do you think that your book may appeal to readers throughout the United States and perhaps other countries? As you consider these questions, be realistic. Sure, you may want to be a guest on *The Today Show*, but is the topic of your book truly of interest to the viewers? To generate the best results from your PR efforts, carefully target the media outlets and approach only appropriate channels, based on the target audience of your book.

After you gather your list of media outlets you want to target, track down the specific journalist, reporter, editor, producer, or talent booker who works for each media outlet and who is responsible for covering the topic you're pitching. For example:

- ✔ If you're looking to obtain book reviews from newspapers, target the book reviews editor.

- ✔ If you've written an autobiography or a book that has a strong human interest element, contact the features editor of newspapers.

Contacting the wrong reporter, journalist, editor, talent booker, or producer not only wastes your time and money, but also wastes the time of the media professionals you contact. The wrong person has no interest in what you're pitching. Don't rely on one person within a media organization to pass along your book and press materials to the appropriate person. You need to research and track down the right person yourself.

Follow these tips for tracking down the right person to hand off your materials to:

- ✔ Contact the main switchboard or receptionist at each media outlet.

- ✔ Purchase an up-to-date media directory (see the next section).

- ✔ When you contact electronic media, such as radio or television shows, pinpoint exact shows that you're interested in being a guest on. Call the production office for that show and ask for the name of a segment producer or talent booker who is responsible for booking guests.

    Don't try to pitch your idea directly to the executive producer or host. At smaller shows, especially at local radio or TV stations, you may discover that the person responsible for booking guests is the show's executive producer or even the host. Unless you know that this information is true, first contact a segment producer or talent booker at a show.

- ✔ Pitch your story through e-mail. One of the most convenient (and least expensive) ways to pitch a story idea to a media outlet is via e-mail. Based on the response you receive from your initial e-mail pitch, you can then send a complete printed press kit and a review copy of your book. You can also direct the media professional to visit your Web site (where your press materials are listed) for more information about the book and you as an author/expert.

Using media directories

A handful of directories, publications, and online databases used by professional publicists contain detailed contact information for every reporter, journalist, editor, and producer at every newspaper, magazine, radio station, and television station. These directories are a starting point for developing your media list.

Before investing in any media directory, determine whether the information is what you need, based on the type of media and specific contact you're looking for. Also, determine how often the directories are updated and verified for accuracy. Any information that's more than six months old contains outdated listings.

Using one or more directory, along with your own research, enables you to develop a comprehensive media list to target places to send your press kit and PR message. Some of the more popular media directories include:

- **Bacon's:** This company offers complete, up-to-date media directories for all forms of print and electronic media. Bacon's also offers a press release distribution service. Contact (866) 639-5087 or www.bacons.com.

- **Book Marketing Update:** For self-publishers, this biweekly newsletter is the ideal PR tool and a must read. In addition to offering informative articles, each issue offers a listing of newspapers, magazines, radio shows, TV shows, and Web sites currently looking to interview authors. Back issues are also available in electronic form. Find out more info at www.bookmarketingupdate.com or by calling (610) 259-0707 ext. 119.

- **Bulldog Reporter's Media List Builder:** This online service helps create a targeted media list based on your unique needs. The company's media database is extensive and kept up-to-date. Visit Bulldog online at listbuilder.bulldogreporter.com.

- **BurrellesLuce:** BurrellesLuce offers a wide range of PR services, ranging from media directories and press release distribution services to comprehensive press clipping services (to help you track the success of your PR campaign). Pick up the phone and dial (800) 631-1160 or hop online at www.burrellesluce.com.

- **Harrison's Guide to the Top National TV Talk & Interview Shows:** This directory includes over 200 major national cable and television shows that interview guests. In addition to contact names, phone numbers, addresses, and e-mails, this directory gives detailed comments on many shows including:

  - Exactly what type of guests these shows do and don't want

  - Who to contact if you want to be a guest

  - How the shows want to be approached

  For more info check out these sources: Phone (800) 553-8002 ext. 408; Web site www.rtir.com/products.htm.

- **PR Newswire:** This company offers a wide range of services to help companies and PR professionals create, execute, and manage a PR campaign. Call (800) 776-8090 or visit www.prnewswire.com.

- **Radio & TV Interview Report:** If you're interested in being a guest on radio and television shows, this newsletter is distributed to producers and talent bookers at all of the major radio and TV stations nationwide. Advertising your book in this publication helps radio and TV stations find you. Check out the newsletter online at www.rtir.com or call (800) 553-8002 ext. 408.

✔ **SourceNet:** This online service helps PR professionals (and authors looking for media attention) contact the media by using a variety of different databases, directories, and services. Surf the Web at www.MediaMap.com.

✔ **SRDS Media Solutions:** This company publishes a series of directories covering various aspects of the media: newspapers, magazines, radio stations, and TV stations. The directories are updated regularly and contain specific contact names for reporters, journalists, editors, producers, and talent bookers. Phone (800) 851-7737; Web site www.srds.com.

✔ **The Radio Mall:** This company offers a complete directory of every radio station in America, categorized by format. For example, you can purchase a list of news directors or show producers at every talk radio station in a specific region, state, or throughout the entire country. Phone (800) 759-4561; Web site www.radiomall.com.

Keeping your budget in mind

Launching a comprehensive PR campaign can become costly. Take a look at the following list of items when considering your budget:

✔ **Creating a professional looking press kit:** $2 to $5 or more per kit.

✔ **Copies of your book with each press kit:** Costs vary.

✔ **Postage and shipping costs:** Costs vary.

Ideally, to get attention from the recipient who receives dozens of press kits daily, send your press kit via U.S. Priority Mail or by using one of the popular overnight carriers (FedEx, UPS, or DHL).

✔ **Phone calls to media professionals:** Costs vary.

Simply sending out a mass-mailing of press materials to media outlets you've never contacted works to some extent, but this approach is more costly than targeting specific media outlets, making introductory phone calls, and then sending out your materials after they're requested.

Follow these money saving tips when sending out your packets:

✔ **Only send out your press release in printed or e-mail form.** Instruct the recipients to request a full press kit and a review copy of your book. This process ensures that you only send complete press kits and books to people who're interested. The downside to this is that you only have your one-page press release to sell your PR pitch to the journalist as opposed to all the content within your press kit and actual book.

✔ **Make preliminary phone calls to each media outlet to determine interest and then send out press kits only to those people who specifically request the information.** Don't harass people working in the media with a constant influx of phone calls, e-mails, or faxes. Media folks work under tight deadlines and have little time for long pitches.

✔ **Target only a handful of media outlets at first and slowly build up and expand your PR efforts.** Consider limiting your approach to 50 major newspapers and magazines to include a review of your book in their Book Reviews section, and 50 talk radio shows you want to be a guest on.

For general information on keeping costs under control, check out Chapter 6.

Paying attention to media lead times

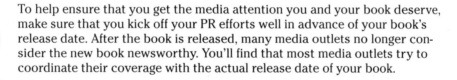

All media outlets work with a lead time, which is the time between when the print article is actually written and when it appears on the newsstand. Some magazines preplan future issues four to six months in advance. Some TV shows book guests a month in advance. Even after a media outlet expresses an interest in reviewing your book, an appearance of your review can take up to three months or longer, so be patient.

Plan your PR efforts based around each media outlet's lead time. If you know that a lead time for a magazine is three months, begin contacting the appropriate writer or editor of that magazine four or five months before the publication of your book.

To help ensure that you get the media attention you and your book deserve, make sure that you kick off your PR efforts well in advance of your book's release date. After the book is released, many media outlets no longer consider the new book newsworthy. You'll find that most media outlets try to coordinate their coverage with the actual release date of your book.

Here are general guidelines for lead times to expect from each type of outlet:

✔ **Newspapers**

- **Major Daily & Local:** These publications have a lead time of between a few hours (same day) and up to two weeks, depending on the section of the newspaper and the topic.
- **Weekly:** Most weekly newspapers have a two to four week lead time.

✔ **Magazines**

- **Weekly:** Plan on at least a two to four week lead time for weekly magazines, unless the topic is extremely timely and newsworthy.

- **Monthly:** The average lead time of a monthly regional or national magazine is about three months.

- **Quarterly:** Because these magazines are only published four times per year, their lead times can be four to six months.

✔ **Radio Shows:** Most radio shows book guests between one day and several weeks in advance, depending on the timeliness of the topic. When approaching radio shows to be a guest, make your availability clear — you can fill in on a last-minute basis or if another guest cancels with little or no notice.

✔ **Television Shows:** Depending on the type of TV show, guests are booked anywhere from a few hours to several weeks prior to airtime. News programs, like the local evening news, may book guests a few hours before the broadcast, while a national talk show may book several weeks in advance, unless a topic is extremely newsworthy or timely.

✔ **Web sites:** Information changes in cyberspace almost instantly. A Web site operator can potentially post information about your book within minutes after receiving your press kit.

Chapter 19

Publicizing Your Book for Free with the Media's Help

. . . .

In This Chapter

▶ Speaking with the media

▶ Putting on a polished appearance

▶ Pursuing book reviews

▶ Setting up author appearances and book signings

▶ Working with a professional publicist or PR firm

. . . .

*A*re you convinced you've written what could become a bestseller? Do you want to see yourself on television, make radio appearances, and have the opportunity to read reviews of your book in your favorite newspapers, magazines, and Web sites? If so, focus on generating free publicity by soliciting the help of the media.

Public relations (PR) is all about utilizing the media — newspapers, magazines, radio stations, TV stations, and Web sites — to generate reviews, articles, feature stories, and interviews about you and your book. As opposed to paid advertising (which I cover in Chapter 20), when a media outlet writes an article about your book, or when you appear as a guest on a TV or radio show, you don't have to pay the media outlet for the coverage. It's free, and it's an extremely powerful tool for reaching potential readers at all levels. People are more apt to purchase your book after spending several minutes reading about you and your book or listening to an interview with you than they are to respond to a paid ad, which they spend just a few seconds at best glancing over.

In Chapter 18, you discover how to create and distribute a professional press kit to help promote your book. But *this* chapter puts the fruits of your labor to work as you promote the publication of your new book. You find out how to speak to (and look good in front of) the media, generate book reviews, and set up special appearances like book signings.

Ideally, if you've never done any type of PR work, you should seriously consider hiring a professional publicist or PR firm to help you develop and launch a comprehensive PR campaign for your book. In this chapter, you discover how to hire a publicist and why this person can be extremely beneficial, assuming you have the budget.

Talk It Up: Saying the Right Thing to the Media

By using your press kit, begin contacting key media outlets and pitching your story (see Chapter 18 for full details about how to do this). Assuming that you do everything correctly, chances are, you start booking interviews with newspapers and magazines, and you may even get invited to be a guest on radio and television shows. Now that you have the opportunity to generate publicity for yourself and your book, make the most of it.

During an interview, make sure to

- ✔ Talk about your book and yourself.

- ✔ Establish yourself as an expert.

- ✔ Convince viewers that your book offers something interesting, informative, entertaining, and/or newsworthy.

- ✔ Note that your book is worth purchasing and reading.

What you say during an interview and how you say it are critical for achieving your objective. Your goal is to ensure that no matter what questions you're asked during an interview that you communicate your PR message accurately, effectively, and hopefully repeatedly.

In the following sections, I explain how to anticipate and prepare for basic questions, stay focused on the message you want to convey about your book, and sprinkle your book's title into your interview. I also give you tips on how to avoid a few common interview blunders.

Here are a couple of things to watch out for before you do any interview:

- ✔ **Avoid being misquoted or taken out of context.** Do interviews in person or over the telephone. Some journalists like to rely on e-mail interviews, in which they send a list of questions and ask you to e-mail back your responses. Try to avoid this type of interview, if possible. It's much easier to gauge what to say to a specific journalist if you're speaking with him or her in person or over the phone.

> ✔ **Make sure that prior to an interview, particularly a TV appearance, you get plenty of sleep.** You want to look well rested. Never drink too much coffee or any alcohol before an interview, either to wake you up or calm you down. Too much caffeine can cause you to shake and look nervous, and alcohol of any kind can impede your ability to think clearly, especially if you're nervous.

Anticipating and preparing for basic questions

After you start doing a bunch of interviews, you're going to notice that whether the interview is for television, radio, or print, the same basic questions keep popping up. Use this to you advantage because you can figure out the very best way to answer each of those questions.

To prepare for interview questions, follow these three steps:

1. **Create a list of 10 to 20 sample questions you anticipate being asked.**
2. **Develop short sound bites that answer each question.**
3. **Practice answering each question by using your sound bite so that your response comes off as natural, engaging, positive, and informative.**

I cover each of these steps in the following sections.

Listing sample questions

The questions during your interviews may vary greatly, but most media folks start off by asking basic questions about you and your book. These questions are easy to anticipate because they typically involve answering who, what, when, where, why, and how.

Here are a few sample interview questions:

> ✔ Tell me about your book. What's it about?
>
> ✔ What inspired you to write your book?
>
> ✔ What initially got you interested in this topic?
>
> ✔ Who would be interested in reading your book?
>
> ✔ When is your book being released, and how can someone obtain a copy?
>
> ✔ What was the most interesting or unusual thing you learned when researching your book?
>
> ✔ How much research went into the writing of your book? What type of research did you do?

✔ What sets your book apart from others?

✔ What are three things someone can learn from reading your book?

As you answer these and other questions, provide information directly from your book as a preview of what readers can expect. This answer helps demonstrate that the content of your book is valuable, relevant, and interesting. Obviously, if you've written a novel or work of fiction, never reveal the ending!

Another easy way to anticipate questions you may be asked: Provide the questions! In Chapter 18, I note that as part of your author bio, you may consider including five or ten sample questions an interviewer can ask you. Don't be surprised if you hear some of those questions come back to you!

Developing sound bites

Most television and radio interviews last only three to five minutes. You need to convey a lot of information, without speaking too quickly. The best way to do this is to speak in what the media industry calls *sound bites.* For every question, provide a comprehensive answer that lasts between 5 and 15 seconds (that's fewer than 50 words).

By anticipating what questions you may be asked (see the previous section) and knowing your subject matter well, you can write answers out ahead of time that communicate the necessary information but that are very concise.

Answering a question in a sound bite means using as few words as possible. In other words, don't babble or ramble on. Answer the question, get your key point across, and wait for the next question. Don't go off on tangents.

Discovering how to speak in sound bites ensures that you can answer the maximum number of interview questions in the time allotted, giving you greater opportunity to promote yourself and your book. Also, when you're participating in pre-taped interviews, speaking in sound bites makes editing an interview easier, and you don't have to cut your answers short or worry about your information being taken out of context.

Practicing your answers

After you create a list of potential questions, think up one or two key points you want to convey as part of each answer. Next, grab a stopwatch and practice answering each question in less than 15 seconds (without simply responding yes or no). It's a good idea to record your responses so you can play them back and hear firsthand how you sound. This method allows you to critique how you responded. Do you sound intelligent, like an expert on the topic? Is your answer informative? By the time you actually start participating in interviews, you should be able to recite answers to common questions flawlessly.

Here are a few additional tips for polishing your answers:

- ✔ **Convey a sense of authority when you speak.** Use complete sentences, using proper grammar. Avoid using slang or words like *umm* or *yeah*. Answer questions confidently and use humor when appropriate.

- ✔ **Repeat the question you were just asked by the reporter and then provide your answer in the form of a sound bite.** For example, if you're asked, "So, what made you write your book?," your response might be, "What inspired me to write my book was . . . " Or, if you're asked, "What's your book about?," your response might be, "[Insert book title] is about . . ."

- ✔ **Answer questions like it's the first time you've been asked.** Even if you're asked the same question 1,000 times, never respond to a reporter by saying something like, "I get asked that question constantly," "People always ask me that," or "You already asked me that." When you respond to any question, even if it's one you've answered many times before, you need to come across to the interviewer and your audience as if it's the first time you've ever been asked that question. Take a second to think about your response (even though you know exactly what it is), and make the interviewer think he's just asked you the most original and intelligent question you've ever been asked. Then, respond with enthusiasm. Also, make sure that your answers don't alienate your audience. For example, offering a strong opinion on a controversial topic or making any kind of insulting or racist comment can easily alienate the audience.

- ✔ **Be prepared to answer uninformed questions.** Often, when someone interviews you, he probably hasn't read your book. He also knows little or nothing about the book's topic. If you're asked what you believe is a stupid question, play along and don't make the interviewer look stupid, but make sure you get your marketing message across to the audience.

Focusing on your PR message

Participating in interviews is fun; however, it's important to focus on the reason why you're doing the interview — to promote your book.

No matter what questions you're asked, it's up to you to ensure that you convey your PR message at least twice or three times during the interview, even if that interview lasts only one to three minutes. Your PR message essentially describes your book and tells people why they should read it. Your PR message can be a one- or two-sentence summary of the unique content your book offers or how the reader will benefit from reading it. (See Chapter 18 for more details on creating a PR message.)

No matter what questions you're asked during your interview, be sure to work in comments like "Well, within my book, I explain . . ." or "As you'll read in Chapter 2 of my book . . ." Even though you're being interviewed as an expert on a topic and you're expected to provide information, your goal in doing the interview is to sell books. Strike a balance between giving away lots of free information during an interview and enticing people to read your book to obtain the information.

Mentioning your book title multiple times

During an interview, you ideally want to mention the title of your book at least three times and mention where the book is available at least twice. This may include promoting your book's Web site address (see Chapter 21 for more about creating a site for your book) or saying that the book is currently available through online booksellers like Amazon.com or Barnes & Noble.com (see Chapter 14 for more about these channels). Typically, when talk show hosts are introducing you, they mention your name and your book title at least once. It's up to you, however, to make sure that you work it into the conversation additional times without being annoying about it.

One easy way to mention your book's title is simply to begin your answers with it. Try out the following examples:

- ✔ "In my book, [insert title], I wrote about . . ."

- ✔ "That's a great question. In chapter [#] of my book [insert title], I discussed that exact topic . . ."

- ✔ "To answer that question, I'd like to tell you a story that I included within my book, [insert title] . . ."

Avoiding common interview mistakes

Your goal during any interview is to promote your book and to come across as an intelligent and well-spoken expert on a topic. You also want to be respected and liked by both the interviewer and the audience or reader. To ensure that you get the best possible response from your interviews, avoid making these common mistakes:

- ✔ **Allowing the interviewer to provoke you into discussing a controversial topic and make you angry or overly emotional about it:** Especially if you're a guest on a morning radio show hosted by "shock jocks," you may come across someone who believes it's entertaining to anger guests or try to confuse them with inappropriate questions. This is showbiz. Your best bet is to go along with the antics, but stay focused on getting your message out to the public. Promote your book, but try to have fun. You always have the option of not answering a question or changing the topic during an interview. Don't get agitated or lash out at the interviewer.

✔ **Coming across as too nervous, unprepared, offensive, or confrontational:** The best way to avoid this is to prepare and rehearse (see "Anticipating and preparing for basic questions," earlier in this chapter). Take deep breaths and speak normally.

✔ **Cutting off the interviewer in mid-sentence as she asks a question, because you're able to anticipate what's about to be asked:** You may be asked the same questions over and over again. Even if you've heard that same question a hundred times, it's the first time that particular interviewer has asked it and the first time that audience will be hearing it. Allow the interviewer to finish, and then respond. Otherwise, you come off as arrogant.

✔ **Mumbling your responses to questions or not speaking with proper grammar and in full sentences:** Never respond to a question by nodding your head or with a one-word answer. Responding "yes" or "no" to a question isn't adequate. Speak with authority and share the knowledge you possess.

✔ **Overly promoting your book, without providing the reader or listener with information about the topic being discussed:** While you want to work in mentions of your book at least two or three times during an interview (see the previous section), you also want to convey information about the topic being discussed. Don't keep replying, "You have to read my book for the answer to that question." You're better off answering the interviewer's question but adding a phrase like, "I go into a lot more detail on that topic within my book."

✔ **Speaking too quickly when answering questions:** Pace yourself and breathe.

✔ **Taking too long to respond to questions or babbling too much about nothing:** Make sure you make proper use of your sound bites as you answer each and every question.

✔ **Telling the interviewer that the question is stupid:** Never insult the interviewer or make him feel inferior. Even if a question is stupid, act as if it's a brilliant question and you're excited to answer it. Remember, you're an expert on a topic. The interviewer may know nothing about the topic, but he's giving you a chance to promote yourself and your book. Use this opportunity to your advantage.

No matter what type of interview you're participating in, make sure that you're introduced or credited appropriately. Develop a one-sentence introduction that the media can use to introduce you. This credit should focus on you as the author of your book and establish your credentials as an expert in your field.

Publicity boot camp: Considering professional media training

If you're doing a lot of interviews, one of the best ways to quickly become media savvy is to undergo intensive media training. Although you can read about how to develop the skills you need, you benefit much more from working with a media training expert. This training involves one-on-one sessions with a skilled PR professional or experienced broadcaster who teaches you everything you need to know about how to be interviewed, how to interact with the media, and how to fine-tune your PR message. Most media training sessions last one or two full days.

To find media training opportunities in your area, search the Internet under *media training* or check your local Yellow Pages under PR firms.

Dress It Up: Looking Good When You Promote Your Book

You're being invited to discuss your book because you've written about a topic of interest to a particular audience. Now, in addition to sounding like an expert, you need to look like one. How you look adds or detracts from your credibility. The following sections focus on what to wear and how to control your body language.

Dressing your best

When you participate in interviews, you want to look your best. Even when interviewing on the radio when people don't see you, looking professional helps boost your credibility and your confidence. (If you're participating in radio interviews by phone from home, you can relax in your pajamas during the interview, and the following sections may not apply to you.)

The following sections contain guidelines to help you perfect your appearance for any event. Here are a couple of quick tips to help you look your best:

- ✓ **Watch the TV program you're going to appear on for several days prior to your appearance.** Pay careful attention to what the hosts and other guests are wearing and dress accordingly.

- ✓ **Don't wait until the last minute to get ready for an interview.** Try out your complete outfit (accessories and hairstyle included) the day before the interview. On the day of the interview, get ready several hours early in case you need to make last-minute adjustments.

Your outfit

Feeling stumped about what to wear? Try the following tips:

- ✔ Choose a stylish outfit, keeping in mind the image you're trying to convey. For example, dress more formally for a business or news-oriented show and casually for an upbeat morning show. Overall, try to dress along the same lines as the host(s).

- ✔ Make sure that everything fits you perfectly and is wrinkle-free and looks good on *you* — *not* just the mannequin in the store.

- ✔ Pay attention to colors and patterns. Never wear busy patterns or solid white on television.

Your objective is to look good, not to make a fashion statement like those celebrities waltzing down the red carpet at an awards show. If necessary, think about what Joan Rivers would say about your outfit if she were to see you on TV and rate your outfit like she does with celebrities. Would you make her best or worst dressed list?

If you're having trouble deciding on an outfit, read a few current issues of fashion magazines and visit a store that offers a personal shopping service to help you choose what you wear. You can also hire a personal stylist to go shopping with you, if it's absolutely necessary. But keep your budget in mind! You can also find good advice from friends and coworkers.

Your accessories

When putting yourself together as a complete package, you may want to consider extra accessories like shoes, hats, scarves, jewelry, and so on. Here are a few things to consider when dressing up an outfit:

- ✔ **Shoes:** Shine your shoes and coordinate them with your outfit and accessories, especially your belt. Don't wear shoes that hurt your feet or that you have trouble walking in just because they look good. Unless you're doing a comedy routine, you don't want to trip on live television.

- ✔ **Add-ons:** The accessories you wear should all complement your outfit and not be distracting. Make sure to wear things that are tasteful and not overbearing from a visual standpoint. Examples include

  - • **Hats:** Refrain from wearing a hat. Hats hide your eyes and interact funky with stage lights if you're on TV.

  - • **Glasses:** Wear them for vision purposes only, not because you think that you look ultra cool. If you wear prescription glasses, either invest in antiglare lenses or wear contact lenses. Regular lenses reflect TV studio lights, which can make you look bad.

  - • **Jewelry:** Choose items such as bracelets, necklaces, earrings, cuff links, or tie tacks that are subtle and complement your outfit. Jewelry that's too sparkly or shiny can be distracting.

Your personal grooming, hairstyle, and makeup

First impressions are important. Shower before your interview and apply any necessary products to control oiliness or dryness on your face and neck. Don't wear heavy perfumes or colognes that may knock out the person next to you. Also, have clean fingernails and be clean shaven.

If you have a hairstylist, make sure that he's consistent with the image you're trying to convey. Some TV shows have a hairstylist on staff who offers to style your hair right before your appearance. This is good in a pinch; however, you should rely on your own stylist to work on your hair prior to the interview. But most people won't have a personal stylist, so plan on arriving to the studio ready to go.

As for makeup (particularly on TV appearances):

- ✔ For men, allow the show's makeup artist to apply the necessary makeup to your face and neck. This application hides blemishes and makes your face look fresh. Don't worry; the makeup won't be noticeable on camera, so your masculinity remains intact.

- ✔ For women, if you choose to apply your own makeup or use your own artist, keep in mind that you look different on television than you do in the mirror. Before your on-air appearance, be sure to check with the show's makeup artist to ensure that you look your best.

Controlling your body language

Most people aren't aware of their own body language, mainly because in everyday life, they don't watch themselves speak or interact with other people. But your body language is something you always have to be aware of and control.

Learning to look comfortable during and interview takes practice. If you have nervous habits, such as tapping your foot, twirling your hair, blinking too much, or waving your arms around wildly when you speak, you need to eliminate these habits.

The best ways to control your body language is to videotape yourself doing practice interviews and then seek out help from people close to you to help you identify potential problems. If you undergo professional media training (see the earlier sidebar "Publicity boot camp: Considering professional media training"), you find out how to control your body language.

Sit up straight, make eye contact with the person or people you're speaking to, and showcase your personality without being over the top or over-emphasizing your gestures.

It's perfectly normal to be nervous before and during an interview. Try the following tips to help you relax:

✔ Make sure that you take deep breaths to calm yourself down; know that you look your best and that you're prepared for the interview, and go into the studio as confident as possible.

✔ Don't pay any attention to the cameras if you're doing a TV interview. Focus on having a discussion with the show's host. The camera operators and show's director makes sure that you look good on television. Don't allow your eyes to wander around aimlessly as you try to figure out which camera you should look into.

Book It: Generating Reviews

Book reviews are a great publicity tool (assuming the reviews your book generates are favorable). When sending out review copies of your book, be sure to include a complete press kit and cover letter (see Chapter 18 for more about these items and about initial contact with the media). It's important that the editor, reporter, or journalist have all of your information in one place. Even if you already sent a press kit and you're following up with a review copy of the book, send another press kit. Editors, reporters, and journalists often receive dozens of press kits per day. Don't assume the original material you sent was kept and is readily available.

If the target publication has a long lead time, it's acceptable to send galleys (laid-out pages) of the book. A reviewer would rather receive an advance copy of the book in galley form than wait until after it's released to the public. Most editors like to time book reviews in conjunction with the book's release, not after it, so plan accordingly.

As you generate positive reviews, reprint copies of them and include them within your book's press kit. You also can use excerpts from positive reviews in your book's advertising (see Chapter 20 for more about book ads) and on your Web site (see Chapter 21 for more about setting up a book Web site).

Show It Off: Coordinating Author Appearances and Book Signings

In addition to generating publicity in the media with interviews and reviews, one free way to let potential readers know your book exists is to participate in author appearances (such as readings) and book signings. These events are fun and allow the author to meet and interact with people interested in the topic. It's a great networking opportunity (and you may sell more books).

Keep in mind that unless you can drive hundreds of people to your event, you may not make a ton of money signing books at a bookstore, but you can use this event as a way to generate local publicity. Many newspapers run a short article announcing a book signing event or author appearance. That publicity is more valuable to you and allows you to reach more potential readers than the actual event.

In the following sections, I explain how to set up an event, conduct yourself professionally, and plan a tour.

Planning and promoting an event

A few weeks before your book's release date, contact a few bookstores in major markets and speak with the store manager about doing a book signing, hosting a discussion, or making an author appearance. Most bookstore managers welcome the opportunity to have authors visit their store because these events drive traffic into the store.

It's always easier to start booking appearances and author signings in your local area, so contact the managers of local bookstores first. Depending on how things go, you can always plan a more extensive book tour later (I cover book tours later in this chapter).

When planning a book signing, make sure that you have an ample number of copies of your books at the location, based on the anticipated turnout. Because your book is self-published, it's up to you to work with the bookstore to ensure that enough books are on hand for your event and that your event is promoted properly.

After you receive a commitment from one or more bookstores to participate, supply the locations with fliers and/or posters to promote the event. Don't rely on the location to promote the event for you. They may not promote it at all, or they could put up fliers that you don't like. You should also contact local media, particularly newspapers and radio stations, to get them to help you promote the event in their calendar or event listings. (You can use some of the press materials I describe in Chapter 18.) Being able to promote a book signing when you're a guest on a local talk radio show is also beneficial.

Setting up an event for smooth sailing

Determine exactly what to expect from the event in advance so that the event itself goes smoothly. Consider the following:

- ✔ Before the event, talk with the store manager to discuss what you'll be doing and what's expected of you. Will you have a podium to speak from? Will you sit behind a table to sign books?

✔ Find out what you need to bring (aside from markers to sign books). Can you distribute promotional materials, like postcards or bookmarks (covered in Chapter 20)?

✔ Decide whether you'll sell your own books or have someone there to handle the money while you interact with readers.

✔ During the actual appearance, smile, be approachable, and talk to the people who come to see you. Try to strike up conversations, answer questions, and come across as a charming and caring individual.

✔ If you're signing autographs, make sure you spell each person's name correctly. If you're not sure of the spelling, ask.

✔ When you sign books, try to incorporate a short message (one sentence maximum) in addition to your signature (if you have time). You can write, "Enjoy the book," "Thanks for your support," or "It was a pleasure meeting you." Be creative and when possible, write something personal, not just "Best wishes."

Taking your act on the road

Depending on your budget (see Chapter 6 for more about money matters), you may decide to embark on a multiple city book tour, which would combine booking signings, author appearances, and interviews with local media in each city you visit. Such a tour requires a time commitment, so be sure that the traveling fits within your schedule.

To get the most out of your investment in a book tour (because you have to pay for your travel expenses to get from city to city), you may be able to book some paid appearances or lectures at schools, universities, or various other types of organizations to help reduce the out-of-pocket expenses. See Chapter 22 for more about becoming a public speaker.

Keep in mind that planning a successful book tour requires a significant amount of pre-planning and coordination. Your overall objective, of course, is to boost awareness of your book and to sell as many copies of your book as possible.

Leave It to the Pros: Working with a Publicist

Based on everything in this chapter and in Chapter 18 about creating a press kit, contacting the media, pitching stories, and participating in interviews, you may decide to leave this type of work to proven professionals. Freelance publicists or PR firms work with you to develop, launch, and manage your book's PR campaign. In the following sections, I discuss a publicist's responsibilities, tips for finding and hiring a publicist, and fees for a publicist's services.

What can a publicist do for you?

Instead of investing your own valuable time doing all the busy work associated with developing, launching, and managing a successful PR campaign (and yes, it requires a significant time and financial investment), hire a publicist or PR firm to get the job done correctly. These associates can

- Create your entire press kit or just write your press release and author bio
- Take the press kit you create and use it to pitch stories to the media and handle all media contact on your behalf, including sending out review copies of your book
- Help you book interviews because most PR professionals already have well-established media contacts and have a much easier time getting you booked
- Help you define and establish your image as a published author and expert in your field
- Provide intensive media training for you
- Schedule paid appearances, lectures, and appearances on your behalf
- Assist you in planning a multiple-city book tour

How do you find a publicist?

Many PR firms and freelance publicists specialize only in promoting authors. Others specialize in promoting experts or companies working in specific industries or cater to only certain types of media.

When looking to hire a publicist (you should do so about two to three months before your book's publication date), the following considerations are important:

- The PR professional has a thorough understanding of what you're trying to accomplish and the audience you're trying to reach
- The person has established contacts with the appropriate media outlets you're interested in
- The publicist or PR firm knows your expectations and timeframe

✔ The PR firm shares your vision for what needs to be accomplished

✔ You need to work well with the account executive(s) or PR professionals

You can find a publicist in many ways:

✔ Check out publishing industry magazines, such as *Publishers Weekly* (www.publishersweekly.com) or *Writer's Digest* (www.writers digest.com), and look for ads from PR firms.

✔ Consult your local Yellow Pages or surf the Internet (search for "literary publicist" or "book publicist").

✔ Contact a professional trade association, such as the Public Relations Society of America (www.prsa.org), and ask for a referral.

✔ Seek out a referral from another author or company you know that's worked with a PR firm.

✔ Visit www.elance.com and solicit bids from freelance publicists based on what services you require.

How much should a publicist cost?

Depending on the services you want a publicist to handle and whether you hire an established PR firm or a freelance PR specialist, the cost varies greatly. Keep in mind that in addition to paying for the publicist's time and expertise, you're also responsible for all expenses (including phone calls, mailing costs, printing costs, travel, and so on).

You can compensate publicist in a variety of ways:

✔ A pre-determined hourly fee (plus expenses)

✔ A flat, per-project fee (plus expenses)

✔ A weekly or monthly retainer (plus expenses)

✔ By scheduled interviews

When your PR person schedules interviews for you, he receives pre-determined rates based on each type of interview. You pay separately for each radio interview, TV interview, or print review/article.

You may pay up to $150 per hour or a monthly retainer of $2,000 (plus expenses) for a PR person. For a publicist to truly do a thorough job with your campaign, she needs between one and three months, due to lead times of various media outlets and the time needed to properly make contact with each media outlet.

Chapter 20

Marketing Your Book with Paid Advertising and Promotional Tools

. . . .

In This Chapter

▶ Recognizing the pros and cons of paid advertising to sell your book

▶ Choosing the best places to advertise your book

▶ Putting together a winning advertising campaign

▶ Using promotional tools to your advantage

. . . .

*I*n Chapters 18 and 19, you discover how to tap the power of the media to generate free publicity for your book and yourself. You can do this by approaching print, electronic, and online media with publicity materials like a press release and getting these outlets to review your book, feature it in editorial coverage, or interview you as an expert on the topic of your book.

Free publicity is wonderful and helps generate sales of your book; however, you seldom have total control over what's written or said about your book or when the coverage actually appears. With paid advertising, however, you have 100 percent control over your advertising message and can decide exactly when and where your advertisements are seen or heard. This control allows you to target your book's potential audience.

This chapter is about how to utilize paid advertising to help sell your book. I cover the pros and cons of paid advertising, help you decide where to advertise, and give tips on planning a successful campaign. I also focus on how to use promotional materials, like bookmarks and postcards, to boost awareness of your book.

I cover the nuts and bolts of paid advertising in this chapter. For more details, check out *Advertising For Dummies* (Wiley) by Gary Dahl. The book features tips on creating ads, working within your budget, and more.

Checking Out the Pros and Cons of Paid Advertising

Paid advertising is when you create an ad. That ad can be a classified or display ad in a newspaper, newsletter, or magazine; a 30- or 60-second radio or television ad; an animated banner ad for the Internet; or a billboard. In the following sections, I explain the advantages and disadvantages of using paid advertising to sell your self-published book.

The benefits

A well-designed ad that appears in the right media outlet has the potential to be seen or heard, and then immediately be acted upon by the consumer, who will (hopefully) call a toll-free number or visit a Web site to order your book, or visit their favorite bookstore to purchase it.

Keep that purchasing power in mind, and consider the benefits of paid advertising:

- ✔ You have 100-percent control over your advertising message.
- ✔ You decide exactly what's said and the frequency with which the ad appears.
- ✔ You can target your book's specific audience by choosing the best places to advertise.

Your objective is to determine your target audience, figure out how to best reach that audience, and advertise in places where your ad is most apt to be seen by those people. (Fear not; I show you how to figure out all this info in the section "Deciding Where to Advertise to Reach Your Target Audience" later in this chapter.)

The drawbacks

Unless you're a multi-million-dollar corporation with a huge advertising budget and the goal of reaching mass-market consumers, there are a few drawbacks to paid advertising you want to consider, as I explain in the following sections.

Your ad may be lost in the crowd

An ad can get easily lost in the bombardment of advertising people are constantly exposed to. Every day, you're flooded with advertising. It's literally everywhere. Companies do just about anything to capture your attention, even for a split second, to promote its message. Because you're exposed to so much daily advertising, many of you may automatically phase it out of your minds. Imagine yourself reading a magazine or newspaper and skipping over the ads or pulling out those little insert cards and throwing them into the trash. When you listen to the radio or watch TV, do you switch the station/channel when the ads come on? Because of these habits, advertisers have an even harder job of promoting their products.

When the roles are reversed and you become the advertiser, you have to find innovative ways to communicate your message so people pay attention to when it's seen or heard. For paid advertising to work, you need to

- ✔ Create a highly effective ad, carefully targeting your audience
- ✔ Have the budget to ensure that your ad is seen multiple times by your audience
- ✔ Choose the best possible media outlets to advertise with

One mistake and the money you invest in advertising may be wasted.

Advertising can be expensive

Mass media advertising can be costly, but you want to reach the most people possible with your campaign. So where do you draw the line and how do you get your name out there?

Many authors and publishers find that paid advertising to promote a book to the public isn't the best way to spend what limited advertising and marketing dollars are available. Niche advertising, in conjunction with a public relations campaign and other grassroots marketing efforts (see Chapters 18 and 19 for more about publicity), often works much better and is a better use of resources. With niche advertising, you find specific magazines, newspapers, newsletters, web sites, or other publications that cater to a small but targeted audience. These publications typically focus on a narrow topic. If you can find a niche outlet that relates to the topic of your book, advertising in that publication virtually guarantees that you reach the perfect audience.

Media outlets have long lead times

Another potential drawback is that most advertising media have a lead time of several weeks or months. A *lead time* is the time it takes for the publication to be written, edited, laid out, printed, and distributed. A magazine's July issue, for example, may have an advertising deadline of April or May. Newspapers tend to have a shorter lead time (typically a few days or a week).

If you want your ad to run in the September issue of a publication, you need to design, place, and pay for the ad up to three months in advance. Then, when the ad comes out, assess the response rate to the ad. See "Tracking the results of your ads," later in this chapter for details.

Deciding Where to Advertise to Reach Your Target Audience

Before launching an advertising campaign for your book, determine exactly who the target audience is for your book, and then figure out the best advertising vehicles to potentially use to reach that audience. To successfully make this determination, you need to understand the daily habits of your audience, know what media they're exposed to, and then determine how you can best spend your advertising dollars to reach those people using the appropriate forms of media.

There is no such thing as an all-in-one solution for creating an advertising campaign or even a single effective ad. Every situation is different, based on the type of book you're trying to sell, the audience you're trying to reach, your budget, the geographic area(s) you're planning to target, and your time frame. If you choose to use paid advertising, focus on what you're trying to accomplish, and then research the best ways to achieve those objectives.

In the following sections, I discuss different media outlets that carry paid advertising. I also show you how to match outlets to your target readers, obtain advertising kits from outlets, and draw up an advertising budget.

Here are a couple of tips to help you start working:

- ✔ Find a successful book or product similar to what you're offering and determine exactly what was done to make it successful in terms of advertising. Discover what's worked in the past without trying to re-invent the wheel.

- ✔ One way to capitalize on free publicity and maximize the impact of your advertising dollars is to run ads with the media outlet(s) that give your book free coverage in the form of a review, article, interview, or profile. This helps ensure that the people interested in the article about your book know exactly how and where to purchase it. For example, when a media outlet interested in reviewing your book approaches you, call the media outlet's advertising department and look into advertising in that same issue or on that same show. (See Chapter 19 for more about working with the media to publicize your book.)

Surveying media outlets that carry paid advertising

Finding potential places to advertise your book won't be a problem. Choosing the best, most cost-effective places to advertise, however, requires extensive research and careful planning. The following sections cover some of the most common places where you can pay for advertising. Check out Chapter 18 for more details on contacting different types of media outlets.

SRDS Media Solutions (Phone [800] 232-0772; Web site www.srds.com) publishes a series of detailed directories covering television stations, radio stations, newspapers, and magazines published throughout the country. In addition to offering information about each media outlet, it also lists average advertising rates and provides contact information. The directories and services offered by SRDS Media Solutions can help you pinpoint the best places to advertise, based on the target audience you're trying to reach and your overall budget.

Print media

Print advertising offers you the opportunity to distribute your book's marketing message to the readers of a specific publication, whether it's a newspaper, a general interest magazine, a niche-oriented magazine, or a printed newsletter:

✔ **Newspapers:** Choosing a newspaper outlet can be a good option if you're looking for an inexpensive way to reach a general audience. Newspapers typically have a short lead time, so you can potentially begin receiving orders for your book much faster than if you were to run a magazine ad. To place an ad, contact the classified ad sales department of each newspaper directly or work with a classified advertising network, which helps you place a single ad in dozens or hundreds of newspapers at the same time. Check out these agencies to help you:

- **Advertising Network of Florida (ANF):** Phone (866) 742-1373; Web site www.national-classifieds.com

- **Classified Nation:** Phone (800) 227-7636; Web site www.classifiednation.com

- **Wide Area Classifieds:** Phone (800) 324-8236; Web site www.wideareaclassifieds.com

You also have several choices when you are looking for the type of paper you want to advertise in. The choices include

- National newspapers, like *USA Today*

- Major daily newspaper (with circulations over 100,000)

- Regional and local newspapers published daily or weekly

Nettizen.com (www.nettizen.com/newspaper) is a comprehensive online directory of newspapers throughout the world. You can use this directory to pinpoint potential publications to advertise in. *Editor & Publisher* magazine is another excellent resource. It's a weekly, industry-oriented magazine that covers the newspaper publishing business. From the publication's Web site (www.editorandpublisher.com), you can subscribe to the magazine or purchase the annual *Editor & Publisher International Directory*, which is a printed directory of newspapers around the world.

✔ **Consumer magazines:** Running an ad in a magazine can be lucrative because magazines tend to focus on a specific topic. So, the people reading it are more apt to be interested in something being advertised that also relates to the topic. Different types of magazines exist:

- **National magazines:** The circulation for these magazines is in the millions. The titles include general interest publications, such as *Time, Newsweek,* or *People.*

- **Special interest or niche-oriented magazines:** These mags have much smaller circulations because they target defined audiences comprised of people interested in specific topics. *New York Dog* magazine, for example, is a full-color, monthly magazine that caters only to upscale dog owners in the New York area.

  Depending on the topic of your book, advertising in a niche-oriented magazine can be very worthwhile. Magazine-Directory.com (magazine-directory.com) is a free, online listing of many magazines published within The United States.

✔ **Industry-oriented magazines:** This type of magazine, also referred to as a *trade journal*, is read by professionals working in a very specific industry. *Billboard* or *Radio & Records* are examples of industry-oriented magazines that cater to people working in the music industry. Depending on the topic of your book, you may be able to target your potential readers by advertising in this type of publication. You can purchase a directory of industry-oriented publications from several different publishers.

✔ **Newsletters:** These publications are shorter than magazines in terms of page count and typically focus on very specific topics. Newsletters are typically an excellent way to reach extremely targeted audiences. Newsletter Access (www.newsletteraccess.com) offers a free online listing of over 5,000 regularly published newsletters.

Electronic media

Not all media outlets involve the printed word. You also can advertise with radio and television:

✔ **Radio:** In addition to AM and FM radio stations throughout the country, you can advertise nationally on radio networks or on syndicated radio programs. There's also advertising opportunities on the XM and Sirius satellite radio networks.

Radio advertising works but only with repetition and if the audience you're reaching is potentially interested in what you're selling. The cost of radio advertising varies greatly, based on the size of the audience, the geographic area, the reach of the station, and the time of day the ad airs.

✔ **Television:** Network television advertising is very expensive, so as a self-published author on a fixed budget, you may want to check into local or regional television and cable TV advertising.

For television advertising to work, you need to produce the TV commercial, and then pay television stations to air it. Just as with radio, TV advertising works best with repetition. Running one 30-second ad on any station or network won't have a huge impact on book sales. Running the same ad at least a few dozen times on one station greatly improves your chances of selling books, but TV advertising is costly.

Online outlets

Online advertising can take on many forms. There's traditional display (banner) advertising, and keyword or search-based advertising, which has become one of the most cost-effective and powerful ways to reach targeted audiences through paid advertising. If you want to target your online-based advertising to any audience you wish and set your own budget, try using a service like Google AdWords (`www.adwords.com`) or Yahoo! Small Business (`smallbusiness.yahoo.com/marketing/sponsoredsearch.php`).

Online advertising, specifically search marketing or keyword advertising, is a great way to initially launch an ad campaign for your book. It's easy and inexpensive, and you can measure the results quickly. For more about using the power of the World Wide Web in promoting your book, see Chapter 21.

Other outlets

Advertising agencies and companies that rely on advertising to generate sales have developed many innovative ways to get their messages out to the public. Wouldn't it be great to see your book advertised on the side of a bus or on a giant billboard as your drive to work? Talk about an ego boost! Here are some options to consider:

✔ **Billboard and outdoor advertising:** If you have the budget, advertising on outdoor billboards, the sides of buses, and outdoor benches is another viable way of advertising a book.

With this type of advertising, you're paying to reach a general, mass-market audience, so it may be suitable for advertising certain types of books that have extremely broad appeal.

✔ **Movie theater advertising:** Advertising in movie theaters has become a popular and somewhat inexpensive way to capture the attention of moviegoers who are a captive audience as they wait for their movie to begin. With movie theater advertising, you can target audiences of specific movies or focus your ads in theaters within specific geographic locations. National Cinemedia (www.nationalcinemedia.com) is one company that specializes in offering in-theater advertising opportunities.

Matching potential readers to specific media outlets

Paid advertising can be used effectively by a self-published author or publishing company if you focus your advertising dollars and resources on niche advertising: finding media outlets that specifically target only those people you believe are potential readers for your book. Sure, it would be a great boost to your ego to see a full-page ad for your book in the *New York Times, Time,* or *People,* but for many self-published authors, this isn't cost-effective or practical.

Niche advertising may include advertising on specific (local or regional) radio or television shows, in special interest magazines and newspapers, and/or within specialized newsletters or Web sites. See the previous section for details on different outlets for advertising.

For example: If you've written a cookbook that teaches the art of Italian cooking, advertising in *Time* magazine or *Business Week* will be expensive and not allow you to reach your intended audience. While some of these magazines' readers may in fact be interested in Italian cooking, you pay to advertise to everyone who reads those magazines, not just the select few who have an interest in what you're advertising. That's a waste of money and resources. Instead, consider finding a special interest cooking or lifestyle magazine to advertise in, so you can better reach your intended audience. The circulation of the special interest magazine may be only 5,000 to 10,000 people, as opposed to several million, but you know the readers of the special interest magazine are far more likely to buy your book.

By figuring out your book's target audience (see Chapter 4 for details on how to do this), you can do research to determine their buying and media habits. Some of this research involves making educated guesses about the forms of advertising that will allow you to reach the most people in your target audience for the least amount of money. For example, are they more apt to listen to a talk radio station on their way to work or read a special interest magazine during their free time?

Obtaining advertising kits

After considering all possible advertising vehicles, choose a handful of what you believe could be the most viable options and contact those media outlets to request an advertising kit (also referred to as a media kit). This kit includes detailed printed information about that media outlet, including its audience and reach, the cost to advertise, the types of ads it accepts, and other information you need to plan your advertising campaign.

Media kits are provided free of charge by the media outlet to potential advertisers. To obtain a media kit, contact the media outlet's advertising sales department. By requesting a handful of media kits from competing media outlets, you can better target your advertising and choose the best advertising opportunities, based on your budget (see the next section) and what you're trying to achieve.

As you read through the various media kits, you may see many technical terms, which are helpful for you to understand. Advertopedia.com (`www.advertopedia.com/advertising-dictionary.htm`) offers a free, online advertising and marketing dictionary, which helps you decipher all the technical jargon related to advertising.

When you contact the advertising sales department at a media outlet, it's the salesperson's job to sell you as much advertising as possible, at the highest possible price. Make sure that promises are backed up with actual documentation, based on past success stories from other advertisers. It's okay to seek out the advice of these advertising agencies in terms of how to best utilize their media outlet to successfully sell your book, as long as you understand their motivation.

Considering your budget

Depending on the readers you're trying to reach and the advertising media you plan to use, a successful advertising campaign can be launched with a few hundred dollars or several million dollars.

As a self-published author, all the money you spend on advertising most likely comes out of your pocket. Therefore, you need to determine, in advance, how much you're willing to spend and in what time frame (see Chapter 6 for more information about sticking to a budget). Then you can figure out the best advertising opportunities available to you.

You pay for advertising in print media outlets based on the size of your display ad or the number of words in your classified ad. For electronic media, like radio and television, you buy time, usually in 30- or 60-second increments. With online advertising, you pay for impressions (the number of people who see your ad) or click-through responses (the number of people who click on your ad to visit your Web site). For specialty outlets like billboards, you pay based on the placement of the billboard and the projected number of impressions it'll make.

Planning a Successful Ad Campaign

Developing a successful advertising campaign is a process with multiple steps. It's not something that can be thrown together haphazardly, especially because you're forking out your hard-earned money for this service. The money you spend on advertising is an investment you're making in the future sale of your books. If the advertising works, you sell a lot of books and make money. If the advertising campaign fails, you wasted the money you spent.

Unfortunately, there are many reasons why an ad campaign could fail. The most common reasons are

- The ad was poorly written or designed and didn't properly address the needs and wants of its audience or didn't capture their attention.
- The message you conveyed with your ad was unprofessional or lacked credibility.
- The ad itself was good, but the media outlet you advertised in was inappropriate for the audience you were trying to reach.
- The timing or placement of your ad was bad.
- Your ad didn't have enough repetition to properly capture the attention of your intended audience.
- There is no market for or interest in what you're advertising.

Developing effective advertising is a skill set that requires learning, research, and experience. Don't try to wing it! Before spending money on any type of advertising, make sure that you know the following:

- Exactly what you're getting
- Who you're reaching
- When the ad appears
- The size or duration of the ad
- How often the ad will run
- What you anticipate the results to be

Throw me a pitch: Hiring an advertising agency

Creating an effective advertising campaign requires an understanding of how advertising works, an intimate understanding of what you're trying to sell, and a strong knowledge about the people you're trying to reach. Working with a reputable advertising agency to help you advertise your book could be an extremely good investment.

An advertising agency has the following roles:

✔ Helps you determine the target audience for your book

✔ Figures out how to reach your audience

✔ Creates an advertising campaign that fits within your budget

✔ Deals with each media outlet directly to coordinate your advertising

✔ Handles the creation or production of your actual ads

Advertising agencies charge different fee structures, depending on the types of services offered. Your best bet is to sit down with several advertising agencies in your area and hear their pitches. In those pitches, you need to look for an understanding of your book and your target audience and how the agency can best utilize your available ad budget to reach this audience. You can find advertising agencies listed in the Yellow Pages, seek out a referral from someone you know, or read agency profiles in publications like *Advertising Age* or *AdWeek*. You can determine an agency's competence based on the work they've done for other clients.

If you have the budget, seriously consider working with an experienced advertising agency to help you design and place your ads effectively to ensure that every dollar you spend on advertising helps you sell the most number of books possible. (See the nearby sidebar "Throw me a pitch: Hiring an advertising agency" for more information.)

In the following sections, I explain how to create an ad, time your campaign wisely, and track the results of your ads to fine-tune your campaign.

To discover more about advertising techniques and trends, read current and past issues of *Advertising Age* (www.advertisingage.com) and *AdWeek* (www.adweek.com). These two industry magazines cover all aspects of the advertising industry and are available from newsstands or via subscription.

Creating your ad

Assuming you've written or published a book you know has a viable market and you understand exactly who your potential readers are, the next step is to create an ad that captures their attention. In the following sections, I provide you with some tips and tricks on crafting effective ads.

Answering important questions about your book

Whichever advertising medium you ultimately use, the advertising message you convey must quickly and powerfully answer the questions: who, what, where, when, why, and how. At the same time, the message needs to focus on the potential reader's wants and needs.

While making sure that your ad appeals to your target audience, the ad must also quickly answer a number of questions. Here are some of those questions:

- **What are you offering?** In this case, you're offering a book. People need to know that.

- **What's the book about?** In one sentence or less, successfully and succinctly summarize what your book is all about.

- **Who will be interested in reading it and why?** Focus on what your book's target audience will want to know about your book.

- **What does the book offer to its readers?** Does your book offer exclusive or valuable content? If so, your ad needs to bring this fact to the attention of potential readers.

- **What's unique about your book?** Focus on why someone should read your book as opposed to another book on the same topic.

- **How will readers benefit from reading your book? What will they learn?** Focus on the value or knowledge the reader will obtain and how your book can help the reader.

- **What information will readers obtain?** List a few specific examples of topics covered in the book. Give readers a taste of what they can expect.

- **What problems can the book help solve?** Be specific and address issues or topics that relate directly to your intended audience. For example, focus on how the book will help your readers overcome a problem.

- **Why should someone buy your book right now?** Create a sense of urgency. Provide one or more reasons why the information in your book should be obtained right away.

- **Where can they obtain a copy of your book? Is the book "Available now from bookstores everywhere!" or "Available exclusively at www.[Web siteURL].com"?** Don't make potential readers search for your book. Tell them exactly where they can purchase it right away.

- **How much does the book cost?** List the cover price of the book. If you've already created a perceived value for the book's content, potential readers should think they're getting a bargain when they see how much the book actually costs.

✔ **Why should the reader trust you as an author? What makes you an expert?** List a few of your key credentials to impress potential readers. This can help add to the book's perceived value.

✔ **Who else thinks your book is incredible?** Many successful book ads utilize excerpts from positive reviews, quotes from celebrities, or awards the book has won.

And, of course, be sure to include basic details such as the book's publisher, author (that's you!), ISBN, and Web site.

Making the most of your chosen medium

Whether you're creating a display ad or a text-based classified ad for a print publication, an audio ad for radio, or a video-based ad for television, you need to use all the tools that particular advertising medium offers to achieve the best possible results. For example:

✔ For classified advertising in print publications or text-based online ads, you have the written word at your disposal. Your ability to create a powerful advertising message relies on how well you use the English language.

✔ When it comes to magazine advertising, you have the ability to use full-color text and graphics to sell your book properly.

✔ If you're radio advertising, you can use the spoken word, music, and sound effects to communicate your sales message.

✔ With television advertising, use your intended audience's ability to see, hear, *and* read your message.

Generating a sense of urgency

The most powerful ads create a sense of urgency. You want the person who sees or hears your ad to believe they must get their hands on your book immediately. Creating a sense of urgency helps encourage the potential reader to take immediate action, such as visiting a bookstore, calling a toll-free number, or surfing a Web site to purchase your book.

One way to create a sense of urgency is to feature a special offer, such as "Order online before a [insert date] and receive 20 percent off the cover price!" People love to save money and receive special offers!

Pulling together text and graphics

After you determine what information needs to go within the ad, figure out the best way to communicate that information, using powerful and attention-getting language. Writing effective advertising copy is a skill that requires training and practice, even for experienced writers and authors.

To convey your message quickly, use powerful words that create excitement, demand, and urgency. You can find great tips for writing copy for ads and other pieces in *Writing Copy For Dummies* (Wiley) by Jonathan Kranz.

Whenever you're advertising in any type of media that allows for visuals, be sure that your book's cover is prominently displayed. People need to know exactly what the book looks like, so they can find it easily on a bookstore's shelves. The cover of your book should be designed to sell itself. (See Chapter 9 for details on putting together an attractive book cover.)

You have only a few seconds to make a positive impression. For a display ad, the headline and the graphics must jump off the page at the reader. The sample book ad in Figure 20-1 uses a bold headline to quickly attract a specific audience's attention (in this case, single guys), and then asks a question to further engage the reader. The book's cover is prominently displayed. The remaining text conveys the relevant information about the book and provides details about its content.

Take a look at ads for other books. Examine the format, the wording used, and the approaches the various ads take. Determine what approach mostly likely works with your book and try to use those same advertising techniques, assuming they apply to your book and your potential audience.

Figure 20-1:
A well-designed book ad uses strong, high-impact language and makes good use of graphics, including the book's cover.

Checking over your ad

Even if you have a professional graphic designer or advertising agency write and design your ad, it's always a good idea to have multiple people proofread it to ensure that it's error free and properly gets your message across in the most efficient way possible. Consider showing the ad to several random people (friends, coworkers, relatives, and so on) and ask for the first impression of the ad to see if it has the desired impact.

Timing your campaign

Timing is a critical component for any ad campaign. If your ads start running too early, before the book is published and readily available, people won't be able to find it right away and could forget about it. Ideally, you want ads for your book to run at the same time the book is available, so when readers order a copy, they can expect to receive it quickly, or they can go to the bookstore and purchase a copy right away.

Proper timing of your paid advertising campaign means coordinating the ads to run around the same time as the free publicity you generate (see Chapters 18 and 19 for more about publicity), as well as in conjunction with any other marketing and promotional activities you're planning. Ideally, readers should be exposed to as many impressions of your book as possible.

As you decide where to place your ads, consider lead times carefully. In terms of print publications, don't get caught up on issue dates. Focus on the street date for each issue. For example, a magazine with an October 2006 issue date often hits newsstands and is mailed to subscribers in early September.

Tracking the results of your ads

It's important to know if the ads you're running are effective and generating the desired response rates. Therefore, it's important to carefully track what ads are running, where they're running, and what the response is from them. This tracking system helps you fine-tune your advertising on an ongoing basis, improve the message, and focus more heavily on the aspects of the paid advertising campaign that are working well. For instance, if you see one ad in a specific magazine or newspaper isn't generating a good response, but your online campaign is generating excellent results, you can reconfigure your budget to put more of an emphasis on the types of advertising that work.

Tracking online ads is extremely simple because you're often provided with useful tools, such as Web site traffic reports and click-through statistics. The Web master of the site you advertise on often provides these statistics. The Web hosting service for your Web site can also help you track visitors to your site (see Chapter 21 for more about setting up a Web site).

Television and radio ads are relatively easy to track as well. You know when an ad runs because you can either pay for specific air times or have your ad run in a random rotation during a specific time period. If you choose the latter (which is cheaper), the TV or radio station tells you exactly when your ad(s) ran. You can then quickly track the results, based on the number of calls, Web site hits, or orders you receive within minutes after the ad(s) air.

Print ads are harder to track because people see them over extended time; the same goes for specialty ads like billboards. If you're advertising in a monthly magazine, for example, you're apt to receive responses from that ad throughout the entire month. For this type of ad, it's useful to include some type of special tracking code for orders. To do this, you can use a unique Web site URL or a toll-free phone number in each ad, or display a code in the ad and ask customers for that code when they place their order.

Effectively Using Promotional Materials

In addition to paid advertising there are a wide range of promotional materials you can use to help spread the word about your new book. If you have an easy and inexpensive way to distribute these materials, you may experience even greater sales success. In the following sections, I cover several different promotional tools: bookmarks, postcards, book excerpts, and book displays.

Bookmarks

Full-color, 2-x-6-inch bookmarks are an ideal and extremely inexpensive way to promote your book. These promotional items can be given away at bookstores, libraries, author appearances (see Chapter 19), or anyplace where you can obtain permission to distribute them to large numbers of people.

For under $250, you can have several thousand promotional bookmarks printed. Design the bookmarks yourself with any graphics program, or have the printing company you use handle the graphic design work on your behalf (which often costs extra.) Whether you're having full-color bookmarks or postcards printed (see the next section for more about postcards), find a competitively priced printer that offers professional offset printing, using ultra-bright, 130-pound paper with 16-point coating (and/or glossy spot UV coating), plus high-resolution, photo-quality, 200-line screen printing (at 2400 dpi), with precise cutting. These specs ensure that the items turn out looking highly professional.

Getz Color Graphics is a full-service printer that specializes in inexpensively producing full-color promotional materials, such as bookmarks and postcards. The company charges $220 for 5,000 full-color bookmarks and has extensive experience working with authors and publishers. You can contact the company at (800) 562-7052 or visit the Web site at www.getzcolor.com.

Promotional bookmarks are just like print ads for your book (see "Creating your ad," earlier in this chapter for details). The front and back of the book-mark both serve a purpose:

✔ **The front of the bookmark:** The front design includes the following:

- The cover artwork for your book

- The title and subtitle using the largest font and type size possible

- The book's publisher, author, ISBN, and cover price

- The Web site along with text stating exactly where the book can be purchased (you may choose to place purchase info on the back)

✔ **The back of the bookmark:** The back can be printed in black and white. Use this area to describe the book in greater detail and who the book appeals to. Be as succinct as possible with the text you use.

Check out a sample bookmark in Figure 20-2 (the front of the bookmark is on the left; the back is on the right). On the front, the book's cover is displayed in full color, and it's big enough to see all of the detail. The headline brings the reader's attention to what the book is about and then provides details about the author, publisher, ISBN, cost, and publication date. At the bottom, the author's Web site is clearly displayed so books can be ordered. The back of the bookmark provides additional reasons why someone will want to read the book and creates perceived value. It also mentions exactly where the book can be purchased.

Postcards

Like bookmarks (see the previous section), full-color postcards are an excel-lent way to promote your book at bookstores, libraries, author appearances, and other events. Having 3-x-5-, 4-x-6-, or 5-x-7-inch postcards printed is inex-pensive when compared to other forms of advertising. The cost is under $100 for at least 1,000 full-color postcards. Prices vary based on the quantity you publish and the printing company you use.

The benefit to using postcards over bookmarks as a promotional tool is that you have more space for your advertising message and they can be mailed, allowing you to target a specific audience through direct mailing. In addition to mailing promotional postcards to friends, family, coworkers, clients, and customers, you can purchase a mailing list comprised of people in your target audience and send out direct mailings to them for less money in postage than sending a first-class letter. (See Chapter 15 for more about mailing lists.)

The Ultimate Guide
For Anyone
About To
Propose Marriage!

Author: Jason R. Rich
Publisher: New Page Books
ISBN #: 1564147177
Price: $13.99 / 224 Pages
Publication Date: Sept. 2003

www.JasonRich.com

Getting Ready To
Pop The Question?

Bestselling author
Jason R. Rich
offers expert advice
on how to propose
marriage and select
the perfect diamond
engagement ring!

This book features
dozens of ideas for
how to make your
proposal romantic,
exciting, and truly
memorable!

Available from bookstores
everywhere, or order
it online today from
Amazon.com or BN.com!

Figure 20-2:
A promo-
tional
bookmark is
a cheap and
easy way to
promote
your book.

Mailing each postcard costs 24 cents. So, for $240 in postage (based on January 2006 postage rates), you can send out a mailing of 1,000 postcards. Be sure to calculate the cost of printing the postcards and purchasing a mailing list when you're figuring your budget.

The content of a promotional postcard should be virtually identical to what you include on a bookmark, only you have more space to get your message across. Instead of cluttering the postcard with more information, use large font sizes and graphics. (Don't forget to leave room on the back of the postcard for the recipient's address and the postage stamp.) Check out a sample postcard in Figure 21-3.

Are You A Single Guy Looking For Answers?

Only $18.95

Read the new book by bestselling author Jason R. Rich

For the first time ever in print...The perfect book for college-bound guys, recent graduates, and recently divorced men!

Published by iUniverse
228 Pages
ISBN 0-595-35593-5
www.JasonRich.com

Now Available From Amazon.com and BN.com, or Order It From Your Favorite Bookstore!

Discover secrets for...

Successful Dating and Finding True Love
Creating The Perfect Bachelor Pad
Dressing Like A Fashion Icon
Finding An Awesome Job
Enjoying Your Free Time
Planning For The Future
Managing Finances
Personal Grooming
...and Much More!

Postage

Figure 20-3:
A promotional postcard can be used for mass mailings or giveaways.

Learn About Products and Services Every Bachelor Should Know About!!

This book is jam-packed with detailed information and answers to common questions that all single guys have as they strive to achieve happiness and success!

Order Your Copy Today From Amazon.com and BN.com

Overnight Prints offers inexpensive full-color printing for your postcards. You can order 1,000 postcards (4-x-6-inch size) online from the company's Web site, for under $49. Contact Overnight Prints at (888) 677-2000 or visit the Web site at www.overnightprints.com.

Excerpts from your book

One fun way to get people interested in reading your book is to offer them a free sample of it. You can create a free, downloadable PDF file and make it available on your Web site (see Chapter 21) and from online booksellers, like Amazon.com and Barnes & Noble.com (see Chapter 14). You can also have excerpts printed as booklets or mini-books and distribute them at author appearances, trade shows, or anyplace else where you can distribute printed materials to the masses.

Excerpts are good, particularly for fiction, for drawing the reader into the story and then encouraging them to actually purchase and read the entire book. For nonfiction, offering an excerpt is always helpful, but a well-written and designed piece of promotional material or ad potentially sells the book just as well to someone who's interested in the topic.

Book displays

As a publisher looking to make a positive and professional impression on booksellers and retail stores that are potentially interested in selling your book, offering a free, cardboard floor or countertop display when they purchase a specific number of books is often a good sales incentive. Plus, if you're promoting your book at appearances or trade shows, a customized retail display helps enhance your professional image.

Corrugated cardboard floor or countertop book displays come in a wide range of configurations, which you select based on the trim size of your book and the number of books you want the display to hold. These cardboard displays can be custom-designed, or you can have stock displays custom-imprinted, based on your needs. As with any type of printing and manufacturing process, the more units you order, the cheaper each display is.

To find companies that manufacture similar displays, use the search phrase *book displays* on any Internet search engine. But here are a couple of my favorites:

- ✔ City Diecutting, Inc. is one of many companies that manufactures custom-designed and custom-imprinted, cardboard countertop and floor displays for books. Depending on size and quantity, countertop displays cost under $8 each and are ideal for retail store displays. Contact the company at www.bookdisplays.com.

- ✔ Displays To Go (www.displaystogo.com) offers a selection of wire book displays in a wide range of sizes and configurations. These displays are ideal for retail or tradeshow settings.

Chapter 21

Maximizing Your Marketing Power in Cyberspace

- -

- -

*T*hanks to the incredible popularity and broad reach of the Internet, marketing a self-published book has never been easier or more cost effective. Although most self-published authors should take advantage of a comprehensive public relations campaign and paid advertising to properly promote their book (see Chapters 18 to 20 for details on these methods), the Internet offers a variety of ways to promote and directly sell books in conjunction with other methods.

Many self-published books are targeted to a niche market. The Internet offers a relatively easy and inexpensive way to target those niche audiences. This chapter focuses on how to use the Internet successfully to promote your book.

The Internet is a powerful marketing and sales tool. Using the Web effectively requires a tremendous amount of planning and creativity. After you decide how to use the Internet, you should develop a well-thought-out plan to ensure that your ideas are implemented and managed properly over the long term. After you create a Web site or blog, for example, update and maintain it regularly. If you accept orders for your book online, fill those orders promptly. This process requires a time commitment. As you investigate the various technologies available to you, determine how you can best use them to reach your target audience and sell books.

Caught in the Web: Building a Promotional Site for Your Book

Simply publishing a book is only one step in actually being successful. After you have books available to sell, promoting, marketing, and advertising the book to its intended audience is crucial. Online-based marketing should be just one facet of your book's overall marketing, public relations, and advertising campaign. Use all the tools and resources at your disposal to reach your book's target market in as many ways as possible.

In the following sections, I explain the benefits of using a promotional Web site, the elements that make up a Web site, and the options you have for creating a Web site.

Why use a Web site to market your book?

Using the Internet as a powerful marketing tool has many benefits:

- ✔ You have the ability to carefully target your marketing efforts and focus exclusively on reaching your book's intended audience. For more about steering target readers to your site, see "If You Build It, Will They Come? Generating Traffic to Your Web Site," later in this chapter.

- ✔ The various online marketing tools available are inexpensive, easy to utilize, and require a very short lead time (unlike paid advertising or other types of marketing). For example, when you send out an e-mail message to dozens, hundreds, or even thousands of targeted recipients, it's received within seconds.

- ✔ You're able to distribute your book's marketing message using text, graphics, photographs, animation, sound effects, spoken audio, and even video when you use a Web site, free downloads, e-mail, a blog, and/or a Podcast as a marketing tool (see "Adding Extra Bells and Whistles" later in this chapter for details).

- ✔ Your message can be changed instantly. It's possible to make edits to a Web site and publish it in minutes.

There aren't many disadvantages to using a Web site for your book unless the site you create is extremely unprofessional and takes away from the credibility of the book itself.

This chapter explores many ways of using the Internet as a marketing tool. Based on your budget, technical knowledge, and goals, use some or all of the online resources available to help you promote and sell the maximum number of books possible. Don't just rely on one or two online marketing techniques.

What are the elements of a Web site?

Web sites are typically divided into individual pages, which are accessed by people who surf the Web by clicking on links or menu options. Keep the design of your book's Web site straightforward, but incorporate the following elements:

- **Author appearances:** If you're participating in a book tour, author signings, or appearances to promote your book, list the dates and details on this page. (See Chapter 19 for more about appearances.)

- **Author's bio:** Tell your Web site's visitors about who you are, what your experience is, and how you gained your expertise. It's a good idea to display your photo to help introduce yourself to readers. Some (potential) readers enjoy seeing who has written the book they plan to read. It can help readers better relate to the material. (See Chapter 18 for details about author bios and photos.)

- **Contact page:** Provide a way for readers, fans, booksellers, the media, and publishing industry professionals to reach you.

- **Free downloadable excerpt:** One way to capture the attention of readers is to offer them a free preview of your book in the form of an excerpt or sample chapter. Create a downloadable PDF file of a chapter and allow visitors to download it for free. (See Chapter 8 for details about how to create a downloadable PDF file using Adobe Acrobat software.)

When you promote your book on a radio or TV show to entice people to visit your Web site, offer them something of value for free:

- • A chapter download of your book

- • A special report that's not included in your book

- • Online excerpts, which make it possible to give readers brief sections of several chapters

- **Frequently asked questions (FAQ):** This section can be used to answer questions about you, your book, your book's topic, and information for potential readers. A FAQ section is typically created in a question and answer format, with a list of the questions included displayed at the top of the document or page for easy reference.

- **Home page:** Think of this page as a promotional brochure for your book. Describe your book in detail. Answer questions like: What's it about? Who should read it? What sets it apart from other books? Where is it available? How much it costs? Be sure to prominently display your book's full-color cover on this page and include prominently displayed links to the other pages of your site. Need help creating content for this page? Utilize the promotional materials you've already created (or plan to create) for your book (see Chapters 18 and 20 for more info).

✔ **Press room:** Create an area where visitors, especially the media, can download or view press releases pertaining to your book (see Chapter 18 for more about press releases).

✔ **Reviews, endorsements, and testimonials:** Offer quotes from published reviews, celebrities, and/or readers that relate directly to your book.

✔ **Shopping cart/Order now:** Allow potential readers to pre-order or order your book online, either directly from your Web site or from an online bookseller, like Amazon.com or Barnes & Noble.com. (See Chapter 16 for more about taking orders for your book; check out Chapter 14 for more about online booksellers.)

What's another item you can sell on your Web site? Try eBooks! For more details on eBooks, see Chapter 12.

Many people use a Web site to promote themselves as authors and experts as well as announce new self-published books. Bestselling author Jamise L. Dames originally launched her Web site (www.jamiseldames.com), shown in Figure 21-1, to promote her first self-published novel, "Momma's Baby Daddy's Maybe." After selling more than 25,000 copies herself, within a year she sold the rights to her book to Simon & Schuster (see Chapter 17 for more about selling your book to a major publisher). Jamise now uses her Web site to promote all her books and her career as a public speaker.

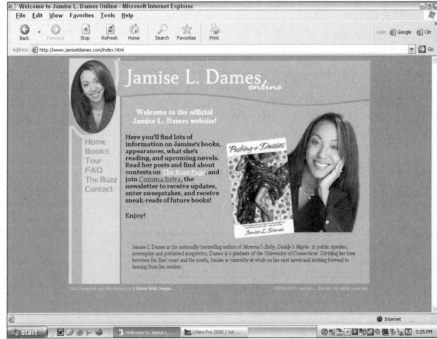

Figure 21-1: Create a Web site to provide information about yourself and your book.

When designing your Web site and creating content for it, first visit several other Web sites developed by authors and publishers. See what's already been done well and learn from other people's mistakes. Don't copy other people's Web sites (because this infringes on their copyrights). Instead, gather ideas for your Web site's overall design, layout, appearance, and content.

How can you create a Web site?

Before your book even gets published, invest the time and effort into developing a promotional Web site for it. This process can begin as soon as you have a concrete idea of what your book is about, who its target audience is, and what content it contains. Ideally, your Web site should have an ordering function or at least point potential readers directly to online bookstores, where they can place their orders for your book. Meanwhile, all of your other marketing, public relations, and advertising efforts should direct people to your book's Web site to obtain more information. The sooner you publish your Web site and make it available on the Web, the better chance you have of getting it established and listed with the various search engines (a process that can take weeks or months).

The goal of your book's Web site is to inform potential readers and the media about the publication of your book and to entice them to order a copy. The Web site you create must look professional and offer the information about your book that potential readers want and need.

Many companies can create and host a Web site inexpensively. These services use online-based Web site design and creation tools that are extremely simple to use. If you hire a professional Web designer to create a site for you, this route is the easiest. You can also create a Web site on your own because it has never been easier, even if you have no programming knowledge whatsoever. Check out *Building a Web Site For Dummies,* 2nd Edition (Wiley) by David A. Crowder. I cover both options in the following sections.

Using a Web site development turnkey solution

For under $30 a month, you can create a professional looking Web site for your book in as little as a few hours, using a turnkey solution. These solutions offer an assortment of online-based Web site design and publishing tools that require no programming knowledge whatsoever. Sites are created using predefined templates that you can customize with your own text and graphics. It's one of the fastest, easiest, and least expensive ways to design and publish a Web site. Try out these businesses:

- Yahoo! Small Business: `smallbusiness.yahoo.com/merchant`

- eBay ProStores: `www.prostores.com`

- GoDaddy.com's Quick Shopping Cart: `www.godaddy.com/gdshop/ecommerce/cart.asp`

Hiring a professional Web site designer

A more expensive option for creating a Web site is to hire a professional Web site designer and hosting company. Hiring a company like this virtually guarantees that your Web site looks professional, and it allows you to incorporate animation, audio, video, or other elements into your site without having to teach yourself Web site programming. A professional Web site designer can also include a shopping cart module to your site, so you can sell books and other products with ease.

The cost of a Web site designer/programmer can vary dramatically. Plan on spending anywhere from $500 to $3,000 for a professionally designed Web site, depending on the time required to design the site and functionality you desire. *Functionality* refers to the specific features you add to your site, whether it's a shopping cart, interactive questionnaire, animation, or other elements to make it more appealing to visitors.

Keep in mind that after your site is designed, it still needs to be maintained. This job can mean an ongoing cost, unless you have the tools and skill to handle updates yourself. If you have the professionals do it, you're also responsible for ongoing Web site hosting charges from the Internet Service Provider (ISP) that hosts your site.

Before hiring someone to develop your site, evaluate the portfolio of work, and ensure that the person you're interested in working with is capable of developing a Web site that meets your needs. Also, surf the Web and find sites you really like in terms of design and functionality. Show these sites to your designer for a better idea of what you're looking for. The more information you provide, the easier creating your Web site can be. Even if you don't have artistic ability, feel free to sketch out ideas for your Web site and share them with your designer. Communicating clearly is important, and it may save you time and money.

Here are a few places to find the best Web designer for your needs:

- Referrals
- The Yellow Pages
- Services like Elance (`www.elance.com`)
- Your Internet Service Provider (ISP)
- Surf the Web

Looking around the Internet for Web sites you really like may help you find a designer. At the bottom of the Web site, typically near the copyright information, you may find a link to the company that designed the site (if it was created by an independent firm as opposed to an in-house staff). Contact the design companies for Web sites you like or that are similar to what you envision needing for you site.

If You Build It, Will They Come? Generating Traffic to Your Web Site

Millions of Web sites exist in cyberspace today and each offers content in an effort to attract people to that site. Just publishing a Web site isn't enough to ensure that people will visit it. It's vital that you inform people of the site's existence.

Developing a Web site to promote an author and a book has become commonplace. Readers expect to be able to find a Web site pertaining to a book and often seek out that Web site before purchasing or reading the book. Therefore, it's important to make sure that your Web site is easy to find.

You can promote your book exclusively to the people you know will be interested in it, often for a fraction of what it would cost you to use other forms of media, like radio, television, billboards, direct mail, newspapers, or magazines. There are many ways of generating such targeted traffic to your Web site. The following sections cover a few common ways.

Choosing an easy-to-remember address and mentioning it everywhere

Your Web site's URL is its address on the Web. For example, the address may look like this: www.[AuthorsName].com or www.[YourBookTitle].com. Make sure that the domain name you choose is obvious so people can find your site easily.

Depending on what you actually wind up doing with your Web site(s), having multiple domain names can be useful. The Web site with the author's name as the URL can be used to promote the author and his/her career, including all their books and work. If you establish a publishing company (see Chapter 6 for details), the publishing company's Web site can be used specifically to promote each book title and accept online orders for the book(s).

To register a domain name, go online and visit a domain registrar site such as www.godaddy.com. The process takes just a few minutes and requires an annual registration fee. Make sure to use the company's full name in the Web site address: Acme Publishing would be www.AcmePublishing.com. Also, be sure to register the author's full name as a Web site domain name if you're going to use a site to promote an author. For example, my Web site URL is www.JasonRich.com.

Within your book and within *all* the marketing and promotional materials, always display your Web site's URL prominently. For example:

- ✔ Display your Web site's URL on your business cards and company letterhead.

- ✔ If you plan to distribute press releases to the media announcing your book (see Chapter 18), be sure to include the Web site's URL within the press release.

- ✔ Whenever you're invited to be a guest on a radio or television show to promote your book (see Chapter 19 for more about interviews and author appearances), always mention the Web site two or three times.

- ✔ When being interviewed for a newspaper or magazine article, specifically ask the reporter to include your Web site address within the article.

- ✔ When lecturing, participating in book signings, or making public appearances as an author, make sure that all attendees know about your Web site.

- ✔ Display the Web site's URL in all paid advertising for the book (see Chapter 20), such as in newspaper and magazine ads.

- ✔ If you distribute promotional bookmarks or postcards announcing the publication of your book (see Chapter 20), be sure your Web site's URL is displayed clearly on them.

Registering your site with search engines and Web directories

Virtually all Web surfers begin each journey into cyberspace using a popular search engine or Web directory, such as Google (www.google.com) or Yahoo! (www.yahoo.com). In order to reach these Web surfers looking for information about your book's topic, be sure to list your Web site on at least the most popular Internet search engines.

To do this, you can either visit each site separately or follow the directions for listing a new site (which is typically free), or you can pay a service to list your site with dozens of the popular search engines on your behalf. These services often offer *Search Engine Optimization,* which means they list your site and take steps to ensure that your site is among the first to be listed for specific search terms or phrases that you predetermine. You can find a Search Engine Optimization service by using any search engine. It's also a service that most Web site development companies provide for an additional fee. The benefit to using this type of service is that they know how to get sites listed quickly. Plus, it saves you time. The cost can be anywhere from $25 to several hundred dollars, depending on the services offered.

Using keyword marketing

Keyword marketing, also referred to as *search marketing,* has become a powerful and inexpensive way to advertise any Web site online. You want to create a short, text-based online ad that displayed every time a surfer enters a search phrase. The online ad should be a headline with two short lines of text. Two companies that can help you create your content include

- ✔ Yahoo! Small Business: Web site `smallbusiness.yahoo.com/marketing/sponsoredsearch.php`
- ✔ Google AdWords: Web site `adwords.google.com/select`

How do these services work? Well, you create the list of keywords and search phrases you believe best describe your Web site and then pay a small fee each time your ad is displayed and someone actually clicks on the link to visit your Web site.

Keyword marketing is extremely cost effective and requires only a very small financial investment (under $50) to get started. This way of generating Web site traffic has become a far more powerful form of advertising than online banner advertising.

Are you wondering what the benefits are? Keyword advertising has many:

- ✔ It launches within minutes and begins generating results quickly.
- ✔ The campaign can be modified in real time to ensure the best results.
- ✔ You can target a variety of different potential audiences for your book using several keyword marketing campaigns simultaneously and continue to tweak your list of keywords that generate the most traffic.
- ✔ You can spend as much or as little money as you want to generate traffic to your Web site.

Linking up with affiliate marketing

By signing up with an affiliate marketing service, you invite other Web site operators (who become your affiliates) to display ads or links to your site on their Web sites. You don't pay upfront for this advertising. Instead, every time someone either clicks a link to visit your site or clicks a link and places an order from your site, you pay that affiliate a predetermined fee. The affiliate marketing service acts as the middle man, tracks traffic, and handles the necessary accounting on your behalf. The cost-per-click ranges from a fraction of one cent to several dollars, depending on a variety of factors, including how targeted the Web surfers are.

Thousands of well-established companies, as well as small online business operators and self-published authors, use affiliate marketing to generate traffic to their sites. For a list of companies that manage affiliate marketing programs on behalf of Web masters, check out the following Web site: www.web affiliatesdirectory.com/affiliate_networks_list.html.

Try out these three companies that manage Affiliate Marketing programs on behalf of Web masters:

- ✔ LinkShare (www.linkshare.com)
- ✔ ClickExchange (www.clickexchange.com)
- ✔ eAdExchange (www.eAdExchange.com)

Becoming an active online participant

As an author looking to promote your book, if you become active online, you may be able to get the word out about you and your book. Here are a few ways to spread the news:

- ✔ **Chat rooms, forums, and message boards:** While blatantly promoting your book may be frowned upon (because you don't want to sound to self-serving), offer advice, comments, ideas, or recommendations as part of your postings and interaction, and then casually mention your book and Web site.

    Find these forums through online searches. Use the topic of your book, for example, as the search phrase. If you're a member of America Online, click the *Community* icon.

- ✔ **Write reviews:** Visit online booksellers' Web sites, and write reviews of other people's books (that relate to your area of expertise or your book's topic). In your reviews, you can casually promote yourself and your book in the process. (See Chapter 14 for more details about reviewing books on online booksellers' sites.)

Adding Extra Bells and Whistles

Internet technology is always evolving. Simple text-based Web sites can be a powerful marketing tool for a book; however, many new technologies now exist that can be inexpensively incorporated into a Web site to make it more engaging and interactive.

The following sections cover a few features, using some of the latest Internet technologies that you can incorporate into your Web site to improve its ability to promote and sell your book.

The first and foremost objective of your Web site and online marketing efforts is to sell your book and promote yourself as an author. Adding fancy bells and whistles, such as visually stunning animations, look great, but they're not always necessary.

Choosing opt-in mailing lists and electronic newsletters

Allowing your Web site's visitors to opt in or subscribe to a mailing list allows you to communicate with those people via e-mail. Many authors and publishing companies find it extremely beneficial to send weekly or monthly e-mails to people on their mailing list. This benefits you by reminding people about your book's existence and providing additional marketing messages on an ongoing basis. For example, you can provide a few informative articles relating to the topic of your book but also include a promotional message or ad about your book as part of the newsletter.

An opt-in mailing list for e-mail is very different from spam. Spam is unsolicited e-mail sent out *without* the recipient's permission. Avoid using spam to market, promote, and sell your book. Uninvited solicitation can damage your credibility and annoy potential readers.

An electronic newsletter can be as short as one page and contain one or more informative articles on a topic that's related to your book and that readers perceive as valuable and interesting. For example, if you've written a how-to book, write an article that lists the top ten tips or common mistakes to avoid.

The company you use to develop and/or host your Web site can help you incorporate an online mailing list and related database. See "How can you create a Web site?" earlier in this chapter for more about finding a company to build your site.

Creating an author's blog

Blogging has become a popular and informal way for people to publish their knowledge, thoughts, advice, and opinions on the Internet. A *blog* is like an electronic diary that's put on the Web and made available for anyone to read. A blog can incorporate text, graphics, photos, and other digital elements.

Many authors create blogs as an informal way to communicate with their readers regularly. Blogging can be used to promote your book but also to help you establish yourself as an expert in your field.

Creating a blog that's tied to your Web site is easy. Many free and inexpensive services exist that you can use to create and maintain a blog. These services require no programming and are extremely easy to use. In fact, after your text is written, you can create and update your blog in minutes.

Some blogging services create separate URLs for blogs. If this is the case, be sure to provide a link from your main Web site to your blog, so people can easily find and access it. For example, my Web site is `www.JasonRich.com`, but, my blog is `jasonrich.blogspot.com`. When you read the blog, you find numerous links back to my Web site (and vice versa).

Many authors have discovered that updating their blog on a weekly or monthly basis is a great way to develop a following and inform potential readers about their book(s).

Figure 21-2 shows my own blog, found at `jasonrich.blogspot.com`. On it, you find information about some of my books and are able to chit-chat about some of the book projects I'm currently working on. The blog is written in an informal style, yet it provides readers with detailed information about my current and upcoming books.

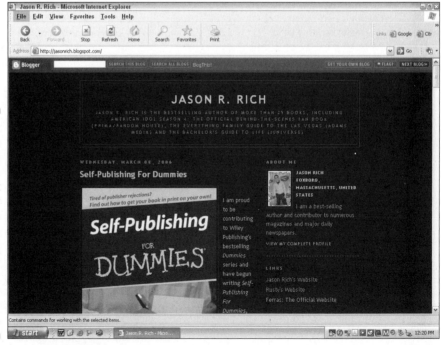

Figure 21-2:
A blog is like an electronic diary that an author creates as an informal way to communicate with readers.

To find out more about blogging and to create your own blog, check out these sources:

✔ www.blogger.com

✔ www.blog.com

✔ www.myspace.com

✔ *Blogging For Dummies* (Wiley) by Brad Hill

Producing a podcast

A podcast is like a prerecorded radio program that can be downloaded and listened to, for free, using any iPod or compatible MP3 player (including computers that can play audio files). A podcast can be an audio-based blog or produced to sound like a professional radio show.

The benefit to a podcast is that you can use audio to generate content of interest to listeners and potential readers of your book. This means that in addition to speaking yourself, you can interview other people, and use music and sound effects to capture the attention of your audience.

A podcast can be recorded by anyone and made available online, through www.itunes.com, from your Web site, or from a growing number of podcast libraries.

Recording and publishing a podcast is relatively easy when you use specialized software, such as GarageBand or QuickTime Pro for Macs or ePodcast Producer for PCs (www.industrialaudiosoftware.com). To understand how to produce a podcast, check out these Web sites:

✔ www.podcasting.com

✔ www.apple.com/itunes/podcasts

✔ www.podcast.net

✔ www.pod101.com

You also can pick up a copy of *Podcasting For Dummies* (Wiley) by Tee Morris and Evo Terra.

Another way to drive traffic to your Web site and promote your book at the same time is to get your book reviewed on other people's podcasts. Go to any blog or podcast directory (such as iTunes) and use the search phrase *book reviews* to find which blogs and/or podcasts to submit your book to in order to get it reviewed.

Hosting an online chat

Just as being a guest on a radio or television show is a great way to promote your book, being a guest on an online chat can be equally productive in terms of selling books. Services like America Online and MSN constantly host live chats with authors and celebrity guests. Plus, you can host your own chats anytime on these and other services. It's even possible to create and host chats from your own Web site.

Online chats are a way for you to communicate with people in real time. E-mail, Web sites, and blogs, require you to publish information for people to read and access later. Online chats are interactive, so people can ask you questions and you can respond instantly. If you want to host your own online chats from your Web site, contact your Web site designer or ISP about adding this functionality to your site. Otherwise, you can work with an existing online chat service or agree to be a guest on other chat sites.

Chapter 22

Expanding Your Income with Spin-Off Products and Services

*C*ongratulations! You've published your book and become an author. But as you may have discovered, the profit potential from selling your book is somewhat limited, mainly because of the relatively low cover price of the book. For most self-published authors, simply publishing and selling a single book isn't an effective get-rich-quick scheme, nor does it allow them to earn a full-time living.

By positioning yourself as an expert in your field, however, you can be hired as a lecturer, instructor, or consultant and potentially earn several hundred dollars per hour (or more). You can also create spin-off products like DVDs or multimedia instructional programs with much higher price tags than the cover price for your book. Your book then can be bundled with these spin-off products and help further boost your credibility.

In this chapter, you discover ways to use your newfound credibility as a published author, not just to sell books, but to create higher-priced spin-off products and services that can boost your revenue by allowing you to repackage and expand on the content in your book.

Most of the time, nonfiction books lend themselves better to spin-off products, and authors of nonfiction books are in higher demand as speakers, freelancers, and consultants.

Considering a Few Important Points Before You Start Down the Spin-Off Road

Creating spin-off products in conjunction with your book can help you generate more revenue over the long term, but initially, doing so requires a significant time and financial investment to develop the products and then properly market and distribute them. You also need to make sure that you choose the right products and services for you and your book. I cover both topics in the following sections.

What kind of investment do you need to make?

Just as you invested the time and money needed to self-publish your book and properly market and promote it, unless you sell the subsidiary rights for your book to another company (see Chapter 17 for more information), an additional investment is needed to develop and sell spin-off products. The goal is to target the audience you've already created for your book and sell those same people (as well as new customers) products and services that relate to your book or its topic.

The actual financial and time investment required depend on the type of products and services you produce.

✔ For example: While you could record, duplicate, package, distribute, and market a CD-based audio book for under $5,000, producing a DVD or video can cost up to $50,000.

✔ The time it takes to develop and manufacture spin-off products depends on a wide range of factors. Typically, each new project takes weeks or months.

Simply publishing your book isn't enough to make it successful. The book needs to be properly marketed, distributed, and sold. The same holds true for any spin-off products you create. Before investing the money to produce any type of product, be sure that you're able to market it to your intended audience and are able to generate enough sales not only to recoup your investment but also to make an ongoing profit. See Chapter 20 to find out the basics of marketing; you also can check out *Marketing For Dummies,* 2nd Edition (Wiley) by Alexander Hiam.

Unless you have a massive budget and the vast resources you need to market your products, start off small and build your product line as demand dictates and new opportunities arise.

Which products and services are right for you?

If you possess knowledge and expertise that others may benefit and profit from, people are likely to pay for that information in whatever form it's made available — a book, DVD, audio book, a live seminar, or a workshop. Having written a full-length book, you clearly have information to share with others. Now that your book has been published, use your business savvy, marketing skills, and creativity to develop new ways to package and sell your information, knowledge, and experience.

As you develop and produce spin-off products that are related to your book and its content, be realistic. If you have no on-camera experience and lack the personality, looks, and the voice to star in your own DVD, don't waste your time and money developing a product that ultimately looks unprofessional and that could hurt your credibility. Furthermore, if you're extremely uncomfortable speaking in front of crowds, don't pursue public speaking opportunities until you've mastered the required skills and confidence. Instead, focus on your own strengths and showcase them in whatever spin-off products you develop and market.

Developing Creative Ways to Repackage Your Content

Taking the same information that's in your book and adapting it to other media allows you to use visuals, audio, and more text to create an even better value. When you wrote your book, you were confined to using just the written word and potentially a few photographs or illustrations. Tap your creativity and come up with a handful of ways to repackage or rework your book's material:

 ✔ If your book featured interviews with experts, in the audio or video adaptation of your book, you could feature those same people, allowing your audience to actually hear or see the interviews.

✔ When adapting content from your book, build on that content and offer something new. Provide additional or expanded examples, new statistics, updated information, or other content not originally included in your book. This helps create a higher perceived value for the new products you're creating, especially among people who have already read your book and want more.

I cover your options, along with the partners you need to create and distribute products, in the following sections.

Surveying potential products

Finding innovative ways to repackage the content in your book and create new types of products is all about creativity. The types of spin-off products that are viable depend a lot on the type of book you've written and its intended audience. While a novel can potentially be developed into an audio book or even a computer game, products based around a work of nonfiction can be transformed into instructional videos or DVDs, audio books, or interactive multimedia applications. In the following sections, I cover several varieties of spin-off product formats.

When deciding how to cater to your potential audience and repackage the material in your book, consider the habits of your target audience and how you can utilize the latest technologies to best communicate with those people. See Chapter 4 for information about determining your target audience.

Audio books

Almost any type of book can be produced into an audio book. However, before investing the time and money into creating this type of product, determine if the type of book you've written is appealing in audio form. In reality, you sell about one audio version of your book for every ten printed copies. This statistic should help you determine if there's a market for an audio adaptation of your book. Ask yourself this: Would someone potentially learn more or be better entertained by hearing your book as opposed to reading it? If so, would they be willing to pay extra for an audio book?

Audio books can be produced in a variety of formats:

✔ Cassette

✔ Compact Disc (CD)

✔ Downloadable digital files (such as MP3s)

✔ Streaming audio files, playable via the Internet

Each of these audio formats requires a slightly different production, duplication, and distribution process. In the past, people listened to CD or audiocassettes, but today, millions of people have Apple iPods and other types of MP3 players that travel with them everywhere.

To find out more info on the audio book industry, contact The Audio Publishers Association (APA) by calling (703) 556-7172 or visiting the organizations Web site at `www.audiopub.org`.

DVDs and videos

Instructional and how-to books often lend themselves perfectly to DVDs and videos. Other types of nonfiction also can be easily adapted to this format, perhaps using more of a documentary style of filming. Of course, if you have a work of fiction, adapting your book into a direct-to-video movie is always an option, but you want to team up with a movie production company.

Multimedia applications

You may want to consider producing an informational or instructional multimedia application (a software package that can be used on a computer via CD-ROM or experienced over the Internet). For example, this application can be an educational program or computer game.

Finding partners and suppliers

Depending on the products you plan to create, you need to line up either publishing and distribution partners or suppliers. In each of the following sections, I show you how to line up people to help with audio, video, and multimedia products.

Audio books

If you plan to produce an audio book, you need to find a recording studio, producer, and someone to "host" or record the audio book. After the master copy is edited and fully produced, it needs to be professionally duplicated, packaged, sold, and distributed. You can either handle all these tasks yourself or partner with an established audio book publisher and distributor. Begin by finding a recording studio capable of producing this type of content. You can find listings in the Yellow Pages or in industry publications focused on the audio recording industry. The studio should be able to help you find the right producer.

If you plan to hire a celebrity host, you need to approach that celebrity's manager or agent. Contact the Screen Actors Guild (`www.sag.org`) or the American Federation of Television and Radio Artists (`www.aftra.com`) for celebrity contact information.

Consider creating your audio book as a digital file. The file can then be sold in different ways:

- **Your Web site:** The file can be sold and downloaded via the Internet through your own Web site (see Chapter 21 for details on building a Web site).

- **Apple iTunes:** This online store sells downloadable audio and video content, mainly for use with Apple iPods and other types of compatible MP3 players. To discover distribution opportunities for audio content such as audio books through iTunes, point your Web browser to www.apple.com/itunes/musicmarketing.

- **Audible.com:** This online store sells a wide range of downloadable audio content for use with MP3 players or a computer. To find out more about becoming an audio content provider for Audible.com, check out www.audible.com.

DVDs and videos

Producing a video or DVD requires a significantly larger time and financial commitment than audio books. Check out the following ways to save time and money and to get your product distributed:

- **Hire a camera crew:** Produce a DVD or video on a smaller scale by hiring a camera crew and producing on a relatively lower budget. A low-budget video might cost $25,000 to $50,000, but costs can vary dramatically. The result may not be a network-worthy TV program, but you can have a professional piece worth selling in conjunction with your live seminars or appearances (see "Generating Revenue with a Wide Range of Services," later in this chapter).

- **Partner with an established producer:** Instead of starting your own video production company, partner with an established producer of instructional DVDs or videos. Find existing products along the lines of what you're interested in producing, and then contact the companies responsible for producing, marketing, and distributing those DVD and video titles.

- **Movie distribution:** After your DVD is produced, make it available to the public. There are a few ways to do this:

  - **Retail stores:** You need to work with one or more distributors or wholesalers that specialize in DVD distribution. Your alternative is to contact the video buyers at retailers that sell DVDs and videos.

  - **Live appearances:** When you make appearances, you can sell your DVD in conjunction with your book, right on the spot.

  - **Rental services:** You can make your DVDs available through rental services, like NetFlix. To find out how to do this, visit the NetFlix Web site at www.netflix.com/SubmitFilm.

Multimedia applications

To create multimedia programs successfully, you need to hire a software development company and potentially a software publisher as well to obtain proper distribution for your multimedia product. One of the best ways to do this is to find a few software products that already exist and that are somewhat similar in style to what you want to produce, and then contact the companies that produced them. You also check out the Yellow Pages in the industry-oriented directories to find multimedia production companies.

Depending on your content, there's typically a much smaller market for multimedia applications than there is for DVDs or audio books. It's important to determine if this type of application is something that your book's audience would be interested in.

Generating Revenue with a Wide Range of Services

One of the best ways that an author can generate additional revenue is to make himself available as a public speaker and offer seminars and/or workshops. Authors can also enter the ranks of the media and become consultants or freelance experts to companies. I cover all these options in the following sections.

Teaching and speaking in public

As a published author and expert in your field, you should take advantage of the wide range of public speaking opportunities available to you. Many of these opportunities pay speakers and instructors either a fee or *honorarium* — a payment given to a professional person for services for which fees aren't legally or traditionally required. Other occasions provide promotional opportunities and the ability to sell books directly to program participants. Public speaking also offers the opportunity to establish yourself further as an industry leader or expert in your field. The following sections focus on ways to use your public speaking skills to generate revenue and sell your book.

Here are some tips to help you get set for teaching and speaking engagements:

✓ **Figure out what you have to say and who'd be interested in hearing you speak.** For example, a fiction author can offer readings from his book or discuss its topic, and a nonfiction author can offer how-to instruction relating to his area of expertise.

   ✔ **Schedule free speaking engagements:** Author appearances and lectures
      at local bookstores or volunteering to speak in front of various nonprofit
      organizations at public libraries or in schools within your community
      are good ways to give you practice speaking in front of crowds.

   ✔ **Join a public speaking organization:** Joining groups such as
      Toastmasters (`www.toastmasters.org`) or the National Speakers
      Association (`www.nsaspeaker.org`) can help you establish your-
      self as a professional public speaker.

Teach through adult education programs

Throughout the country, community colleges and other organizations spon-
sor hundreds of organized adult education and continuing education programs. These programs hire experts, authors, and industry leaders to teach a
wide range of classes, workshops, and seminars.

Students register and pay for your class, which can be a one-time seminar or
a class that spans three to eight weeks (based on your topic). In addition to
being paid to teach the class, you can sell your book to students who use
that book in the class, and you benefit from the exposure you receive by
being promoted as an instructor in the course catalog, promotional mailings,
and advertising done by the adult education program.

Some authors even create one course or workshop curriculum based on their
book, and then they work as an instructor for multiple adult education programs in various regions, ensuring an ongoing income stream.

To become an instructor for an adult education or continuing education program, contact the school or adult education program organizer directly and
inquire about the process for proposing a new course or workshop. A written
proposal and an in-person meeting are typically required to pitch new course
ideas. Become familiar with the types of programs already being offered and
pitch an idea based around your book that you believe potential students
would be interested in and could benefit from.

The Learning Annex is a well-established adult education program around the
country. Each year, it hires and pays hundreds of experts and authors to
teach more than 8,000 classes and seminars on a wide range of topics.
Contact the organization at (212) 371-0280 or `www.learningannex.com`.
The Learning Annex has also developed a comprehensive DVD seminar if you
want to understand how to become a professional speaker. The $195 course
is available from the organization's Web site. See — even it's making money
with a course on how to teach a course.

Host your own seminars

Hosting a seminar is another great way to draw people into your audience
base and increase your revenue. If you want to host your own seminars, consider the following steps before getting started:

1. **Develop a half-day or full-day seminar curriculum.**

   If you have experience public speaking, putting together a seminar based on content from your book probably won't be too difficult.

2. **Rent a conference room at a hotel or small theater.**

   The venue should provide the audio/video equipment you need and ample space for participants to sit comfortably for the duration of the seminar.

3. **Invite participants to attend the seminar.**

   Charge $25 to $500 a person (depending on the topic, the length of the seminar, and your target audience). As you start figuring out how to price and coordinate your events, consider hiring someone with event or seminar planning experience to help you plan and market your seminars properly.

4. **Put together a direct mail piece or heavily promote your event through the media.**

   In your marketing plan, to help you gauge how many people may attend a seminar, offer an early-registration discount to encourage people to reserve their spot in advance. (See Chapter 20 for details about advertising.)

Getting enough people to attend your seminars to make them financially worthwhile may seem a bit challenging, but start off small, with relatively low expectations. For your first few seminars, plan on attracting a dozen or so paying attendees. If your small seminars are well planned and worthwhile, those attendees may spread the word and your following may expand, which means your paying audience expands as well.

Lecture at colleges and universities

Many colleges and universities (as well as organizations and clubs affiliated with schools) have budgets to bring in guest speakers and lecturers. If you're an expert on a topic that college or graduate-level students are interested in, consider contacting local schools and making yourself available as a guest lecturer. If you're a fiction author, perhaps you can speak about the creative writing process to English or literature majors.

If you're prepared to make a larger time commitment, you could become a visiting faculty member at a college or university and teach one or two classes. To do this, however, you have to commit to being available at least for one full semester and holding classes one or more times per week. (See "Teach through adult education programs," earlier in this chapter, for more about teaching classes.)

Speak at trade shows and conferences

Industry trade shows and conferences always utilize guest speakers and lecturers. Depending on the trade show, these gigs are often paid. Even if the trade show doesn't pay its speakers, these gatherings provide an excellent opportunity to further position yourself as an expert in your field and sell books to your target audience. They're also a great way to promote yourself as a consultant or freelancer within your industry (see "Becoming a consultant or freelancer," later in this chapter).

You can find trade shows or seminars to speak at by reading industry trade publications that focus on your area of expertise. If you can't get invited to be a speaker at a trade show, you can still promote yourself by setting up a booth and selling your book or by distributing promotional materials about your book (and your consulting services) to attendees.

Work with a speaker's bureau

A speaker's bureau is an organization that matches speakers with venues and organizations looking for people to host lectures, seminars, or workshops. The group promotes you as a public speaker, schedules speaking gigs on your behalf, and then takes a commission based on the revenue you generate from the appearances.

To sign up as a client with a speaker's bureau, most agencies request that you first submit a video or audiotape of yourself speaking, along with a copy of your book and related promotional materials. You can find reputable speaker's bureaus to work with online or in the Yellow Pages under *Speaker's Bureaus* or *Public Speaking*.

Entering the ranks of the media

As an expert in your field, one way to share your knowledge and attract attention is to become a contributor to newspapers or radio. The following sections focus on these options.

Write a newspaper column

Writing a daily or weekly newspaper column focusing on your area of expertise is a great way to promote yourself and your book, and generate an ongoing income. First, contact a few local newspapers in your area (both daily and weekly newspapers) and see if they're looking to hire columnists. Chances are, you may not earn much initially, but after the column is established, you can syndicate it to dozens or hundreds of newspapers. Through syndication you can earn a serious income. And remember to promote your book regularly within your column.

As an established author, one way to syndicate your column is to work with an established newspaper syndication company. To find out more about the newspaper industry and the syndication process, subscribe to *Editor & Publisher* magazine or visit the publication's Web site at `www.editorand publisher.com`. *The Editor & Publisher 2005 Directory of Syndicates* is an excellent resource for contacting newspaper syndication companies.

Host a radio program

Talk radio is extremely popular on AM, FM, and satellite radio. Local radio stations, programming syndication companies, and radio networks are always looking for innovative new programming. To become a radio personality, you must

- ✔ Establish yourself as an expert in your field
- ✔ Have a great voice
- ✔ Exhibit an outgoing personality

After developing a concept for a talk radio program, contact the program director at a few radio stations to discuss your idea. After that, you may develop a strong following in a local market, and you can always syndicate your show nationally or team up with a national radio network.

As a radio show host, you can regularly promote your book on the air, and you can potentially earn a salary as a radio host. Some stations let you sell your own advertising and keep some or all the revenue generated by the show.

Most talk radio shows appeal to a broad audience and have mass appeal. Therefore, if your book and area of expertise is extremely narrow, interest in your program ideas may be limited.

Becoming a consultant or freelancer

If a company can benefit from your expertise, consider offering yourself as a consultant or freelancer and charging by the hour or the day for your services. Consultants with specific areas of expertise can earn $100 to $500 per hour to share their knowledge and help companies solve problems, increase sales, train employees, or overcome challenges.

In addition to being an expert on a topic, consultants also must

- ✔ Work well with others
- ✔ Be good educators and trainers
- ✔ Be self-motivated

- ✔ Value organization
- ✔ Generate highly creative ideas
- ✔ Possess extreme professionalism
- ✔ Be responsible enough to be their own bosses
- ✔ Promote the consulting business
- ✔ Handle day-to-day operations
- ✔ Manage the company's finances
- ✔ Cater to the clients' needs

Effectively mastering the above skills may ensure success right from the start.

Check out *Freelancing For Dummies* (Wiley) by Susan M. Drake for full details on starting down the path to successful consulting and freelancing.

Don't just quit your day job to become a consultant. Building up a successful consulting business can take months or even years. Sure, being a published author and recognized expert in your field helps enhance your reputation, but establishing a large enough client base to support yourself financially takes time and hard work. Consider starting off working as a part-time consultant and building up your clientele before giving up your steady paycheck and job-related benefits.

Part VI
The Part of Tens

The 5th Wave   By Rich Tennant

@RICHTENNANT

Is this the "self—published authors sweat out their aggressions" aerobics class?

In this part . . .

No *For Dummies* book is complete without the Part of Tens! This part lists pitfalls to avoid as you embark on your publishing project. You also find a list of additional resources to get more information and guidance when it comes to writing, designing, printing, distributing, marketing, and selling your book.

Chapter 23

Ten Self-Publishing Mistakes to Avoid

*I*f you're about to self-publish your first book, you can make a handful of mistakes that can mean the difference between a successful publishing venture and a total bomb. Careful planning and implementing your own common sense are two ingredients that can help guarantee your success. This chapter focuses on ten common mistakes inexperienced self-publishers often make and offers advice on how to avoid making these often costly mistakes.

Not Targeting Your Audience Appropriately

In addition to ensuring that the content within your book is appropriate for your intended readers, craft the language and vocabulary to appeal to your readers and to be easily understandable. A fun, upbeat book about how to create a scrapbook or plan a family vacation shouldn't read like a history textbook or scientific research paper. Know your audience and write specifically for those people. See Chapter 4 for more about target audiences.

Inaccurate Information, a Lack of Organization, and Poor Writing

Providing inaccurate, incomplete, outdated, or misleading information to your reader damages your credibility and takes away value from your book. Avoid this mistake by doing proper research. Even if you're writing fiction, you want your plots and characters to be realistic or believable. Chapter 4 has more information on research.

Proper organization makes your book easier to read. The content flows in a more logical order and it's easier to understand by the reader. The trick to developing a well-organized book is to begin by developing an extremely detailed outline *before* you start writing (see Chapter 4 for more details).

Just because you've decided to write a book doesn't automatically mean that you're a talented writer. Many authors spend years fine-tuning their craft. If you feel that you don't have the skills to create a well-written, full-length manuscript, seriously consider hiring a co-author who's a professional writer, a ghostwriter, and/or a really good editor (see Chapter 5) to work with you.

A Lack of Attention to Detail and Editing

A well-written book contains absolutely no spelling mistakes, grammatical errors, inaccurate information, misprints, incorrect details (such as incorrect names, phone numbers, Web sites, statistics, chapter references, facts, or figures), or mislabeled figures and captions. In addition to proofreading your own work, hiring a professional editor to review your manuscript *before* it goes to press is crucial. See Chapter 5 for more about working with an editor.

Inefficiently Using Money and Resources

As a self-published author, all the expenses related to creating, editing, laying out, printing, distributing, advertising, marketing, and promoting your book come out of your pocket. Careful budgeting and knowing what expenses you may incur during each stage of the self-publishing process helps you best utilize the money that you have available when it comes to publishing your book. See Chapter 6 for details on creating a business plan and a budget.

Implementing Poor Cover Design and Copy

Having a well-written book with a poorly written and designed cover or a bad title has a negative impact on sales. Conversely, having an amazing cover and catchy title on an otherwise average book may dramatically improve sales. And hiring a professional graphic artist or experienced book cover designer to create your book's cover is an essential piece of your puzzle. Unless you have professional graphic design experience, hire someone who does! Chapter 9 goes into detail about book covers, including design and the absolute importance of having a catchy title and subtitle.

Choosing the Wrong Printing Method

For many self-published authors, Print-On-Demand (POD) publishing offers the perfect solution. It's inexpensive, relatively quick and allows virtually anyone with a good book idea to get published. POD (described in Chapter 11) has many benefits, but it's not the ideal publishing solution for everyone. Other traditional printing options, such as offset printing and eBook publishing opportunities, may be more appropriate based on your goals. Chapters 10, 11, and 12 focus on your printing options.

A Lack of Comprehensive Distribution

In addition to writing an awesome book and heavily promoting it, the third key ingredient for success is making sure that your target audience can find and buy it. Based on how you're going to publish your book, figure out the best and most achievable distribution methods, and then make full use of them. Part IV focuses on various distribution methods and opportunities available to self-published authors.

Wasting the Potential of Online Distribution

Online sales, whether it's through your own Web site or the well-established online booksellers, such as Amazon.com and Barnes & Noble.com, are extremely cost effective and powerful distribution channels that can't be ignored by self-publishers. These days, more and more people are Internet savvy and finding ordering books online convenient.

As you discover in Chapter 14, however, simply getting your book listed on an online bookseller doesn't generate sales. Ways do exist, however, to promote your book heavily on online.

Improperly Planning the Publicity and Marketing Campaign

Writing what can potentially be a bestseller and publishing it is certainly important, but making sure that potential readers know about your book's existence is equally important when it comes to generating sales. Many self-published authors do an excellent job creating and publishing their book, but inadvertently they forget about marketing and advertising, or they don't realize the importance of these efforts.

A comprehensive and well-timed advertising, marketing, and public relations campaign is crucial for a book's success. If you don't have the advertising, marketing, and PR savvy to create, launch and manage an effective, well-planned, and comprehensive campaign, hire experienced experts to help. Check out Part V for more on publicity and marketing.

Bad Timing throughout the Self-Publishing Process

As you complete the various steps in the publishing process, pay careful attention to scheduling, lead times, and deadlines. Rushing steps, cutting corners, or taking shortcuts is a surefire way to failure and making costly mistakes. See Chapter 1 for a brief timeline of steps in the self-publishing process.

Timing also refers to when your book actually gets published and becomes available to readers online or at retail. Is there a specific date, season, holiday, or time of year when interest in your book may be stronger? Choosing the most appropriate release date is essential, especially if the book somehow ties into or relates to a specific date, holiday, or season. Most people aren't going to buy a Christmas cookbook in July. See Chapter 7 for tips on selecting your book's publication date.

Chapter 24

Ten Useful Resources for Self-Publishers

· ·

In This Chapter

▶ Finding helpful books and print publications

▶ Surfing the Web for help

▶ Contacting professional associations

· ·

*A*s you embark on your self-publishing project, you don't need to reinvent the wheel and find new ways of accomplishing each step involved with the process. Work from what many others before you have done and rely on the companies that have established expertise in the book publishing field. This chapter describes a handful of awesome resources self-publishers can use to get questions answered, find referrals, and discover more about various aspects of book publishing.

Books for Writers Worth Reading

The following are books written specifically for authors, writers, and journalists. These books come in handy when they're added to your personal reference library and referred to during the writing process.

The Chicago Manual of Style, 15th Edition

Published by the University of Chicago Press, *The Chicago Manual of Style,* 15th Edition offers more than 1,000 pages of information designed to help writers properly use the English language. This book is a reference book that every writer should have on his desk. The manual is also available on CD-ROM and portions of it can be accessed for free online. Check out the resource online at www.press.uchicago.edu/Misc/Chicago/cmosfaq.

Other great reference books

To round out your reference library as a writer, grab a copy of *Merriam-Webster's Collegiate Dictionary,* 11th Edition (Merriam-Webster) and *The Elements of Style,* 4th Edition (Longman) by William Strunk, Jr. These resources are excellent books for quickly answering common questions (like "How on earth do I spell this word?").

Helpful Print Publications

The following print publications are targeted to people in book publishing. These magazines and newsletters offer information articles about trends in the publishing industry and how-to articles of interest to writers. They also provide valuable advice on how to write or publish all types of material.

Booklist

The American Library Association publishes a well-respected resource that librarians and booksellers often refer to when choosing new titles to purchase and inventory. This resource is called *Booklist,* and it comprises primarily new book reviews along with advertising from publishers. For people working in the publishing field, a positive review from *Booklist* gives you and your book a lot of credibility. The subscription rate is $295 per year. Visit www.ala.org/booklist for more information.

Book Marketing Update

Book Marketing Update is a biweekly newsletter targeting self-published authors and small publishing houses. The newsletter focuses primarily on inexpensive ways to market a book to the general public and the media. In addition to informative articles, each issue includes contact information for at least a dozen media outlets interested in receiving books to review.

For more information or to subscribe, call (610) 259-0707 ext. 119 or visit the publication's Web site at www.bookmarketingupdate.com. The basic subscription rate is $19.95 per month. This fee includes access to over 60 back issues of the newsletter online and new issues mailed to you biweekly.

Other publications to check out

The following monthly special interest magazines for writers and publishers are available from newsstands and larger bookstores that sell magazines:

- *The Writer Magazine* (www.writermag.com/wrt)
- *Writer's Digest* (www.writersdigest.com)
- *Publishers Weekly* (www.publishersweekly.com)
- *ForeWord Magazine* (www.forewordmagazine.net)
- *Independent Publisher* (www.independentpublisher.com)

Powerful Online Resources

The Internet offers a vast resource of information for self-publishers and can be a powerful research tool for writing and fact checking, as well as for uncovering information about the publishing industry and gathering referrals for companies and freelancers to work with on your publishing projects. Check out the following company Web sites to get started.

BooksInPrint.com Professional

Operated by R.R. Bowker, the BooksInPrint.com Professional Web site offers access to the BooksInPrint.com database of over five million in-print, out-of-print, and forthcoming books being published by recognized publishing companies. This site is used by booksellers, libraries, and other companies to determine what books to order and sell. But as an author, you can use this database to research other books with a similar topic to yours and find out about trends in the publishing industry. You also want to make sure that your book gets listed in this publication to help you spread the word of its availability to key buyers. Access to this database is provided on a paid subscription basis. Call (800) 526-9537 or visit www.booksinprint.com for more information.

BookWire

Also published by R.R. Bowker, *BookWire* is the most comprehensive online portal into the book industry. The site, located at www.bookwire.com, contains over 18,000 links connecting book titles to consumers, librarians, booksellers, and book enthusiasts all over the world. The company's sites offer various advertising opportunities that can help you promote your book directly to booksellers, distributors, wholesalers, and key industry buyers.

Elance and Guru.com

Certain steps in the self-publishing process, such as editing your manuscript or designing your book's cover, require the expertise of someone with specialized skills and experience. Web sites such as www.elance.com and www.guru.com help you find the best people to hire. Simply post a listing describing your specific needs and budget. Within hours, you start receiving e-mails from experienced professionals interested in being hired for your freelance project. You can then evaluate their portfolios and negotiate fees.

Two additional Web sites focusing on writing and publishing-related specialties are www.manuscriptediting.com and the referral service provided by the American Society of Journalists and Authors (www.asja.org).

Trustworthy Professional Associations

The following professional associations offer a variety of services. In addition to providing educational materials, these and other similar associations can help you find referrals for freelancers, printers, and distributors. They can also help you sell your book to booksellers and other retail outlets.

The American Booksellers Association

The American Booksellers Association (ABA) is a professional association comprised mainly of independent booksellers throughout the country. The association offers small publishers several advertising and editorial opportunities to reach buyers from over 1,000 independent booksellers in order to educate them about your new book title(s).

The organization also publishes *Book Sense,* which is an innovative strategic marketing, branding, and bookselling campaign created for the independent, storefront bookstore members of the American Booksellers Association.

To find out more about The American Booksellers Association, visit www.bookweb.org or call (800) 637-0037. For advertising opportunities available online and through *Book Sense,* point your Web browser to www.bookweb.org/booksense/publisher/3311.html.

PMA, the Independent Book Publishers Association

PMA, the Independent Book Publishers Association is a trade association comprised of independent publishers. The organization's mission is to advance the professional interest of independent publishers by offering a wide range of cooperative marketing and educational programs designed to assist small publishing companies and self-published authors compete with the major publishing houses when it comes to marketing, distributing, and selling their book titles.

Membership fees start at $109 per year. For more information give them a call at (310) 372-2732 or visit online at www.pma-online.org.

Index

• *P* •

BUSINESS, CAREERS & PERSONAL FINANCE

0-7645-5307-0

0-7645-5331-3 *†

Also available:

- Accounting For Dummies †
  0-7645-5314-3
- Business Plans Kit For Dummies †
  0-7645-5365-8
- Cover Letters For Dummies
  0-7645-5224-4
- Frugal Living For Dummies
  0-7645-5403-4
- Leadership For Dummies
  0-7645-5176-0
- Managing For Dummies
  0-7645-1771-6

- Marketing For Dummies
  0-7645-5600-2
- Personal Finance For Dummies *
  0-7645-2590-5
- Project Management For Dummies
  0-7645-5283-X
- Resumes For Dummies †
  0-7645-5471-9
- Selling For Dummies
  0-7645-5363-1
- Small Business Kit For Dummies *†
  0-7645-5093-4

HOME & BUSINESS COMPUTER BASICS

0-7645-4074-2

0-7645-3758-X

Also available:

- ACT! 6 For Dummies
  0-7645-2645-6
- iLife '04 All-in-One Desk Reference
  For Dummies
  0-7645-7347-0
- iPAQ For Dummies
  0-7645-6769-1
- Mac OS X Panther Timesaving
  Techniques For Dummies
  0-7645-5812-9
- Macs For Dummies
  0-7645-5656-8

- Microsoft Money 2004 For Dummies
  0-7645-4195-1
- Office 2003 All-in-One Desk Reference
  For Dummies
  0-7645-3883-7
- Outlook 2003 For Dummies
  0-7645-3759-8
- PCs For Dummies
  0-7645-4074-2
- TiVo For Dummies
  0-7645-6923-6
- Upgrading and Fixing PCs For Dummies
  0-7645-1665-5
- Windows XP Timesaving Techniques
  For Dummies
  0-7645-3748-2

FOOD, HOME, GARDEN, HOBBIES, MUSIC & PETS

0-7645-5295-3

0-7645-5232-5

Also available:

- Bass Guitar For Dummies
  0-7645-2487-9
- Diabetes Cookbook For Dummies
  0-7645-5230-9
- Gardening For Dummies *
  0-7645-5130-2
- Guitar For Dummies
  0-7645-5106-X
- Holiday Decorating For Dummies
  0-7645-2570-0
- Home Improvement All-in-One
  For Dummies
  0-7645-5680-0

- Knitting For Dummies
  0-7645-5395-X
- Piano For Dummies
  0-7645-5105-1
- Puppies For Dummies
  0-7645-5255-4
- Scrapbooking For Dummies
  0-7645-7208-3
- Senior Dogs For Dummies
  0-7645-5818-8
- Singing For Dummies
  0-7645-2475-5
- 30-Minute Meals For Dummies
  0-7645-2589-1

INTERNET & DIGITAL MEDIA

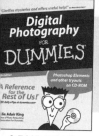

0-7645-1664-7

0-7645-6924-4

Also available:

- 2005 Online Shopping Directory
  For Dummies
  0-7645-7495-7
- CD & DVD Recording For Dummies
  0-7645-5956-7
- eBay For Dummies
  0-7645-5654-1
- Fighting Spam For Dummies
  0-7645-5965-6
- Genealogy Online For Dummies
  0-7645-5964-8
- Google For Dummies
  0-7645-4420-9

- Home Recording For Musicians
  For Dummies
  0-7645-1634-5
- The Internet For Dummies
  0-7645-4173-0
- iPod & iTunes For Dummies
  0-7645-7772-7
- Preventing Identity Theft For Dummies
  0-7645-7336-5
- Pro Tools All-in-One Desk Reference
  For Dummies
  0-7645-5714-9
- Roxio Easy Media Creator For Dummies
  0-7645-7131-1

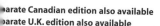

Separate Canadian edition also available
Separate U.K. edition also available

Available wherever books are sold. For more information or to order direct: U.S. customers visit www.dummies.com or call 1-877-762-2974.
U.K. customers visit www.wileyeurope.com or call 0800 243407. Canadian customers visit www.wiley.ca or call 1-800-567-4797.

SPORTS, FITNESS, PARENTING, RELIGION & SPIRITUALITY

0-7645-5146-9

0-7645-5418-2

Also available:
- Adoption For Dummies
  0-7645-5488-3
- Basketball For Dummies
  0-7645-5248-1
- The Bible For Dummies
  0-7645-5296-1
- Buddhism For Dummies
  0-7645-5359-3
- Catholicism For Dummies
  0-7645-5391-7
- Hockey For Dummies
  0-7645-5228-7

- Judaism For Dummies
  0-7645-5299-6
- Martial Arts For Dummies
  0-7645-5358-5
- Pilates For Dummies
  0-7645-5397-6
- Religion For Dummies
  0-7645-5264-3
- Teaching Kids to Read For Dummies
  0-7645-4043-2
- Weight Training For Dummies
  0-7645-5168-X
- Yoga For Dummies
  0-7645-5117-5

TRAVEL

0-7645-5438-7

0-7645-5453-0

Also available:
- Alaska For Dummies
  0-7645-1761-9
- Arizona For Dummies
  0-7645-6938-4
- Cancún and the Yucatán For Dummies
  0-7645-2437-2
- Cruise Vacations For Dummies
  0-7645-6941-4
- Europe For Dummies
  0-7645-5456-5
- Ireland For Dummies
  0-7645-5455-7

- Las Vegas For Dummies
  0-7645-5448-4
- London For Dummies
  0-7645-4277-X
- New York City For Dummies
  0-7645-6945-7
- Paris For Dummies
  0-7645-5494-8
- RV Vacations For Dummies
  0-7645-5443-3
- Walt Disney World & Orlando For Dummi
  0-7645-6943-0

GRAPHICS, DESIGN & WEB DEVELOPMENT

0-7645-4345-8

0-7645-5589-8

Also available:
- Adobe Acrobat 6 PDF For Dummies
  0-7645-3760-1
- Building a Web Site For Dummies
  0-7645-7144-3
- Dreamweaver MX 2004 For Dummies
  0-7645-4342-3
- FrontPage 2003 For Dummies
  0-7645-3882-9
- HTML 4 For Dummies
  0-7645-1995-6
- Illustrator cs For Dummies
  0-7645-4084-X

- Macromedia Flash MX 2004 For Dumm
  0-7645-4358-X
- Photoshop 7 All-in-One Desk
  Reference For Dummies
  0-7645-1667-1
- Photoshop cs Timesaving Technique
  For Dummies
  0-7645-6782-9
- PHP 5 For Dummies
  0-7645-4166-8
- PowerPoint 2003 For Dummies
  0-7645-3908-6
- QuarkXPress 6 For Dummies
  0-7645-2593-X

NETWORKING, SECURITY, PROGRAMMING & DATABASES

0-7645-6852-3

0-7645-5784-X

Also available:
- A+ Certification For Dummies
  0-7645-4187-0
- Access 2003 All-in-One Desk
  Reference For Dummies
  0-7645-3988-4
- Beginning Programming For Dummies
  0-7645-4997-9
- C For Dummies
  0-7645-7068-4
- Firewalls For Dummies
  0-7645-4048-3
- Home Networking For Dummies
  0-7645-42796

- Network Security For Dummies
  0-7645-1679-5
- Networking For Dummies
  0-7645-1677-9
- TCP/IP For Dummies
  0-7645-1760-0
- VBA For Dummies
  0-7645-3989-2
- Wireless All In-One Desk Reference
  For Dummies
  0-7645-7496-5
- Wireless Home Networking For Dumm
  0-7645-3910-8